D0992304

THE SUPREME COURT
AND THE
AMERICAN FAMILY

Recent Titles in
Contributions in American Studies
Series Editor: Robert H. Walker

The Bang and the Whimper: Apocalypse and Entropy in American
Literature
Zbigniew Lewicki

The Disreputable Profession: The Actor in Society
Mendel Kohansky

The Formative Essays of Justice Holmes: The Making of
an American Legal Philosophy
Frederic Rogers Kellogg

A "Capacity for Outrage": The Judicial Odyssey of J. Skelly Wright
Arthur Selwyn Miller

On Courts and Democracy: Selected Nonjudicial Writings of J. Skelly
Wright
Arthur Selwyn Miller, editor

A Campaign of Ideas: The 1980 Anderson/Lucey Platform
Clifford W. Brown, Jr., and Robert J. Walker, compilers

Dreams and Visions: A Study of American Utopias, 1865–1917
Charles J. Rooney, Jr.

Mechanical Metamorphosis: Technological Change in Revolutionary
America
Neil Longley York

Prologue: The Novels of Black American Women, 1891–1965
Carole McAlpine Watson

Strikes, Dispute Procedures, and Arbitration: Essays on Labor Law
William B. Gould IV

The Soul of the Wobblies: The I.W.W., Religion, and American
Culture in the Progressive Era, 1905–1917
Donald E. Winters, Jr.

Politics, Democracy, and the Supreme Court: Essays on the Frontier
of Constitutional Theory
Arthur S. Miller

THE SUPREME COURT

AND THE

AMERICAN FAMILY

Ideology and Issues

EVA R. RUBIN

CONTRIBUTIONS IN AMERICAN STUDIES, NUMBER 85

GREENWOOD PRESS

New York • Westport, Connecticut • London

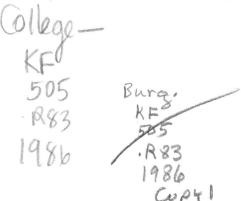

Library of Congress Cataloging-in-Publication Data

Rubin, Eva R.
  The Supreme Court and the American family.

  (Contributions in American studies, ISSN 0084–9227 ;
no. 85)
  Bibliography: p.
  Includes index.
  1. Domestic relations— United States. 2. Sex
discrimination against women— Law and legislation—
United States. 3. United States. Supreme Court.
I. Title. II. Series.
KF505.R83   1986   346.7301′5   85–21865
                     347.30615
ISBN 0–313–25157–6 (lib. bdg. : alk. paper)

Copyright © 1986 by Eva R. Rubin

All rights reserved. No portion of this book may be
reproduced, by any process or technique, without the
express written consent of the publisher.

Library of Congress Catalog Card Number: 85–21865
ISBN: 0–313–25157–6
ISSN: 0084–9227

First published in 1986

Greenwood Press, Inc.
88 Post Road West, Westport, Connecticut 06881

Printed in the United States of America

The paper used in this book complies with the
Permanent Paper Standard issued by the National
Information Standards Organization (Z39.48–1984).

10 9 8 7 6 5 4 3 2 1

To Shirley Sanders

Contents

Introduction

In 1959, a woman named Gwendolyn Hoyt killed her husband with a baseball bat and was tried and convicted of second degree murder. The Florida jury that convicted her was all male. The homicide had occurred during a marital dispute and the defendant appealed her conviction, claiming that women jurors would have been able to understand her act and would have been better able to assess her defense of temporary insanity. The fact that the jury was all male was not, under current constitutional doctrine, sufficient to make it unrepresentative. Defendants are not constitutionally entitled to be tried by juries that include members of their own particular class, race or gender. If a jury is chosen by an impartial, non-discriminatory procedure and no group of citizens is excluded outright, it cannot be challenged as violative of due process of law.

But the composition of Gwendolyn Hoyt's jury was not a matter of the "luck of the draw." At the time of her trial, the state of Florida gave women an automatic exemption from jury duty. Women were not forbidden to serve on juries, a responsibility that most citizens consider a rather onerous civic obligation; their names could be added to the jury lists if they registered with the clerk of the circuit court and indicated their desire to serve. At the time of Hoyt's trial only 220 women out of a total of about 46,000 registered voters had claimed their privilege to serve on juries, and of these only a few names were added to the jury list each year. In challenging her conviction Hoyt claimed that the all-male jury violated her right to due process and that there had been a systematic, discriminatory exclusion of women.

In 1961 the Supreme Court was the Warren Court, a liberal, activist Court that had already handed down the *Brown v. Board of Education* decision that outlawed school segregation by race. The Court was in the process of forcing legislative reapportionment and was beginning to supervise the administration of criminal justice in the states. Yet by a unanimous decision this Court denied Hoyt's constitutional claim, finding neither systematic exclusion of women nor a discriminatory denial of due process or equal protection in Florida's jury procedures. Justice John Marshall Harlan's opinion explained that the Florida legislature had reasonably concluded that women, rather than sitting in courthouses, should be at home with their families, and that an automatic exemption from jury service for women was therefore constitutional. Because women were still regarded as "the center of home and family life," it was not constitutionally impermissible to relieve them from a general responsibility for jury service.[1]

Two decades later, after increasingly perceptive examination of the subtleties of gender discrimination, it is clear to readers of this opinion that it contained a whole list of unexamined assumptions about women's roles and that the Court's ruling reinforced a number of classic stereotypes about female behavior. The basic premise that the opinion reflected is that women's proper place is in the home. Because women belong at the center of family life and are responsible for family maintenance and child care, the opinion assumed they should be excused from civic obligations. According to this theory, legislation that protects women and enhances their family roles is beneficial to them. Because any woman is likely to become a mother, all women can reasonably be exempted from jury service. General legislation that includes the whole group is justifiable. Law should be used to protect the family and the home and may legitimately do so by exempting women from public duties and obligations.

Issuing their ruling in 1961, the Justices did not appreciate that a case might be made for the opposite point of view. Today it is almost axiomatic that so-called protective legislation may actually burden women by treating them as inferior workers, as less competent people and citizens, and, by tying them tightly into traditional female roles, may deny them the power and the rewards of public life. By assigning all women to the private world of the family and the home, women as a group are denied the status of full citizens which they should have assumed when they gained the right to vote. In 1960 33.4 percent of the civilian labor force was female. The Court did not take judicial notice of this figure. The facts were available, but they simply were not seen as relevant. The Court and the Florida legislature defined women as they had always been defined in the traditional ideology of the family.

The Hoyt decision was handed down by a unanimous Court and was properly decided in terms of prevailing constitutional doctrine. Precedent and traditional equal protection rules dictated the result. The Court held, as it had before, that equal protection of the laws did not forbid the differential treatment of men and women as long as a rational basis for a gender classification was asserted.

Since *Hoyt v. Florida*, the Supreme Court has increasingly been confronted not only with disputes presenting claims of gender discrimination but also with legal problems that involve, as *Hoyt* itself did, the role of women in both family and society. The Justices are no longer as naive as they were a quarter of a century ago. Twenty-five years of political demands in the legislature, twenty years of litigation over equal rights and the campaign for the Equal Rights Amendment have been highly educational. Feminist lawyers and political scientists have produced increasingly sophisticated analyses of the interplay of law, family configurations and gender assignments.[2]

Even so, individual judicial decisions still reveal a great reluctance to examine traditional stereotypes about the family, even as social and economic pressures are causing monumental changes in the family itself. The law, precedents and statutes, assumes a familiar family pattern, as well as settled traditional male and female roles. Judges and justices are deeply attracted to the familiar pattern. Their own family experiences and training have created deep psychological commitments to certain family forms. In addition to personal and political convictions about what family life should be, their institutional obligation to apply time-honored legal principles colors their judgments even when these views conflict with new social facts. It is clear from facts and figures now being collected about American families that very few families actually conform to the preferred model, a model that is perhaps largely mythological.

Constitutional doctrine does not provide the Court much guidance in handling family cases, most but not all of which present claims based on equal protection or due process of law. Both of these concepts are very broad. Neither provides clear, unequivocal guidelines to constitutional decision. Because they are abstractions, they have no firm meaning of their own apart from the factual situation being evaluated. Concepts of equality and fairness are not self-defining, but require weighing and comparisons: equal to what? fair or not fair under what circumstances?

If equal protection requires no more than "equality before the law"—that existing law be applied without favor and does not require that courts ask whether the substance of the rules promotes equality—then the clause can be as much a means of perpetuating inequalities as it is a means of guaranteeing equality. Legal rules often freeze persons and things into unequal positions.[3] Equality, in a substantive sense, must always be evaluated in the context of specific social situations. The 1954 *Brown* decision is the example *par excellence* of this proposition. Segregated school systems were not perceived as blatantly unfair in the context of the nineteenth-century South, where public schools were few and closely tied to local financing and political control and the important issue was the provision of education for the Negro, not integration. But the whole underlying social situation had changed by 1954, and the national need to dismantle the Southern system of segregation raised serious constitutional questions about the retention of systems of separate, inferior schools.

Due process means procedure that is either fair or not fair in a particular context. The factual situation again determines the outcome. Proper application of both constitutional standards depends, therefore, on a realistic understanding of social facts rather than a picture of society that is biased and distorted by being viewed through outmoded stereotypes. Although the Supreme Court knows that its duty is to decide cases on the basis of constitutional principles rather than social science data, its assessments of constitutional fairness and equality will be invalid if they are not based on some degree of understanding of social facts. This does not mean that a court must undertake an independent inquiry in order to understand the underlying substance of a dispute. Most cases dealing with social issues now present some documentation in the briefs.

Just as *Brown* illustrates the relationship between constitutional doctrine and shifting social facts, so also it illustrates one of the important roles of the Supreme Court—that of a facilitator of social change. Popular institutions, charged with the task of keeping the law in tune with new conditions, are sometimes immobilized, checked, balanced, fragmented, and efforts to introduce new policies become stalled in wars between opposing forces stagnating behind permanent Maginot lines. The Supreme Court, as self-appointed guardian of the Constitution, has some responsibility in its own right for keeping legal rules in harmony with fundamental principles. In many of the great conflicts of the past, it has accepted the obligation and changed the law to bring it into line with new circumstances and perceptions. In these crucial cases, "pivotal cases" like *Brown*, it is possible to see the Court acting not as a maker of law, but as a remover of obstacles to the proper functioning of the political process. Reaching back to reinvigorating constitutional principles, the Court breaks a stalemate, cuts the Gordian knot and frees a new alignment of political forces to work out a new political solution. The initial problem is not necessarily "solved," but the terms of the conflict are redefined and the battle is resumed on different grounds.

Between 1968 and 1973, the Supreme Court decided several pivotal family cases that had this facilitating consequence, clearing away the debris of old doctrine. In all of these cases the Court overturned legal doctrines that were impeding the adjustment of law to changes already well advanced. *Levy v. Louisiana* overturned the venerable use of legitimate/illegitimate birth as a classifying device. *Roe v. Wade* restricted state power to pass criminal abortion laws and established a woman's right to limit reproduction. *Reed v. Reed* forced a reexamination of the relationship between the Equal Protection Clause and gender classifications and, for the first time, overturned a state law giving an automatic preference to males. *Stanley v. Illinois* extended some parental rights to unmarried fathers. All four of these cases had immensely important implications for family law, many of which the Justices did not immediately recognize. What the Court did, however, was to sweep away a vast amount of traditional legal doctrine, making room for arrangements more in tune with vexing social problems. The task of the Court in deciding these cases was not easy. Constitutional doctrine is not entirely congenial to family problems because it is primarily concerned with the relationship of individuals to the state. The categories of constitutional law, which assume that individuals are autonomous political persons with rights against government, do not always supply suitable solutions to family problems, where individual rights are intertwined and the family itself has a certain collective personality. In its traditional form, the family was neither an egalitarian nor a democratic institution. Its organization was hierarchical and paternalistic. It was buttressed by legal controls, but it was left to function largely independent of government. Yet in the past, even though individual families were organized along undemocratic and hierarchical lines, it was possible to fit this organism into the constitutional order because it was seen as a small government in its own right, an independent social entity intended to operate largely free from government regulation. The social programs of the last fifty years have occasioned substantial intrusions by government into the internal workings of the family itself—bringing disputes between the state and the family, and disputes among family members themselves, into the courts. But as soon as courts begin to fiddle with relationships within the family unit, to allocate rights and responsibilities to individuals (as in the abortion cases, for example, or in cases involving children's rights), the integrity of the unit is threatened and dangers of family destabilization arise. There are also unique problems in areas where family functions have been parcelled out to the state. Whose rights prevail and what constitutional standards should apply, for example, when a mother seeks to commit an uncontrollable child to a mental institution? The law seeks to solve some of these problems on a due process model, but it may not be the most useful model to use in multi-party conflicts where child, parents, professionals and the state all have linked, often conflicting interests.

The Supreme Court's family-related decisions—and these include not only gender discrimination cases but also the whole range of legal problems related to sex, reproduction, child care, marriage and divorce, custody and foster care, education and the socialization of children, legitimacy and parental rights—provide a fascinating context in which to observe the institutional interplay of law, courts, legislatures and political forces.

Adding to the complications presented by conceptual difficulties, "the family" has become a political issue. Political controversies, some with religious overtones, now rage around family concerns. Although it is clear that some of the older legal rules governing family relationships are obsolete—laws penalizing illegitimate children were ripe for reexamination by 1968—judicial modification of these rules is often seen as itself destructive, and the courts are attacked as enemies of the traditional family. Attacks made on the Court after its decision in the abortion case, *Roe v. Wade*, made the Justices more cautious, more aware of the underlying implications of their decisions for the family structure. Indeed, by this time, the family had become deeply embroiled in politics. In the "war over the family," forces representing demands for new legal and social perspectives and policies in family-related matters are arrayed against traditionalists who seek to protect and bolster familiar patterns. One side is willing to accept and accommodate change (although it is frequently unsure about the direction public policy should take); the other side wants emergency damage control to "save" the troubled family and, if possible, to turn back the clock to simpler days.

All of the Justices of the Supreme Court support the traditional family and accept the ideology supporting it, so it would be inaccurate to give them labels indicating pro- or anti-family positions. It is more accurate, perhaps, to label them tentatively as traditionalists and individualists. The traditionalists do not want to interfere with settled rules of law; they prefer to defer to state legislatures and decide cases as narrowly as possible. Even when some changes in direction are necessary, their preference is to limit the impact of change with fine distinctions and rationalizations. Within the more traditional position there are various reasons for resisting change; subgroups might be labeled ideologues, deferrers and minimalists. The individualists also look back to traditional values, but they are likely to look to theories of individual rights for doctrinal direction, rather than to the family ideology. Several of the Justices approach new social problems pragmatically and, at least in some types of situations, are willing to begin the task of adjusting constitutional doctrine and redefining it to develop orderly avenues along which changes can occur. But differences among the Justices are subtle, and there is a great deal of basic agreement on the Court about what families should be and do, and none of the Justices strays too far from the traditional ideology.

The chapters that follow examine a number of the more familiar Supreme Court decisions that deal with matters relating to families. This analysis shows that there is a well-defined *ideology* of the family that has been stated in opinion after opinion, in a line of decisions stretching back to 1888. It is an ideology because it is a consistent and well-articulated set of principles that defines the kind of family recognized by our law and outlines the relationships that are expected to exist within the family. It is also clear that the Court does not always scrutinize family relationships with a cool, neutral and unbiased eye, but frequently bases its decisions on stereotypical views of what the Justices think the family should be like. Use of the term *stereotype* here indicates a cognitive function. The Justices, looking at real men, women and children through lenses colored by the traditional ideology, often see, not surprisingly, what they expect to see.

But can it be demonstrated that this ideology actually affects decision-making? One of the theses developed in this book is that there is perhaps more resistance to introspection and self-awareness in this area of law than in others. Unlike political and economic biases that can be identified and discounted, preferences for particular family forms touch very deep psychological currents and do not easily lend themselves to inspection. Failure to recognize conflicts and to understand the nature of these conflicts often prevents clear analysis and allows unexamined assumptions to creep undetected into the decision-making process. Although it is not always possible to demonstrate how such a subtle set of influences affects decisions, it is easy to show that the opinions often use language that indicates where the preferences lie. It is also possible to demonstrate that many of the opinions fail to examine the underlying assumptions that appear to be involved in the reasoning. And it is possible to show that some of the Justices are more willing than others to look at facts presented by the parties which contradict the traditional assumptions about family life. The language in three cases in particular, *Wisconsin v. Yoder*, *Carey v. Population Services* and *Moore v. City of East Cleveland*, reveals the decisional motivation of the Justices.

In the chapters that follow, I hope to show that, although many of the specific decisions appear to be based on constitutional principles—equal protection, due process, the right to privacy, freedom of religion—the Court often uses these doctrines to protect a different fundamental value—a traditional ideal of the American family that no longer characterizes the reality of what family life often means in the United States of America today.

1

The Ideology of the Family

We are told about the world before we see it. We imagine most things before we experience them. And these preconceptions, unless education has made us acutely aware, govern deeply the whole process of perception.

Walter Lippmann[1]

The ideology of the family may be what holds it together.

Judith Mitchell[2]

In recent years the Supreme Court of the United States has been inundated with social and family issues. It has been forced to decide cases dealing with sex, marriage, living arrangements, abortion, contraception, conflicts between parents and their children, and allied matters.[3] For the Court to handle the constitutional issues in this area has proved difficult—in part, perhaps, because the Justices, like other federal judges, are inexperienced in family law, but at least as much because this is an area where it is very hard to avoid accepting stereotyped views of men's and women's roles and the nature of the family, and to look objectively at such matters as marriage, procreation and sexual standards.

Most people have strong beliefs about the family, what it is and what it should be, because they have been thoroughly accustomed to accept traditional and familiar arrangements as inherent in the institution. The Justices of the Supreme Court, aware that personal beliefs and prejudices influence decision-making, try to avoid reading their personal predilections into the law, but attitudes and emotions about this family realm are rooted in such unconscious layers of the mind that it has been particularly difficult for them to recognize their own hidden biases.

Although family-related cases on the Court's docket present legal and constitutional problems, they also provide a sampling of the social problems generated by major changes taking place in the structure of American life in a time of "cultural disintegration and social transformation." If, as Arthur S. Miller has remarked, "law is only a memorandum," legal rules incorporate the formulas for handling conflicts that society accepts at any given time.[4] In order to provide a basis for handling conflicts effectively, however, the solutions that the law offers must be relevant to society's real problems and give answers in line with contemporary expectations. When the older, traditional solutions contained in the law are no longer acceptable to society at large, legislatures and courts must change or reinterpret the legal rules. There has been very rapid change in family life and in standards of personal behavior in the last forty years, but as yet no consensus has been reached as to what is happening, where we are going or what we are ready to accept as the norm. The traditional rules covering many social relationships no longer reflect settled patterns of behavior, and, as one might expect, conflicts between what the law posits and the way people actually behave frequently end up in the courts.

State law has always regulated the basic patterns of marriage, divorce, sex, morality and even some aspects of child-rearing and living arrangements, although there has also been an unspoken agreement that the state should leave some things to private negotiation and not intrude too deeply behind the domestic curtain. The old rules favor the family as a social and economic unit. But the basic fact is that the role of the family in American society today is in flux.

Until recently federal courts have stayed largely out of family law. But two developments have operated to change this situation. The promulgation by the federal government of comprehensive social welfare programs affecting the family (such programs as social security, food stamps, AFDC—Aid to Families with Dependent Children) has forced federal courts to decide statutory and administrative law questions that have great impact on family structure and functioning. Provisions of federal tax law such as deductions for dependents and joint returns for married couples also affect families significantly even though they are not aimed directly at family issues.

The second development has been the elaboration of constitutional law in the areas of due process, equal protection and the right to privacy. *Brown v. Board of Education* opened the possibility of attacks on family laws under the Equal Protection Clause,[5] first in racially related cases like *Loving v. Virginia* (interracial marriage)[6] and then in challenges to classifications other than race in such cases as *Levy v. Louisiana* (illegitimacy).[7] The articulation of a right to privacy in *Griswold v. Connecticut* laid the basis for an attack on state abortion laws and state laws regulating sexual practices.[8] Due process requirements of procedural regularity have been gradually extended to deprivations of new kinds of property, such as entitlements to welfare payments,[9] and have been held to require high standards of care in child custody and parental rights hearings and commitments to mental and correctional institutions.[10] The concept of substantive due process was revived by *Griswold* and *Roe v. Wade*, where several of the Justices asserted that rights to reproductive choice were fundamental personal liberties protected from unnecessary governmental intrusion by the Constitution.[11] Due process requirements that state legislation be rational, reasonable, neither arbitrary nor capricious, and necessary and appropriate for the public welfare[12] supply litigants with a means to challenge some of the more obsolete state regulations as well as some of the newer statutes which are supposed, in theory, to preserve or restore traditional family patterns.[13]

Since *Brown*, too, groups who find the state legislatures inhospitable to their demands for change have resorted more and more frequently to litigation as the best means of attacking obsolescent state policies. The National Association for the Advancement of Colored People (NAACP) and the American Civil Liberties Union, among other organizations, actively supported court challenges to state miscegenation laws and legitimacy/illegitimacy classifications. Between 1943 and 1968, Planned Parenthood brought a series of cases attacking state statutes restricting the sale and use of contraceptives and finally succeeded in overturning one of them in *Griswold v. Connecticut*.[14] Women's groups mounted dozens of assaults on criminal abortion laws during the late 1960s and early 1970s and won a major victory in 1973 in *Roe v. Wade*, which legalized early abortions.[15] Welfare rights organizations such as the Mobilization for Youth (MFY) and the National Welfare Rights Organization (NWRO) began to use the courts to question state and federal regulations that intruded oppressively on the living patterns of people on public assistance, and succeeded in getting judicial decisions that modified some of the more objectionable practices.[16] Success in landmark cases such as these encouraged other organizations to use the courts rather than take the legislative route to law reform.

Once the doctrinal bases for constitutional challenges had been established, it was inevitable that increasing numbers of family-related cases would appear on the appellate dockets of the Supreme Court. Not surprisingly, the Supreme Court has been as hesitant about overturning laws that represent long-accepted legal compromises as have state courts and state legislatures, even where outmoded patterns of legal regulation provide so loose a fit with the facts that they have become basically unfair. The Court has never been reluctant to extend constitutional protections to the family; the problems have come in deciding what kind of creature this constitutionally protected family is.

Textbooks on sociology delineate the model of the conventional family that has been dominant since the mid-nineteenth century. The following description, accepted both by lay persons and by social scientists, is taken from Arlene and Jerome Skolnick's *Family in Transition*, published in 1971. The popular stereotype, as these scholars depict it, contains these propositions:

1. The nuclear family—a man, a woman and their children—is universally found in every human society, past, present and future.

2. The nuclear family is the building block of society. Larger group-ings—the extended family, the clan, the society—are combinations of nuclear families.

3. The nuclear family is based on a clear-cut, biologically structured division of labor between men and women, with the man playing the "instrumental" role of breadwinner, provider and protector, and the woman playing the "expressive" role of housekeeper and emo-tional mainstay.

4. A major "function" of the family is to socialize children; that is, to tame their impulses and instill values, skills, and desires necessary to run the society.

5. Unusual family structures, such as mother and children, or the ex-perimental commune, are regarded as deviant by the participants, as well as the rest of the society, and are fundamentally unstable and unworkable.[17]

This family type is as much an ideal, an idea of what ought to be, as it is a description of existing reality, past or present. It is part of a system of beliefs about male and female roles, about the correct relationships between men and women, parents and children, as well as about the structure and functions of family units, and it represents a vision of the family that developed and matured in the nineteenth century. Alexis de Tocqueville saw, or thought he saw, this model of family life when he made his tour of the United States in 1831–1832. He called it the "dem-ocratic" family and found that it differed in important ways from the "aristocratic" family of Europe, a genus that emphasized lineage and duty to the family's future and deemphasized the individual. In American families, the nuclear unit was more important than the family line. Choice of partners and romantic love made for more amicable relations between men and women, but men and women still inhabited separate spheres. Men were oriented toward the public world of commerce and government; women belonged in the home. Morality belonged in the female world, a realm protected from exposure to the crude practices of the marketplace. The parts that women played were impor-tant, and American women were strong, chaste, virtuous, in-dependent and energetic, but they played supporting rather than leading roles. Men were no longer the civil rulers, kings, judges and priests of their clans as they were in Europe; here the male was primarily the economic provider. But even though authority within the family was less stern, and relationships between fathers and sons more democratic and affectionate, the father was still the head of the family.[18]

The decisions of the Supreme Court, when they touch on family matters at all, articulate a family ideology that embodies many of these principles. In the early years only a few family decisions, as such, came to the Court, but taken together they present a well-articulated picture of the traditional family taken from common law doctrines, American legal writers, dominant Protestant ideology and American popular thought. The classic Supreme Court cases dealing with the family, beginning with *Reynolds v. United States* in 1878, *Maynard v. Hill* in 1888 and *Meyer v. Nebraska* and *Pierce v. Society of Sisters* in the 1920s emphasize a cluster of basic principles drawn from legal writers such as William Blackstone, James Kent and Thomas M. Cooley as well as from the Court's perception of the essential nature of American family life.[19] The family accepted by the Supreme Court in these early cases is clearly the ideal Victorian family. The family unit is a small government in its own right, authoritarian and paternalistic, with women and children in a subordinate position. The rearing and education of children is its most important function. Although wives and mothers are respected and should be consulted on family matters, there is little internal democracy. Parents speak and act for children, discipline them and determine what their education will be. Families educate and socialize children. When families fail, it is not surprising to find that the children turn out badly, turning to antisocial behavior and ultimately to crime.

Individual cases illustrate the special characteristics of American families. In the *Reynolds* case, upholding the conviction of Mormons for bigamy against a claim of religious freedom, the Supreme Court told us that the family in our law is the monogamous family of Western Europe, not the polygamous or tribal family of Africa or Asia.[20] Other cases elaborate the basic ideology of the family. The family unit is the basic institution of Western society. It is formed by marriage, and it is within the union so arrived at that sexual activity, procreation and child-bearing take place. The rights to marry and have children are basic rights of man. "We are dealing here with legislation which involves one of the basic civil rights of man. Marriage and pro-creation are fundamental to the very existence of the race."[21]

The institution of marriage creates a private realm which the state should not enter.[22] Privacy includes the right to make pri-vate choices free from state interference; private choices include the decision to have children, but also decisions to use contra-ceptives or to have abortions if children are not wanted. The state may not act to deprive persons of the right to marry or to take away their ability to have children, nor may it forbid the use of contraceptives or abortion.[23] The private realm of family government has never been thought of as entirely immune from state regulation. The state has always laid down the basic rules for family formation by regulating marriage and divorce, and has checked family power by passing laws requiring that chil-dren be supported and educated and that other traditional duties of the family be carried out. But except where indigent families are concerned, it has had little reason to interfere in the internal management of family life, barring criminal abuse or failure to perform basic responsibilities. The principle of non-interference in what goes on behind the "domestic curtain" is well estab-lished. An early North Carolina decision supporting husbands' prerogatives to beat their wives in order to maintain order and authority in the home describes this principle:

. . . family government is recognized by law as being complete in itself as the state government is in itself, and yet subordinate to it; and that we will not interfere with or attempt to control it in favor of either husband or wife, unless in cases where permanent or malicious injury is inflicted or threatened or the condition of the party is intolerable. For however great are the evils of ill temper, quarrels, and even personal conflicts inflicting only temporary pain, they are not comparable with the evils which would result from raising the curtain and exposing to public curiosity and criticism the nursery and the bed chamber. Every household has and must have a government of its own, modeled to suit the temper, disposition and condition of its inmates.[24]

Sometimes the Justices have waxed lyrical about marriage and the family, institutions that seem to take on an almost mystical aura as they are described in the opinions of the Court. An early opinion caroled about "the foundation of the family and society, without which there would be neither civilization or progress."[25] Justice William O. Douglas' opinion in *Griswold v. Connecticut* is a virtual hymn to marriage, which he describes as "a coming together for better or for worse, hopefully enduring, and intimate to the degree of being sacred. It is an association that promotes a way of life, not causes; a harmony of living, not political faiths; a bilateral loyalty, not commercial or social projects. Yet it is an association for as noble a purpose as any involved in our prior decisions."[26]

The Supreme Court also accepts the proposition that the primary function of marriage and family life is the bearing and raising of children. The home derives its preeminence from the part it plays as the abode of the family.[27] The individual has a right to marry and establish a home in order to bring up children. Parents have the responsibility for raising and educating their children, and this responsibility brings with it the power to control the children's actions. Writing for the majority in a case dealing with the rights of minor children to contest their parents' decision to commit them to mental hospitals, Chief Justice Warren E. Burger repeated the emphases of earlier cases on parental responsibility and control. Our jurisprudence, he wrote, accepts Western civilization's view of the family as having broad authority over minor children. The family has the "high duty" to prepare children for their responsibilities in society, to "socialize" them. The parents have this extensive authority over the child because they have what he or she lacks, "the maturity, experience, and capacity for making life's difficult decisions."[28]

Raising children is a private, family matter, not a communal task. Although government does have power to step in and protect children when parents abuse their authority, the Court has explicitly rejected the idea that the state can ever replace the family. In *Meyer v. Nebraska*, Justice James C. McReynolds criticized Plato's utopian state for taking the control of children away from their parents.[29] There are limits to what the state can do to foster citizenship. The "statist notion" that government should supersede parental authority because some parents act wrongly is repugnant to American tradition. Even though there are aberrant parents who abuse or neglect their offspring, parents usually act in the best interest of their children. The family is the ideal place for the socialization of children. But the state is deeply concerned with the manner in which families fulfill their responsibilities because they are producing potential citizens, teaching them morality and religion, training them for work and preparing them to function in society.

The perception of women's roles that dominated judicial thinking until fairly recently also derives from American middle-class Protestant thinking. The world of work and the world of domesticity are separate spheres. Women belong in the domestic world, where they exercise moral leadership and exert a civilizing influence on men. They should be socialized to accept their proper function as that of caring for a good husband, providing domestic tranquility and bearing, nurturing and instructing children. The common law subordinated the married woman to her husband. Popular American Protestant thought placed her in the home and sentimentalized her role as wife and mother.[30] In this setting, the home is envisioned as a walled garden, an inner sanctuary presided over by a loving, selfless mother who soothes and comforts those who have returned to the garden after venturing into the cruel, outside world.[31] If the mother dominates the home, however, she does not do it by right or legal position, but because of the power of love. She does not need equality of rights, because her husband will protect her. It does not matter that she cannot vote, join the professions or occupy an equal place in the economic system. She is not suited for the turmoil of public affairs; her domain is the domestic world. Since *Reed v. Reed*, in 1971, the Justices have moved away from the view of woman's role which this ideology accepts, but the traditional view can be seen in earlier cases such as *Bradwell v. Illinois* and *Minor v. Happersett*.[32]

The traditional family is a kinship group and is connected by ties of blood and marriage. It is monogamous, based on a male-female pair, although the concept of family is broad enough to include relatives and in-laws.[33] Natural families that have not formalized their relationships by marriage still have some constitutionally protected rights. The parents of illegitimate children may have ties with their offspring which are "warm, enduring and important." The state may not disregard these family ties but should try to strengthen them whenever possible; it should not remove children from the custody of fit parents, although it may take children away from unfit parents. The right of the natural parent to the companionship and care of his or her child is a fundamental right protected by the Constitution. Unrelated individuals or foster families, although they may perform some basic family functions, are not in the same position as natural families. Surrogate parents and foster parents have an important service to perform, but their interests are not protected as fully as ties to the natural family.[34]

Even though most families perform their tasks well, the Court has recognized that not all families measure up to the ideal and that family life may have a darker side. Parents may neglect or abuse children, or may fail to provide proper homes for them because of poverty or illness.[35] It has always been accepted that the state may legislate to protect children and may even intervene in family affairs in the child's best interests.[36]

This, then, is the basic ideology of the family which lies behind many of the Supreme Court's domestic relations decisions. The family is monogamous, marital, a sacred, private relationship, a small government within the larger social unit of the state, paternalistic, patrilineal, justified by its primary function of procreation and the raising, socializing and education of the children.

Five of the Justices sitting on the supreme bench in 1985 were born between 1906 and 1908. The younger Justices fall into two groups. Justice Potter Stewart, who retired in 1982, was born in 1915 and Justice Byron White in 1917. Justices John Paul Stevens, William Rehnquist and Sandra Day O'Connor were born in the 1920s. All of the Justices have middle- or upper-middle-class backgrounds and were trained and educated in the society that existed before World War II. They have come to the Court with much of the classic family ideology firmly in place and view the changes that have been revolutionizing family relationships through the lenses of these traditional stereotypes. It is not surprising to find that their preconceptions about what family life should be often appear to influence their decisions.

Patterns of living that may have seemed settled and immutable to persons growing up in the 1930s and 1940s have now begun to shift and reform in subtle ways. To many observers these changes in style, organization and function represent threats to "the family" itself. There is very little agreement about where many of these changes are leading us. But if there is agreement on little else, there is substantial agreement among all observers that the American family is undergoing significant change.

Concern about the viability of the family is nothing new; as Christopher Lasch put it in his book *Haven in a Heartless World: The Family Besieged* (1977), "the family has been slowly coming apart for more than 100 years."[37] After a relatively stable period between 1900 and 1950, family structure and the role of the family in society have been changing very rapidly. According to demographic historian Edward Shorter, the two biggest changes are loss of control over children and the weakening of the couple; " . . . the reshaping of the family currently underway has two main components; an inherent instability of the couple itself and a loss of control by parents over adolescent children."[38] These are big, visible changes. Marriage is becoming less stable, and parents are finding it increasingly difficult to maintain authority over older children, especially over their sexual activities. An additional factor affecting family life in important ways is the drift of women out of the home into paid employment.[39] The sociologists and the census reports fill out some of the details of these developments. Some of the changes and a few of the pressing social problems stemming from or related to these changes are detailed in a 1984–1985 report of Family Service America, the headquarters for a number of local family service agencies. The report notes that:

1. The traditional nuclear family with the husband working to support his dependent wife and children has become the exception rather than the rule and is now typical of fewer than 10 percent of all households.

2. Marriage patterns have been changing. Although 90 percent of all Americans still marry, the marriage rate is dropping. Divorce and remarriage are becoming part of a typical pattern of serial marriage. The divorce rate for first marriages is between 40 and 50 percent.

3. The number of working women is increasing, and if trends continue, men and women will soon be in the labor force in equal numbers. Married women including those with young children are now more likely than not to be employed. With increased educational opportunities available, the number of women in professional and technical jobs is increasing.

4. There has been a consistent upward trend in out-of-wedlock births, in part because of the decrease in births legitimated by marriage. Teenage births now comprise a large proportion of total births. The rate of births to unmarried black women is now more than five times greater than the rate of births to unwed white women, although this gap is now beginning to close.

5. The proportion of one-parent families has almost doubled since 1970. Divorce and out-of-wedlock child-bearing have increased the number of families headed by females, and there is a high incidence of poverty among female-headed families. There has been a phenomenal increase in the number of one-parent families headed by unwed women.

6. There are other changes in family patterns and life styles in addition to the increase in unwed single-parent families. With the loosening of religious, social and legal taboos, cohabitation has increased, as have homosexual partnerships and single-person households.

7. Population changes affect family relationships. The population is growing at a slower rate; it is also aging, and the children born in the ''baby boom'' of the 1950s and 1960s are now approaching middle age. There are a number of geographical shifts. Population is shifting geographically from the North and Midwest to the South and West, from cities to suburbs and is increasingly mobile.

8. Many social and technological changes are having a direct impact on family structure. These include such things as medical technology that allows artificial insemination, in vitro fertilization and heart transplants, makes it possible to save premature babies and those with severe birth defects, and increases the life expectancy of adults. New methods of blood testing allow the accurate determination of paternity. Television, computerization and other innovations work both direct and indirect, drastic and subtle, changes on society and on the family unit.[40]

Not only are family forms changing, but so are basic family functions. Some of these have been delegated or abdicated to other social institutions, especially to governmental entities. Harry

D. Krause, one of the leading scholars in the family law field, has attempted to enumerate the important social functions which marriage and the family fulfill. According to his listing, they provide (a) an orderly setting for sexual activity, (b) stable circumstances for procreation, and (c) an agency for the socialization of children, (d) companionship and psychological support for the couple, and (e) rudimentary economic security which permits role division (for child-raising and homemaking), and (f) economic security for old age.[41] Yet it is clear that even traditional families often fail to perform many of these assignments.

Family units do not exist in isolation but are parts of an intricate, interrelated social system. As the forms and functions of families have evolved, some of the social controls that once reinforced a particular family model have become inappropriate, unworkable, no longer rationally related to newer conditions. Many of the older controls were imposed by custom and by the community or by the churches rather than by government, although these institutions were themselves supported and bolstered by the law. State support for marriage and strict control over divorce, church and community disapproval of both divorce and extramarital sex reinforced each other, encouraged family formation and discouraged marital breakdown. Now changes in the law have made divorce easily available, and although public opinion and religious institutions generally disapprove of extramarital sex, there are countervailing influences, especially in the media and the world of entertainment which advertise it as a positive value. Although in some states adultery and fornication are still crimes "on the books," such statutes are rarely enforced and have in effect been repealed by disuse.[42] At one time, strong sanctions in these areas were necessary if women were to be kept psychologically and economically dependent, with reproduction and mothering as their primary roles. Fear of pregnancy also deterred women of all ages from engaging in unmarried sexual relations, and laws forbidding contraception and abortion were accepted, in part, because it was feared that the ability to control reproduction would loosen these inhibitions. Because reproduction was seen as a function of the family, it was not surprising to see sanctions of various kinds placed on unmarried motherhood and penalties and disabilities on illegitimate children. Preferential treatment of legitimate children was thought necessary to protect legal families, and the law offered little protection to the children of unmarried parents.[43]

The fact that women's access to higher education was limited and their place in the workforce low in status also encouraged them to stay in the home. For lower income families this was often not possible; black and immigrant women and other women from marginal economic groups were routinely forced to work by economic necessity, and in fact were expected to take low-paying jobs as domestics and menial workers even if it meant leaving dependent children.

Many of the supports that buttressed the family are now being relaxed. Reproduction can now be regulated by contraception and abortion, freeing women to leave the home and take jobs. Guarantees of equal employment opportunity have increased access to all parts of the working world, and promises of equal pay have made jobs outside of the home more desirable. The increasing entry of women into the workforce has accelerated change in the traditional patterns of family life. Although it is not clear that employment outside the home itself increases the possibility of divorce, it is clear that economic self-sufficiency makes divorce possible, that employed women are more likely to divorce and that the decreasing dependency on the male often allows him to justify his leaving the family. The new economic freedom also allows women to desert their families, and run-away wives are a new social phenomenon.[44]

Teenage sexual activity, a topic that is another matter of intense public concern, is also tied into the changing role of the family. The nuclear family unit, with the husband in a position of dominance, was responsible for support and education of the children and was able to exercise some control over their sexuality as well as to supervise their marriages. Teenagers today are socialized as much by their peers as by their families, and are much freer from rigid parental control than their counterparts in the past.[45] In addition, a bewildering array of governmental programs, policies and services affect adolescents directly, and experts of all kinds offer specialized advice and support that sometimes conflicts and undercuts family authority.[46]

In the opinion of many people, government, instead of protecting and promoting a preferred style of family living, has been a prime cause of the instability of the family unit. Although reforms in the law of marriage and divorce have been enacted in response to popular demand, there is also a widespread fear that the removal of these legal supports to marital regularity fatally undermines traditional family life. Some people also believe that by proliferating services to families and individuals in families, government itself has undermined family cohesion. The courts have been blamed for chipping away at the cement that holds families together by requiring improvement in the status of women, and by emphasizing individual rights in various family settings. The Supreme Court's involvement with these problems has been at the outer edges of family law. The greater part of this subject matter is still the responsibility of state legislatures and state courts. But the cases that do raise constitutional (or federal statutory) questions, even though they appear in a haphazard order, manage to provide a fairly representative sample of the problems that are afflicting contemporary families. Groups of cases cluster about three subjects in particular: illegitimacy, reproductive control and the treatment of pregnant women in the workforce. All three of these areas are related to the two key developments isolated by Edward Shorter: the coming apart of the couple and the family's loss of control of its adolescents.

In 1968, in one of its first major incursions into the area of family relationships, the Supreme Court began a reexamination of the venerable legal rules on illegitimacy that impose disabilities on non-marital children and to reexamine the claim that these rules strengthen the family and deter promiscuous sexual activity. In this category of cases, the Supreme Court was asked to decide whether it was still constitutionally permissible to use legal classifications based on illegitimacy, given the fact that they were of little use in protecting the traditional family, but had a whole range of deleterious side effects.

The abortion decision handed down in 1973 is perhaps the central family issue because it is related at so many points to the internal structure of the family. It is difficult for women to achieve political and social equality unless they can regulate and control reproduction, but assumption of reproductive control threatens many traditional family arrangements. This decision became a focal point for conservative opposition to the many kinds of changes taking place in family life.

A third sequence of cases involved the employment rules that restricted pregnant women in the workforce—sending them home on mandatory maternity leave until their children were a certain age, or denying them benefits under employee disability plans. These rules were challenged as involving a subtle form of sex discrimination contributing to the inequality of pay and benefits for working women. They also represented certain assumptions about the roles of women which were becoming obsolete. In these cases the Justices had a hard time detaching themselves from the traditional stereotypes about women at work and about pregnant women generally.

In another group of cases the Court examined laws that seek to curb the sexual activity of the young: controls on the availability of contraceptives, laws requiring parental notification before minors can have abortions and statutory rape statutes that impose criminal penalties on persons having sexual relations with minors. In most of these cases the Court was willing to defer to legislative solutions which were at an arm's length relationship with reality, rather than trying to make neutral appraisals of the actual impact of legislation and whether it was rationally related to any goal the legislature might sensibly adopt. Massive increases in the number of unmarried teenagers having babies were, for example, a legitimate cause of public concern over teenage sexual activity but it was at best questionable to try to cope with pregnancy and the birth of illegitimate children by denying access to contraception and abortion.

A number of other cases touched on family issues: schooling and religious education, custody, the termination of parental rights and the involuntary commitment of children to mental institutions. Claims to family protection by new quasi-family forms also began to seek a hearing by the Supreme Court.

Many of these cases involved problems of due process or equal protection, or both. Others anchored their claims in other sections of the Constitution. But all of these subjects brought before the Justices, in the guise of constitutional conflicts, clashes between traditional rules and values and the changes that are taking place in American families.

2

Legitimacy and Illegitimacy

"Why Bastard, Wherefore Base?"

King Lear, Act I, Scene 2[1]

Family law has traditionally been the domain of state government. When the Constitution was written, it was the common understanding that the states, not the federal government, would regulate domestic relations. None of the powers granted the central government was regarded as conferring any authority on Congress to invade a realm that had always been regulated by state law.[2] State laws did and still do regulate the structure of family life: marriage, divorce, abortion, contraception, sterilization, legitimacy, illegitimacy, child abuse, adoption, custody arrangements, child support, inheritance and so forth. The sprinkling of early decisions in the Supreme Court Reports that touch on this area of the law are designed to demonstrate that the concept of liberty enunciated in the Fourteenth Amendment protects individual, almost "natural" rights, to marry, conceive, raise and educate children, form family relationships and retain a modicum of marital privacy. But beginning in 1968, the Supreme Court has made a deep and comprehensive incursion into one aspect of family law, in effect federalizing the whole law of illegitimacy.[3]

The Law of Bastardy, as it is still called in some states, is older than the nuclear family; it is medieval and feudal in origin. Under the old English common law, the illegitimate child was *filius nullius*, the child of no one, and because it was born outside the legally recognized family constellation, it was denied the rights that derived from the family relationship. The legitimate child had a right to the family name, could inherit property and had a right to food and education. The bastard could not inherit from his father or use his name and had no legal relationship to his mother. Neither parent had a right to custody or the guardianship of such children.[4] In medieval society, the incapacity to inherit was the most important legal consequence of this status.

The act of marriage obligated parents to feed and support their legitimate children, but at common law the "putative father," as he is designated, had no duty to maintain his bastard children.[5] The problem of support for illegitimate children as well as for foundlings and abandoned children became a public issue after the passage of the English Poor Laws in the sixteenth and seventeenth centuries, when responsibility for their support fell on the parish. The parish authorities on whom this burden descended were, of course, anxious to shift part of the cost of supporting bastards back onto the natural parents.[6] In later centuries, various statutes allowed the mother, after a "filiation" hearing, to seek payment of a weekly sum for the maintenance of the child.

American law generally followed the English pattern in placing some disabilities on illegitimate children, although marriage generally legitimated children already born to the couple, a deviation from English law. The egalitarian spirit of the New World influenced the treatment of children of irregular marriages. Virginia passed a statute drafted by Thomas Jefferson in 1785 making the children of any marriage, valid or not, legitimate, and at least twenty-five states picked up and followed this early lead.[7] The treatment of legitimacy and illegitimacy varied from state to state, with most states retaining rules based on the common law. In 1921 Arizona declared all children to be legitimate children of their natural parents, entitled to support and education, but such reforms were unusual. As late as 1973, Texas still denied an illegitimate child the right to claim support from his natural father.[8] Statutes more generally allowed an unwed mother to claim support after an adjudication of paternity. But it also seems to be true that as the law moved toward treating non-marital children more liberally, the process of claiming paternity, or "filiation," was made more difficult.[9] Improvements in blood-testing procedures and other scientific means of determining paternity have now made complicated legal battles over this factual issue irrelevant. The law governing illegitimacy has, however, been slow to change, and state law is often a jumble of archaic and inconsistent rules.[10]

Modern students of family law are generally in favor of doing away with the label of illegitimacy as such, of considering all children as legitimate and of changing the focus of the problem from "labeling" the children, to making sure that all children have adequate levels of care. Certainly, giving children the status of illegitimates even when they have on-going family ties to their biological fathers is no longer acceptable public policy, for it harms the children psychologically and weakens rather than promotes family ties.

The concern underlying proposals to discard the label of illegitimacy is partly fair treatment of the children involved, who have had no choice in their birth status, but it is also partly a matter of pressing public policy. It was becoming increasingly clear by mid-century that the use of legitimate birth as a basis for allocating legal rights and benefits raised serious social problems; the distinction was not only punitive but it was basically unjust, for it could be used to deny a child rights or public benefits because of a condition that was not his or her fault. It is also psychologically damaging to a child to be labeled illegitimate. The burdens of this kind of classification fall unevenly; because of different marriage patterns among the poor and the black, legitimacy classifications are in some situations almost racial classifications. In the past, welfare programs often denied necessary help to non-marital children because their mothers were "immoral." Many welfare rules were used, at least in part, to control or punish the mother's sexual conduct and incidentally punished the child also.[11] Acceptance of common law marriage once alleviated some of the harshness of the law, for the children of stable, non-marital relationships were recognized as legitimate. Today, only one-fourth of the states recognize common law marriage; abolition of this traditional institution has, in effect, increased illegitimacy.[12]

But in addition to the concern about labeling children, there is also a growing problem of public policy in the area of child support.[13] Illegitimate children are not the only children who end up on the AFDC rolls; divorcing and deserting parents also have had a major part to play in the increasing number of single-parent families, usually headed by women, that have had to turn to public agencies for support. When added to the crisis caused by parental desertion and post-divorce child support failures, the rising rate of illegitimacy has caused the burden on the public of supporting dependent children to become acute. At least one expert argues that if child abandonment and illegitimacy continue to increase at present rates, the welfare system will break down completely.[14]

By 1968, the date of *Levy v. Louisiana*, the first major Supreme Court ruling on this subject, it was clear that illegitimate births were increasing. In 1950, 4.0 percent of all births were illegitimate; in 1978, 16.3 percent of all births were out-of-wedlock. Mothers under fifteen years of age numbered about 3,200 in 1950, but the number had risen to 9,400 in 1978. Mothers in the teenage bracket, fifteen to nineteen, rose from 56,000 in 1950 to 239,000 in 1978. The teenage pregnancy problem was particularly visible because of the declining fertility in older women, the increasing reluctance by teenagers to marry and the greater inclination of this group to keep their babies rather than put them up for adoption. The increase in illegitimacy was especially striking among minority groups. By 1967, 29.4 percent of live births for blacks and 4.9 percent of live births for whites were illegitimate; this was a substantial increase from the 1950 figure, when 1.7 percent of all births to white women and 16.8 percent of all births to black women were out-of-wedlock. By 1979, 9.4 percent of all white births and 48.8 percent of all black births were illegitimate.[15]

Family law in this country is middle-class law and does not

always meet the practical realities of situations in which the poor live, and state laws requiring formal marriage penalize minorities more heavily than segments of the majority.[16] A case can even be made for the proposition that the application of the traditional rules of marriage inevitably produces class and race discrimination. Because patterns of marriage are so different, classifications by legitimacy/illegitimacy approximate racial classifications, with the prevailing law denying one-fourth of all black children legal relationships with their biological fathers.[17] This is true even when the father lives with and supports the mother and child.

With increasing rates of illegitimacy and a greater number of divorces, separations and desertions, the single parent family headed by a female has become increasingly visible as a category meriting special concern. There was a sharp increase in these families between 1970 and 1980, from 9 percent to 12 percent for whites and from 28 percent to 40 percent for blacks. In 1983 an estimated 11.4 million children lived with their mothers only. Female-headed families were among the most economically vulnerable; the median income of these families was about 45 percent of that of married-couple families.[18]

Poor women with children have always been among the most poverty stricken in society and most in need of government aid for themselves and their families, but these women frequently have been penalized by rules that deny them welfare, housing and other forms of support. Females with children born outside of wedlock have been punished in many ways, and the children have been stigmatized, even taken from their mothers because of their illegitimate status. Recent feminist writers have directed attention to the view that discriminatory treatment of the nonmarital child is also sexist in that it promotes a patriarchal concept of society in which legitimacy and status derive from the dominant male. Karen De Crow, a former president of the National Organization for Women has written, "Our society can't seem to make up its mind about motherhood. Women have been persecuted and died, for generations, in trying to terminate unwanted pregnancies. Women who do have their babies are also punished."[19]

CHANGING THE LABELS

In 1968, using the Equal Protection Clause, the Court over-turned the use of an illegitimacy classification. Since the land-mark *Levy* case, the Justices have handed down over twenty related decisions.[20] The Court's performance has not always been entirely consistent nor its doctrines clearly articulated; in fact, Gerald Gunther once called this course of decision "unpredict-able," "inarticulate," "uneasy," "zigzag, or (to put it mildly) a wavering one."[21]

On first glance the decisions do seem to be wildly inconsistent, with about half of them overturning illegitimacy classifications on the grounds that they deny equal protection of the laws, and the other half sustaining such distinctions as an appropriate basis for provisions in both federal and state statutes.[22] But while there is not a clear, conscious, well-articulated theoretical basis to these decisions, there is both direction and cautious incremental change.

Levy v. Louisiana, and several later cases, *Stanley v. Illinois*, *Caban v. Mohammad*, *Quilloin v. Walcott*, *Parham v. Hughes* and *Lehr v. Robertson*,[23] illustrate some of the assumptions and some of the uncertainty with which the Supreme Court has ap-proached legal distinctions based on legitimacy and marital status.

In *Levy v. Louisiana* (1968) the U.S. Supreme Court overturned a Louisiana statute which denied illegitimate children the right to recover for the wrongful death of their mother, a right that legitimate children were accorded. The mother in this case was a domestic worker who had been misdiagnosed and incorrectly treated at Charity Hospital in New Orleans and who subse-quently died.[24] The children had been living with their mother and were dependent on her for support. They brought suit for her loss in the state courts, but the case was dismissed on the grounds that illegitimate children could not bring this action. The Louisiana Court of Appeal affirmed, holding that "child" in the article of the Louisiana Code providing for such suits meant "legitimate child," and that the denial to illegitimate chil-dren of the right to recover was based on the general welfare and promoted morality by discouraging the bringing of children into the world out-of-wedlock.[25] The Supreme Court of Louisiana denied *certiorari*.

By a 6 to 3 vote, the Supreme Court reversed the state courts, holding that such a statute denied the children equal protection of the laws. In his opinion for the Court, Justice William O. Douglas emphasized that there are no clearly discernible differences between illegitimate children and other persons. These children are, or will be, subject to the responsibilities that all other citizens have to pay taxes, serve in the armed services and perform other civic duties. By claiming the right to recover for the wrongful death of their biological mother, they are asking the law to allow them to claim reimbursement for the loss of their source of nurturing, food and shelter and family life. There is no rational basis for denying them the right to make this claim merely because they are illegitimate; they themselves are in no way at fault for their status, and the distinction in the law based on the marital status of their parents is discriminatory. Douglas focused on the needs of the children, reasoning that it makes very little sense to allow private parties to deprive children of care and economic support when the entire burden may then be thrown on the public. Presumably an award of damages would provide the orphaned children with some financial assistance. Reasonable legislation should be based on the principle that when wrongful acts deprive children of support and protection, the tortfeasors should not be freed of the responsibility for repairing the damage.

The Court's decision, then, recognized for the first time that a rationale such as that put forward by Louisiana was socially disfunctional in view of the increasing number of illegitimate children being born. Indeed, it is doubtful that laws denying rights of recovery for wrongful death have ever discouraged anyone from bringing illegitimate children into the world. Most of these laws drawing lines on the basis of legitimate birth were part of a traditional pattern of dealing with the inheritance of property in a patrilineal society, although they also reflect the medieval church's interest in promoting marriage as a religious sacrament.[26]

In his opinion in *Levy*, Justice Douglas gave the Court a clear guideline to follow: the non-marital child should not be denied rights merely because of his or her birth out-of-wedlock. The law's first interest should be the welfare of the child, and this principle requires that legitimate and illegitimate children be treated alike.

In a companion case to *Levy* the rights of the errant mother, not those of innocent, illegitimate children were at stake. In *Glona v. American Guarantee & Liability Insurance Co.* (1968), the mother of an illegitimate child contested a state law that denied her the right to recover for the wrongful death of her child in an automobile accident.[27] The Court held that there was no rational basis for withholding relief from the mother simply because the child was born out-of-wedlock. Such a law in no way inhibited sin but merely provided a "windfall to tortfeasors" in automobile accident cases. The Court noted that Louisiana law dealing with illegitimates was a jumble of inconsistent rules, some based on archaic doctrines. Both common law wives and married mothers, for example, could sue for the wrongful deaths of illegitimate children, but unmarried mothers could not. Louisiana made no distinction between legitimate and illegitimate children, however, where incest was involved. A mother could inherit from an illegitimate child whom she had acknowledged, and vice versa. A mother could sue someone who killed her illegitimate child's horse, if the child also died, and could recover if a child died in an industrial accident, but she could not recover damages if the child was killed in an automobile accident.[28] In the context of Louisiana's other laws relating to illegitimacy, it was clear that there was no rational, underlying legislative policy.[29]

Rules like that in the Louisiana Wrongful Death Statute were premised, at least in part, on the idea that laws which discriminate against illegitimates are an effective check on immorality and promiscuity, a view that is not only not supported by any factual data, but that is now repudiated by the public at large.[30] In 1977, this view was specifically repudiated by the Supreme Court in *Trimble v. Gordon*, where the Court stated that laws making legitimacy classifications must have stronger reasons behind them than the tenuous "promotion of legitimate family relations."[31]

It was clear from the dissents in *Levy*, however, that some

Justices were reluctant to abandon the traditional legal employment of legitimacy as a classifying device and were concerned about the consequences of changing the existing rules. Classifications based on legitimacy had always been useful in a variety of legal contexts. The dissenters also disliked interfering with state law in an area normally considered the preserve of state government, upsetting the delicate balance of the federal system. Because of the difficulty of determining paternity, laws keeping illegitimate children from inheriting except by will were, they asserted, practical and rational. Workmen's compensation and wrongful death statutes properly require a legal relationship between father and child. Legitimacy gives the courts a clearcut rule for deciding who may bring wrongful death suits, and without such a yardstick it might be difficult for a court to determine, among scores of possible claimants, which were actually dependent on a dead parent or which deserved to inherit because of ties of affection and dependence. Personal relationships ("affection and nurture and dependence") are far too evanescent for courts to evaluate. According to this view, if the state wishes to handle the problem by allowing only legitimate children to sue, there should be no constitutional obstacle, because this classification serves legitimate state needs. Legal relationships as well as biological realities provide a rational basis for determining who may sue and who may not, and are much easier to ascertain.

In *Levy*, however, although the dissenters stated their case in terms of the tasks facing the courts, it is clear from the language in the opinions that the underlying premise is that people choosing to ignore the formalities of marriage are ignoring reasonable and normal community rules, and cannot complain when they are penalized. Justice Harlan's dissenting opinion expresses the view that these laws are morally correct as well as legally useful:

If it be conceded, as I assume it is, that the State has power to provide that people who choose to live together should go through the formalities of marriage and, in default, that people who bear children should acknowledge them, it is logical to enforce these requirements by declaring that the general class of rights that are dependent on family relationships shall be accorded only when the formalities as well as the biology of these relationships are present.[32]

Labine v. Vincent, decided three years later (1971) by a 5 to 4 vote, indicated that the Court was unwilling to extend the principle announced in *Levy* to the law of inheritance, where legitimacy had for centuries been recognized as a proper basis for determining the disposition of property after death.[33] Justice Hugo Black, who now switched positions, wrote an opinion for the Court. For Black, the allocation of responsibilities in a federal system was an important consideration, as was the preservation of traditional state law governing inheritance. He rejected the idea that illegitimacy could *never* be used as a classifying device. The opinion is noteworthy for the use of language that indicates a deep attachment to basic family ideology. The world of the traditional law, and seemingly also the world of several Supreme Court Justices, was populated on one side by chaste females and responsible males, wives and husbands and regular marital relationships, and on the other by bastards and concubines, illicit and meretricious relationships, adulterine and incestuous children, unknown fathers and irresponsible parents. Laws allowing the disposition of property following the death of a family man, to his legitimate heirs, seemed to this group to be a rational method of strengthening and preserving family ties.

In its decisions in *Levy* and *Glona*, the Supreme Court indicated a growing awareness that legitimacy and marital/non-marital classifications were now of decreasing usefulness. As greater numbers of illegitimate children are born and require public support, there is pressure for changes in the law which will regularize non-marital relationships and force all parents to take responsibility for their offspring. Social pressures in modern society have made traditional attitudes toward illegitimate children untenable, but there are still excellent social reasons for encouraging men and women to marry before they have children. Unless the state is to take over part of the responsibility for reproduction, it has an interest in promoting stable families that are able to support their children adequately. Instead of relieving unmarried fathers of their responsibility to support their natural children, as did the common law doctrine of *filius nullius*, there are strong policy reasons for putting pressure on them to deliver what support they can. In 1973 in *Gomez v. Perez*, using the Equal Protection Clause, the Supreme Court rejected a state policy based on the older doctrine. In Texas, legitimate children could claim support and have their claim enforced by the courts, but illegitimate children were denied a judicially enforceable right to support from their natural father, even after a state court finding that the child needed support and maintenance and that the man was indeed the child's biological father.[34] Texas' attempt to limit the impact of the *Gomez* decision by putting a one-year statute of limitations on the filing of paternity suits was later overturned in *Mills v. Hableutzel*,[35] and a similar Tennessee statute of limitations was declared invalid in *Pickett v. Brown*, decided in 1983.[36] In the 1982 *Mills* case, for the first time, several of the Justices explicitly recognized that, although states have an interest in "seeing Justice done" and in preventing stale and fraudulent claims of paternity, there is a countervailing public interest in having all children supported by their parents and in reducing the "number of individuals forced to enter the welfare rolls."[37] The Court, however, was still reluctant to outlaw traditional state use of legitimacy classifications.

In 1968, when the Court handed down the *Levy* decision, only a few states had taken any steps to equalize the status of legitimate and illegitimate children; most state laws still reflected the traditional attitudes described in Justice Harlan's dissent. The decision in *Levy v. Louisiana* mandated a standard of equality but left each state legislature free to apply its own interpretation of the decision. State legislatures have been slow to enact new laws that meet the constitutional standard. Some challenges in the courts have resulted in the overturning of discriminatory statutes, but most state codes retain a residue of the old doctrines, even though they are now of doubtful constitutionality.

In order to encourage states to modernize their laws on this topic, in 1973 the National Conference of Commissioners on Uniform State Laws promulgated a "Uniform Parentage Act," and the American Bar Association approved the Uniform Act in 1974. By 1983, ten states had adopted the act. It abandons the concept of illegitimacy and requires full equality for all children, whatever their parents' marital status. Where the child's parents

are not married, it establishes a series of presumptions and procedures for identifying the father. The adoption of the Uniform
Act by all states would complete a broad, comprehensive change
in public policy. It would also bring equality to all children in
matters of inheritance, workman's compensation and wrongful
death actions, bypassing the need for specific statutes making
these changes.[38]

Previous doubt about the possibility of accurate determination
of paternity, one of the reasons for laws treating illegitimates as
a special class, has now been eliminated by improvements in
blood-testing techniques and other scientific tests. Unmarried
fathers can now be identified with almost 99 percent accuracy.[39]
There are also pressures on unwed mothers to name the fathers
of their chldren, and some recent statutes make government
benefits conditional on maternal cooperation in naming their
partners. These developments come in the wake of compelling
social reasons for finding and identifying fathers, reasons that
were not present in the past.

EQUALIZING THE RIGHTS OF BIOLOGICAL
FATHERS

One of the consequences of identifying non-marital fathers
and making them responsible for the support of their children
has been a demand by men that their rights to custody and
association with their children be equalized. The removal of
gender classifications has also required changes in legal rules
which treat unmarried men and unmarried women differently.
Now that the courts regard gender as well as legitimacy classifications with suspicion, there must be a convincing rationale
behind sex-based distinctions.

Stanley v. Illinois, decided in 1972, marked the end of constitutional indifference to unwed fathers.[40] The decision shifted the
emphasis from the equal treatment of children to the rights of
unmarried parents, the Court holding that the state of Illinois
was barred from taking custody of the children of an unwed
father without giving him a hearing and without finding that
he was an unfit parent.[41] A confusing decision that could have
been grounded in either the Due Process or Equal Protection

clauses, the *Stanley* case was handled as a problem of procedural due process. The Court held that "irrebuttable presumptions" (here the presumption that all unmarried fathers are unfit parents) were unconstitutional because they did not give individual men an opportunity to rebut charges of unfitness. This is a charge that the statute denied due process. But, in holding as it did, the Court obscured the basis of the decision, combining due process and equal protection; by giving unmarried fathers fewer procedural rights than other parents would have had, the state, the Court held, had denied them equal protection. The decision could just as easily have been made solely on equal protection grounds inasmuch as Stanley, the father, had argued that by treating unmarried fathers differently from married fathers or unwed mothers the state discriminated against them. Under Illinois law, an unmarried mother's right to care for her children was not questioned, but an unmarried father was presumed incapable and was not given a hearing to see whether he was, in fact, able to care for his children. This decision was handed down toward the end of President Richard M. Nixon's battle with the Senate over replacements for Justices Hugo Black and John M. Harlan, and the newly appointed Justices, Lewis F. Powell, Jr., and William Rehnquist, did not participate in the case. It is possible that the Court used this procedural analysis because it wanted to avoid any expansion of equal protection doctrine until the new Justices were able to participate.

The holding that irrebuttable presumptions deny both due process and equal protection surfaced in a few other cases during the 1972–1975 period, but the "brief and troubled life" of this doctrine ended in 1975. It seems clear that the cases decided on this basis were all equal protection claims where the legislative classification was unduly burdensome, but where the Court did not want to extend equal protection analysis to new categories.[42] In the *Stanley* case, for example, an equal protection holding would have put both marital classifications and gender classifications in a "suspect" category.

Although the ruling in *Stanley* was narrow, the Court holding only that a state may not use an adverse presumption based on a gender classification to deny unwed fathers all rights to their natural children, the decision created a number of new problems, especially where adoption was concerned. If unwed fathers have rights of any kind, they must be identified and notified of proceedings in which their rights are in jeopardy. This meant that the states would have to develop procedures for informing them of impending custody and adoption hearings. Once this problem was recognized, it was obvious that it would be impossible to notify all biological fathers of non-marital children—some distinctions would have to be made. The immediate legislative response to this decision was to limit the notice requirement to fathers who had acknowledged their children, filed notice of intent to claim paternity, lived with the mother after the birth of the child, or helped support the child. Wisconsin adopted a scheme of notification by mail or publication, but procedures of this sort raised "right to privacy" problems.[43] There were also questions about how much interference with established procedures in custody and adoption cases must now be tolerated; once the father was given a protected right to participate in custody and adoption proceedings, he might make demands that conflicted with the child's best interests, and there was a risk that the child might be hurt. Time-consuming procedures for identifying and notifying fathers could have adverse effects on adoption. If the father could block adoption, he might prevent the relocation of the child in a permanent family relationship. Thus, the protection of the father's relationship to his natural children could not be in any sense absolute but must be balanced against the children's interests in being legitimate members of stable families.[44] The broad question left open by this decision was whether the Equal Protection Clause forbade all differences in the treatment of married and unmarried parents in custody and adoption proceedings. The decision also raised the possibility of gender discrimination claims where judges followed the traditional practice of awarding custody of minor children to their mothers, as well as other legal procedures that treated unwed mothers and fathers differently.

It is possible to argue that the *Stanley* case raised more questions than it decided. In three later cases, the Court was forced to come to grips with a number of these unresolved issues.

CHILDREN'S AND PARENTS' RIGHTS IN
CONFLICT

Quilloin v. Walcott (1978) answered several of these questions, holding that the equal protection principle did not require that the law treat married and unmarried fathers alike in all situations.[45] Unmarried fathers do have substantive rights to the care and company of their non-marital children, but these rights can be overridden when the child's best interests are at stake. The Georgia law at issue in the case required the consent of both parents before a child born in wedlock could be adopted, but where the child was born out-of-wedlock, only the mother's consent was necessary, unless the father had legitimated his child. No question of fitness or unfitness was raised by the Georgia law; it quite simply treated married and unmarried fathers differently. The Court held that where there was a judicial finding that the child would be best served by allowing it to be adopted, a natural father's objections could be overridden without infringing on his parental rights.

Although Justice Thurgood Marshall's opinion, for a unanimous Court, rejected the equal protection claim, it recognized the parent-child relationship as a constitutionally protected area, finding *dicta* to this effect in a number of the earlier decisions. He cited *Prince v. Massachusetts*, a 1923 decision, for its statement that "the custody, care and nurture of the child reside first in the parents, whose primary function and freedom include preparation for obligations that the state can neither supply nor hinder." He also noted that opinions in previous cases had asserted that the family unit itself, as well as freedom of personal choice in matters of family life, were part of the substance of liberty protected by the Due Process Clause.[46] The Court's decision in *Quilloin*, however, recognized that the child's interest in belonging to a stable family might be in conflict with the "parenting rights" of its mother or father, whatever their marital status.

But in *Caban v. Mohammad*, decided the following year, ruling on a New York statute that required the consent of both parents to the adoption of a child born in wedlock but the consent of the mother alone where the child was illegitimate, the court came to an opposite conclusion.[47] The difference between the two cases lay in the relationship between the father and his children. In the *Quilloin* case, the father did not have a personal relationship with his child. In the New York case, the father had lived with the mother and children for several years, had helped with their care and provided some of their support. When the mother married another man and petitioned for formal adoption, the father, Abdiel Caban, sought to block the adoption. The Court accepted his claim of gender discrimination. Caban could not adopt his children without their mother's consent, and he could not prevent their adoption by withholding his consent. The majority opinion, written by Justice Powell, found the law objectionable because it accorded unmarried fathers no rights in adoption proceedings; hostile or alienated mothers could arbitrarily cut loving, caring fathers off from their children. The law thus left men powerless since even marriage was precluded if the woman would not agree. In *Parham v. Hughes*, another case involving unwed fathers that was decided the same day, Justice Powell elaborated on this insight. His concurring opinion in *Parham* complained indignantly that, "To require marriage between the father and the mother often is tantamount to a total exclusion of fathers, as marriage is only possible with the consent of the mother."[48] If the ghosts of unwed mothers could have read Supreme Court opinions, there would have been peals of laughter at the irony of this statement.

Gender distinctions, to be valid, must serve important governmental purposes, and the Court could not see that any necessary purpose was served by a classification that automatically treated unmarried men and women differently. Although mothers are closer than fathers to their newborn infants, an unwed father may have a strong and affectionate relationship with his children when they are older. Caban had established such a relationship; in the contrasting factual situation in the *Quilloin* case, the father had demonstrated very little interest in his child until adoption was imminent. These decisions placed the parent-child relationship within the group of values protected by the Due Process Clause and confirmed that unmarried men as well as married men have parental rights. But the *Quilloin* decision emphasized that there are still differences between parents who are married and those who are not, differences that the law may recognize.

In *Stanley v. Illinois* the Court had opened the door to the recognition of the rights of unmarried fathers, and by doing so it had held that in some circumstances at least the biological connection between father and child takes precedence over rules based on the formal legal status of their relationship. But the *Stanley* decision revealed a conflict between two tenets of the family ideology. The family ideology recognizes the importance of blood ties and accepts the proposition that parents should be held responsible for their reproductive activities. It also accepts the idea that children should be nurtured in families and that families, not the state, should raise and care for children. If all parents, married or not, are to be made to shoulder responsibility for their children, blood ties must be recognized. However, conflict can arise between this proposition and the principle that children should be raised in a family environment and that the integration of a child into a working family unit is the proper goal of public policy. Where adoption is the best means of providing a secure family for a child, it may be necessary to ignore the claims of a biological parent. After *Caban* the Court quickly became aware of the contradictions that could arise from these two principles in adoption cases. In order to reconcile the conflict, it was necessary to limit the *Stanley* rule and to mandate equal treatment only for those fathers who had developed a substantial relationship with their children, a subclass of the larger class.

Parham v. Hughes, decided the same day as *Caban v. Mohammad*, reopened the issue of the right to sue for wrongful death that had been considered in *Glona v. American Guarantee & Liberty Insurance Co.* Like *Glona*, *Parham v. Hughes* questioned whether a state could refuse non-marital parents the right to bring suits for the wrongful deaths of their children. The *Glona* case concerned a mother, and the Court had held there that the state could not forbid a claimant who was clearly the mother from suing for the wrongful death of her child; such a state law denies equal protection of the laws. The *Parham* case involved a father, and the Court found that fathers who have not legitimated their children may be denied the right to file suits for a child's wrong-ful death.[49] Eleven years after the initial decision, the Court's composition was considerably changed, but there was still dis-agreement among the Justices on the constitutionality of clas-sifications based on marital status. Although a majority was willing to follow *Levy* where discrimination was aimed at the children themselves and was even willing to recognize that un-married fathers have some parenting rights, the Court as a whole was still not ready to abolish all distinctions based on the reg-ularity of the marital relationship.

Under Georgia's wrongful death statute, unwed mothers were entitled to sue following a child's death, but the state withheld this right from unwed fathers unless they had taken formal steps (under state law) to legitimate the child. The case thus raised equal protection questions on two levels: a legitimacy classifi-cation was involved, and men and women were treated differently.

Curtis Parham, however, was not a father who had appeared in court only when his child was dead, after having ignored the existence of the child in life. Even though he had never taken steps to legitimate his child or marry its mother, he had ac-knowledged the child and signed its birth certificate, contributed to its support and visited it on a regular basis. Like Abdiel Caban, he had established a relationship with his offspring.

Four members of the Supreme Court voted to uphold Geor-gia's law, and Justice Stewart wrote the plurality opinion. He found that there was no discrimination against the child. Nor did the state law discriminate against the father, since the law's requirements that the father establish his relationship by legi-timating his child were reasonably related to the state's interest in proving paternity and preventing fraudulent claims. There was no gender discrimination; men and women were not sim-ilarly situated because it is easier to establish maternity than paternity. Therefore, there is no equivalent situation between mothers and fathers. The only real categories to be compared here are "fathers who have legitimated their children and those who have not." (Compare Justice Stewart's classification of preg-nant women and non-pregnant persons in *Geduldig v. Aiello*, discussed in Chapter 4.) But in spite of this set of careful legal distinctions, it seems clear that several Justices still believed, as Justice Harlan had in the earlier case, that people who choose not to follow the regular pattern of family relationships accepted by society have no reason to object when society treats them as pariahs. Fathers who choose not to marry and refuse even to legitimate their children (when a procedure is clearly provided for doing so) have no right to benefit from a child's death. Justice Stewart's opinion expressed the traditional view that laws penalizing people who ignore society's interest in marriage are justifiable.

Legitimation would have removed the stigma of bastardy and allowed the child to inherit from the father in the same manner as if born in lawful wedlock. Unlike the illegitimate child for whom the status of illegitimacy is involuntary and immutable, the appellant here was responsible for fostering an illegitimate child and for failing to change its status. It is thus neither illogical nor unjust for society to express its "condemnation of irresponsible liaisons beyond the bounds of marriage" by not conferring upon a biological father the statutory right to sue for the wrongful death of his illegitimate child.[50]

Parham was decided by a 5 to 4 vote. In *Caban* Justice Powell had agreed with Justices White, Brennan, Marshall and Blackmun that the state law denied unwed fathers equal protection of the laws, and had written the opinion of the Court. His switch in this case altered the result. He seems to have believed that the Georgia law was constitutional because it did not totally exclude fathers, leaving them avenues through which they could assert their interests.

The four dissenters in *Parham v. Hughes*, now in the minority, thought that this law, like the one in *Caban*, used an invalid gender classification to discriminate against unwed fathers, but they also objected to the Court's assessment of the underlying realities. They did not believe that there would be serious problems of establishing paternity in the few cases of this type that found their way to the courts. On the other hand, there were probably a great many fathers who had substantial relationships with children whom they had not legitimated, who would suffer real loss if those children were killed. It was also unrealistic to

assume that the formal legitimatization procedure provided by
Georgia law would be accessible to most of these fathers.

For the first time, in a footnote to the dissent in this case,
Justice White recognized explicitly the extent of the racial differential created by the concept of legitimacy; in 1977, 15.5 percent of all children and 51.7 percent of the black children born
in the United States had unmarried parents.[51] Although scholars
have found that urban lower class blacks generally have the same
attitudes toward marriage and the family as do lower and middle-class whites, unemployment rates are so high for black males
that they may not have the jobs or incomes that make marriage
a practical possibility. Insofar as legal rules discriminate against
non-marital families and illegitimate children, they may burden
blacks disproportionately.[52]

It was still not clear from these decisions how far the Justices
were willing to go to protect the bare biological relationship
between unmarried fathers and their children. *Lehr v. Robertson*,
decided in 1983, confirmed the principle that had been announced in *Quilloin v. Walcott*, that the biological link alone would
not be protected if the father had not taken available steps to
turn it into a meaningful family relationship.[53] The factual situation in the Lehr decision lay somewhere between that in *Quilloin* and that in *Caban v. Mohammad*. Although the facts were
disputed and Lehr had not had an opportunity to present his
case in court, it seems likely that he had tried to make contact
with his daughter but had been rejected by the mother. He had
cohabited with the mother before the child was born and was
acknowledged to be the father of the child. After the *Stanley*
decision, New York had enacted legislation describing the relationships that would allow a father to assert his rights, and
providing a procedure by which additional fathers could be included if they filed their names on a "putative father registry."
Lehr met none of the statutory requirements and had not registered; the question the Court had to decide was whether, under
these circumstances, he could block the adoption of his daughter
by initiating a paternity action.

The Supreme Court ruled against Lehr by a 6 to 3 vote, with
Justice John Paul Stevens, a dissenter in the *Caban* case, writing
for the majority. The Court reasoned that the "mere existence
of a biological link," without more, did not merit constitutional

protection. There are a number of other interests involved in adoption proceedings, including the child's well-being and the state's interest in placing children in stable, formal families which outweigh the simple biological relationship. If it were to require notification of fathers who have not supported their children, legitimated them, married their mothers, established important relationships with them or even taken certain minimal steps to acknowledge the relationship required by state law, the Court would uphold formal due process requirements at the expense of a number of more essential social values.

Dissenting Justices White, Marshall and Blackmun took the position that the Constitution should be interpreted to protect the interest of a natural parent in his or her child, that the biological connection is the basis of family life and is the relationship that creates the protected interest. It is the "nature" of the claimed right, not the individual parent's particular claim, which is important. The dissenters emphasized the biological basis of the natural family. The family which the law accepts and protects is the natural family, with ties of blood as well as marriage. The ties that bind children to their natural parents are important, even when steps to legalize the relationship have not been taken, and these Justices are unwilling to allow the state to ignore them, without the rudimentary requirements of notice and hearing.

The majority was willing to protect the unmarried father's claims to his children where a linkage had been established between parental right and parental duty, where the father had some significant "custodial, personal or financial" relationship with the child. Under the traditional family ideology, the biological, unmarried father is ignored; a protected status is accorded to the family, once established, whether after the prescribed ceremonies or by common law. The family is protected in large part because its functions include not only reproduction, but also the support and education of the resulting children.

CHILD SUPPORT: THE NEW CRISIS

On both state and national levels, public policy has been moving toward insistence on the enforcement of child support obligations against all biological parents, whether married, unmarried or divorced. In the last two decades increasing rates of divorce, family abandonment and illegitimacy "have combined to leave unprecedented numbers of children in single parent homes, typically without adequate support from either parent."[54] Rising welfare costs have made child support a political issue, but the problem is much broader, encompassing all children whose standard of living drops dramatically after "economic abandonment" by one or both parents.

In an attempt to bring some coherence to the hodgepodge of state laws and overlapping jurisdictions and to force deserting fathers to pay for the support of dependent children, Congress promulgated and the states ratified an interstate compact, the Uniform Reciprocal Enforcement of Support Agreement Act of 1950 (URESA). URESA was substantially revised (RURESA) in 1968, and the revised version has been accepted by about half of the states.[55] The agreement commits states to cooperate in locating child support delinquents and in collecting payments from them. It allows actions for child support to be initiated in one state and tried in the state where the delinquent parent actually resides. But the benefits accruing to illegitimate children from these new procedures have been limited, because the act applies to support payments for illegitimate children only if the state has created a statutory duty of support. RURESA has been only marginally effective. Some states do not have the funds to bring the necessary prosecutions. Where a second family has been formed, the state of residence may be wary of requiring support payments which could force the second family to seek public assistance.

An enforcement mechanism that is potentially more effective was created by the Child Support Provisions, added to the Social Security Act in 1975.[56] These amendments set up a federal enforcement unit (Federal Office of Child Support Enforcement) within the (now) Department of Health and Human Services (HHS) to help the states collect support payments. Before this program was enacted, the enforcement of child support obligations was the sole responsibility of the states. The program is now a joint federal-state enterprise. Child support agencies (known as Title IV-D agencies) have been established in the states, and a Parent Locator Service is authorized to obtain data from the files of HHS and other agencies of the U.S. government to help locate absent parents.[57] In order to receive financial aid, welfare recipients are now required to assign their support rights to the state, to identify the father if the child was born out-of-wedlock and to cooperate in any legal proceedings brought against the absent parent. In addition, the law has provided positive incentives for state compliance with the new rules and increased supervision of state enforcement programs. If necessary, the Internal Revenue Service can now be used to collect support obligations assigned to a state. The primary purpose of the program is to reduce expenditures for public aid by requiring the parents of children who receive AFDC to contribute to their support, whether the children are legitimate or illegitimate, and whether or not there is an outstanding support order.[58]

Even with the provision of this machinery for collecting child support, only 35 percent of the 8.4 million women bringing up children with an absent father receive any payments at all. New legislation passed by Congress in 1984 and signed into law by President Ronald Reagan has the potential for revolutionizing the current child support situation by requiring the states to withhold child support payments from wages and other sources of income. The Child Support Enforcement Act amends the Social Security Act to require states to establish procedures for mandatory withholding of wages of parents in arrears on child support.[59] It also allows states to withhold state income tax refunds and could, in its final form, also allow the interception of federal income tax refunds. The states are given incentives, in the form of monetary awards, for improving child support collections—for both welfare and non-AFDC families.[60] This legislation reflects growing public opinion that parents should be responsible for their children and that the government should not be required to support families thrown into poverty by divorce and desertion, or to subsidize non-marital families. With 12 million children now living in female-headed families, more than 50 percent of whom are below the poverty line, what was once a private moral and legal problem has become an urgent question of public policy. Yet, although the nation still subscribes in theory to the view that responsibility for child-raising belongs with the individual and the family, it is clear that a certain amount of erosion of that principle is occurring in practice. Judith Cassetty, a scholar working in the field of child support, has written about "a general rejection of the notion of personal responsibility for the consequences of one's procreative activities," pointing out that the responsibility for raising children now falls on people other than natural parents—or, in last resort, on the state.[61]

As the number of children on public assistance has increased, pressures on state treasuries have stimulated state legislative experimentation with various means of ensuring parental accountability. A Michigan statute, for example, required unmarried fathers-to-be to file a prior notice that they were about to become fathers and to acknowledge their support responsibilities, or lose any further claims to the child. Professor Harry D. Krause, an authority on family law, suggested that this requirement might be called a "notice of fornication," and he pointed out a number of serious legal and constitutional problems with the statute.[62] Some of the state schemes are of doubtful constitutionality, although only a few have been examined by the Supreme Court. The "putative father registry" maintained by the state of New York allows a man to demonstrate his intent to claim paternity of a child who will be born out-of-wedlock by mailing in a postcard. By registering with the state, he insures that he be notified about any legal proceedings affecting the child.[63]

An ingenious attack on the child support problem by the Wisconsin legislature forbade fathers who were under court order to support their non-marital children from contracting marriages in the state and voided any marriages that were made in violation of the law. This ban on marriage could only be lifted by a court determination that existing children were not public charges and were not in danger of needing public assistance. After this law was invalidated by a Supreme Court decision in 1978, the Wisconsin legislature passed a law that set standardized guidelines for determining child support payments and tied support agreements to the ability of the absent parent to pay.[64] Payments are made to the clerk of the court who then disburses them to the parent. The state is now considering a minimum guaranteed benefit for each child who has absent parents. The parent would be responsible for $3,500 for one child, $5,000 for two children and $6,000 for three children. Both parents would contribute, and the state would make up the difference if necessary.[65]

The Supreme Court's landmark decisions in *Levy*, *Glona* and *Stanley v. Illinois* put pressure on the states to make changes in the traditional relationships between parents and their non-marital children and laid the basis for government enforcement of child support responsibilities for both married and unmarried parents. Even though the 1968 decision in *Levy v. Louisiana* opened the door to equal protection challenges of legitimacy classifications, the Court still has not been willing to hold that illegitimacy is a suspect classification requiring "strict scrutiny." It has adopted an intermediate level of review "with teeth" which requires more than an arguable rational basis for a state's differential treatment of legitimate and illegitimate children and their parents.[66] Using this test, it has examined over twenty cases that involve statutory use of the classification and has held that the classification was wrongly used in about half of them.[67]

Equal protection doctrine, however, does not really provide a clear basis for understanding these decisions. It is hard, for example, to see that there is a substantial reason for accepting a state law that rejects the inheritance rights of acknowledged illegitimate children whose father has died intestate,[68] but refuses to allow a state to discriminate against the illegitimate children of intestate fathers, when these children have gone through a court proceeding to prove their paternity.[69] Surely, acknowledgment by the father is as clear a proof of paternity as the completion of a court procedure. There also seem to be inordinately fine distinctions in the construction of social security statutes that set up various categories of children who can receive social security benefits.[70] Where federal spending statutes are involved, the Court's decisions seem to be influenced more by the wish to allow Congress to establish guidelines that can be administered effectively than by reasoned assessments of the substantiality or the equal impact of legitimacy classifications. For example, in *Califano v. Boles* (1979), the Court upheld a provision of the Social Security Act which restricted "mothers' insurance benefits" to widows and divorced wives of wage earners, and excluded the mothers of wage earners' illegitimate children.[71] The Court decided that this section of the Social Security Act was intended to benefit dependent spouses rather than children, and that marital status could be reasonably used as an "index" of dependency in order to facilitate the allocation of funds. The dissenters disagreed with this reading of the statute and thought that the denial of resources to the mothers of illegitimate children inevitably discriminated against the children themselves.

One is inclined to agree with Justice Rehnquist as well as with some critics in the law schools who see much equal protection analysis as "froth," and to look for a different explanation for the Court's handling of these cases.[72] If the practical results of the decisions give us a clue, the matter that concerns the Court (except for inheritance cases where the Court is reluctant to disturb long-accepted state rules governing the inheritance of property) is the actual access of children to support. Because illegitimacy and poverty go hand-in-hand, and these children begin life with a social stigma and with very little chance of success, it seems unreasonable to deny them access to resources (various kinds of welfare payments, entitlements and the father's resources) simply because of their irregular status. There is also a public interest in making the parents of illegitimate children responsible for them whenever possible, forcing parents to provide essential aid rather than relying on public funding. But public funds should be available to non-marital children on the same terms as they are to legitimate children.

The conclusion from the Court's handling of these cases seems to be that, although the Supreme Court will no longer accept illegitimacy classifications that damage the innocent child, it is not yet willing to use the Equal Protection Clause to invalidate all possible uses of the classification. Under the careful distinctions, one senses a residue of the old concern that the equalization of marital and non-marital child-parent relationships for all purposes would, in effect, reward irresponsible persons who flout society's rules and would discourage the formation of strong, two-parent families. In the past, legitimacy classifications bolstered the regularity of marital arrangements. But the other side of the coin was that no one was legally accountable for children born out-of-wedlock, and the responsibility for their care often fell on private charity or, increasingly, on the state. With ever-greater numbers of children on the welfare rolls, it becomes urgent to adjust legal sanctions to encourage fathers to provide for their children regardless of whether they are married to the mothers. Middle-class marriage rules have never been entirely appropriate to the circumstances in which many lower class and minority families live; therefore, policies that penalize such families for failing to conform to middle-class standards may be at best useless and at worst counterproductive. Traditional due process and equal protection analysis has not always been entirely satisfactory in giving the Court doctrinal guidance in solving these problems. Neither doctrine quite fits the subject matter. There are too many conflicting interests intertwined in family cases. When it remedies gender discrimination against non-marital fathers, the Court is likely to penalize children by making their adoption and the regularization of their status more difficult. Strictures against gender discrimination are also troublesome to apply, for it is extremely unlikely that, for most purposes, unmarried mothers and unmarried fathers are similarly situated. The responsibility for child care and support invariably falls to the mother if the father cannot be identified, cannot be found or deserts the family.[73] All in all, it is not surprising that the Court has been split in these cases, that traditional constitutional principles have been difficult to apply consistently and that the course of decision has been uneven.

3

Abortion as a Family Issue

The norms of reproductive institutions motivate persons to bear children, and they control sexual behavior to this end. If the connection between sexuality and the bearing of offspring were entirely broken, then a powerful factor in the motivation to procreate would be lost. . . . Our taboos against abortion and contraception are at one with our taboo against extramarital intercourse—they both function to maintain a motivational connection between sexual gratification and procreation.

Kingsley Davis[1]

Roe v. Wade, decided in 1973, marked the second major excursion of the Supreme Court into family law. In spite of their theoretical underpinnings in individual rights to liberty and privacy, abortion rights cases are, *au fond*, family cases. A careful inspection of the ramifications of these cases illustrates both the overlapping, interconnected nature of family relationships and some of the difficulties that emerge when courts attempt to settle family controversies in terms of the rights of autonomous individuals and the traditional categories of constitutional law.

Abortion is a family issue because reproductive control undermines traditional family structures. If one starts from the proposition that the family is the principal reproductive institution of our society and that law has customarily tried to ensure that reproduction will take place in such a unit, one that has the economic and emotional resources to invest in the raising of children, it becomes evident that laws restricting contraceptive practices and abortion, like the penalties on illegitimacy, are part of the legal infrastructure designed to ensure that sexual activity resulting in reproduction takes place within marriage. Sexual opportunities outside of marriage decrease incentives for individuals of both sexes to take on the responsibilities and burdens of marriage and child-raising. Reproductive control by married couples changes the dynamics of family relationships and subtly changes the rationale behind marriage.

Marriage ensures that men will work to support the family unit while women devote their attention to reproduction and child-raising. In traditional, patriarchal families the father assumes, along with the economic burden, the power to control his dependents. Common law doctrines reinforced the subordination of women and children to the father's authority. Social and legal sanctions that penalize women who bear children outside of marriage link sex, marriage and procreation and encourage women to insist on a permanent marital relationship and to accept the restrictions on their freedom which marriage imposes. Unmarried mothers and children born out-of-wedlock are stigmatized by society. Abortion and contraception interfere with the structure and dynamics of this reproductive institution in many ways. By separating sex from its natural consequences, they discourage family formation. A large number of marriages have always been undertaken because of pregnancy. Reproductive control also undermines the structure of husband-wife relationships within marriage, because it allows women a degree of sexual freedom and makes them less dependent on male support. As soon as they can plan children and find permanent, well-paid employment outside the home, the internal pressures to keep the family together as an economic unit are reduced. Divorce becomes an option, as does single parenthood.

There is thus a clear connection between accepted patterns of sex, marriage, reproduction and the ties that bind women to their traditional roles in the paternalistic family. In this broad sense, abortion is a family issue indeed. Women's sexuality, the authority of the father, his control of his wife and children, parental control over children and the sexual activity of minors are all related to this matter in some fashion, and all these relationships are undergoing monumental change at the present time.[2] If family means the traditional, patriarchal family, social conservatives are quite correct in linking reproductive control to the loosening of family ties, and in rejecting birth control and abortion as being in conflict with the coherent belief system that supports the family, an ideology that lies behind social and legal sanctions against reproductive control.[3] The traditional ideology of the family insists that men and women are intrinsically different and have different roles in life. Men are best suited for the public world and women for rearing children, managing the home and caring for their husbands. Women are emotionally unsuited for the competitive world of work, and employment outside of the home shortchanges the family. Both contraception and abortion are wrong because, by giving women control over their fertility, they break up "an intricate set of social relationships between men and women that has traditionally surrounded (and in the ideal case protected) women and children."[4] Sex is part of the procreative process, and not an end in itself; according to this view, it is profaned and degraded when it is taken out of the family context in which it belongs.[5]

When abortion is available, the decision to have an abortion is likely to evoke conflicts and opposing interests within the family structure. Individual family members may perceive themselves affected in different ways. From the woman's point of view, the decision should be hers because her bodily integrity and safety, and even her life, can be endangered by child-bearing. Her physical health and her emotional well-being, her ambitions and desires as an individual, can be destroyed by unwanted pregnancies. She will also undertake a long-term child-rearing assignment that may conflict with other plans and ambitions. The husband, however, especially if his wife decides to have an abortion without his consent, may feel that his position as head of the family is compromised. Because in the past the father spoke for the family—indeed represented the family in all important matters—to assign an independent right to limit reproduction to the mother involves a serious reversal of traditional roles. From the point of view of many men, fertility is a source of prestige and power, and interference with their procreative virtuosity is extremely threatening.[6] But a husband may also have reasons to propose an abortion, in opposition to his wife's wishes to bear the child. There can be benefits or disadvantages for other family members as well. Limiting family size may well be a positive move for everyone. It should also be remembered that abortion often prevents the conclusion of unstable or unsuitable marriages and allows couples, married or unmarried, to avoid family responsibilities. In each abortion decision, therefore, there are likely to be both individual and communal interests of varying intensities at stake.

The conflicts between parents and children caused by the availability of birth control devices and the possibility of electing abortions have been especially troublesome. Teenagers who have access to contraceptives or the option of abortion if they become pregnant are freed from some inhibitions against sexual experimentation. Families may thus regard access to abortion and contraception by teenagers as a major factor in the loosening of the family's controls over its children, especially if parental permission to acquire contraceptives or to undergo abortions is not required. Because most parents believe they have both the right and the responsibility to protect and advise their children, they are likely to have serious misgivings about public policies that allow minors to decide to end their pregnancies without consulting family members.[7] But minors who are old enough to have children justifiably believe they should be allowed to make decisions that have such important long-range implications for their lives. Disputes over reproductive rights are thus likely to reveal opposing interests within the family itself. This intrafamily conflict is most clearly symbolized by the irreconcilable interests of an unwilling mother and a fetus.

Because families are social institutions their problems and internal arrangements present issues of public policy, and the demand by women for the right to control reproduction has become the subject of political contention. Fertility control did not become a matter of general public concern until methods became safe and reliable enough to give females a large measure of real reproductive choice. At this point, control over fertility

became a matter of interest to the medical and political estab-
lishments because it posed the possibility of women themselves
taking control of the reproductive process and managing it in
their own interests. Men generally, and physicians in particular,
who were in control on the knowledge and techniques that made
contraception possible, did not believe that women were competent to make responsible reproductive decisions themselves.
Among the many rationalizations that were offered in explanation, the most common were that women were ignorant and
uninformed about biological facts and would indulge themselves
by refusing, for frivolous reasons, to accept their natural roles
as child-bearers. The situation was not improved by the fact that
contraception was associated with vice, obscenity and lowered
moral standards rather than with family planning and hygiene,
goals that later made it seem more palatable. The systematic
suppression of information about contraception by the medical
profession which occurred in the last decades of the nineteenth
century was partly motivated by concern about its impact on
family life.[8] "Medical attitudes toward birth control were shaped
less by the practical or ideological needs of the profession than
by the commitment of doctors to the maintenance of social order
as they understood it." "Since the family might be weakened if
sex was too easily separated from procreation, physicians believed that they had a social obligation to manage carefully the
dissemination of birth control."[9] Abortion was part of the same
picture. By the 1880s advances in technology had made it less
dangerous, and a growing number of professional abortionists
were willing to perform the operation.[10] In response to a serious
moral and legal crusade against abortion mounted by physicians,
legislatures passed statutes that tightened legal restrictions to
the point that almost all abortions were prohibited except those
performed by physicians for pressing medical reasons. Changes
in the law made in the period between 1880 and 1900 that resulted in the prohibition of most abortions[11] "medicalized" the
operation, placing the control of abortions that remained legal
in the hands of the medical profession as a "treatment" rather
than under the control of women who needed a means of limiting reproduction.[12] Neither an effective means of contraception
nor abortion was now available for fertility control. Even though

abortion had become reasonably safe, male doctors and legislators controlled its availability; women were left with little power
to decide for themselves as to when or whether they wished to
assume the burdens of reproductive activities. The legislation
prohibiting contraception and abortion reinforced male control
within the family through the legal authority of the state.[13] It
also coincided with pro-natalist policies, which were thought to
serve society's best interests by maintaining population, reducing the need for immigration and promoting economic
expansion.[14]

When the availability of abortion re-emerged in the 1960s as
a political demand of the women's movement, its connections
with more general "family" concerns were downplayed or ignored. Most pro-abortion rhetoric emphasized individual rights
and personal freedom—"the right to control our own bodies,"
the "right to choose" or the right to "abortion on demand"—
fighting slogans appropriate to movement politics. There was
some writing about "compulsory motherhood" and about laws
that made women reproductive slaves of the state, formulations
that suggested a need to examine the connections between law,
reproduction, the family and the growing demand of women
for political and social equality. But in general the movement
identified abortion as a personal right to freedom from unjust
government control.

ROE V. WADE: PRIVACY AND LIBERTY

In its principal abortion decision, *Roe v. Wade*, the Supreme
Court of the United States accepted the proposition that constitutional protection of personal privacy covered the right to
choose an abortion. The Court did not immediately see the connection between reproductive rights and family structure or re-
alize that by protecting even a limited access to abortion it would
be accused of undermining the family itself.

What the Court saw before it was a complex weighing problem
involving the competing rights of three separate entities: the
woman, the fetus and the state. The right accorded the woman
was a very limited right: the right to choose, during the first
three months of pregnancy, not to bear a child. This right was

tied to and limited by the opposing interests of the developing fetus. The right was also limited in time; it was dominant only during the first trimester. The temporal point the Court accepted as the outside limit of the woman's unimpeded right to choose was "viability"—the ability of the growing child to survive after being removed from its mother. At this point the child's right to survival was clear and could be overridden only if its mother's life was at risk. The definition of viability depended, of course, on medical technology, and ever since the *Roe* decision was handed down in 1973, technology has dramatically improved the survival chances for extremely premature births. Although Justice Sandra Day O'Connor recently criticized this sliding scale as setting the rights of a woman and a fetus on "a collision course" as medical science extends its capability of providing for the "separate existence of the fetus," there is reason to believe that the possibility of extremely early fetal survival is not unlimited and that perhaps the limits have been reached.[15] During the last three months, when many fetuses are capable of independent survival, the Court held that only a threat to the mother's life or physical well-being justifies abortion, and that state legislatures can forbid abortions in this period except when the mother's life is in danger.

The concept of state police power, the traditional power that entitles state governments to regulate conduct in order to protect health and the general welfare, was also in opposition to women's claims to unconditional abortion rights. The Court held that during the second three months of pregnancy, in order to protect the mother's health, the state was free to regulate the conditions under which abortions might take place.

The rights of the fetus and the police powers of the state were not the only other interests accommodated in this delicate balancing process. The interests of the medical profession in retaining control of the abortion procedure, which it had kept since the passage of restrictive legislation in the last century, was also included in the balance. Justice Blackmun's opinion formulated the pregnant woman's right as that of deciding in favor of an abortion during the first three months of her pregnancy—after she had discussed the problem with her doctor. By phrasing the right in these terms, the Court emphasized that abortions should still be subject to a degree of medical control and that abortion was still to be regarded as a medical procedure. There are echoes here of some of the old stereotypes about females and their behavior. Women need to be protected from their own mis-judgments and guided and controlled, if not by men, at least by professionals. The Justices were not willing to assume that women could or should make responsible reproductive decisions entirely on their own.[16]

Apart from the fact that it diminishes as pregnancy continues, the right created in this case was an odd sort of right. In some ways it resembled the right to counsel as it stood at the time of *Betts v. Brady* in 1942.[17] The right to counsel guaranteed to crim-inal defendants at that time was severely limited. It attached only at the trial stage, and indigents in state courts had no right to assigned counsel except in capital cases. In other criminal cases the right was available only where serious injustice would occur without it—unless, of course, the defendant could pay for legal help. Similarly, a pregnant woman was entitled to an abor-tion only if she could find funds to pay for it; this was settled in the abortion funding cases in 1977. Abortion rights cases are similar to right-to-counsel cases in another respect; the right is not one that claimants can exercise by themselves. It is a right to demand professional assistance—a right that cannot be ex-ercised without the help of a paid professional.

Although the right to choose an abortion identified by the Court was a narrow right with many qualifications, it is surely correct to recognize, as Professor Sylvia Law has recently noted, that "Nothing the Supreme Court has ever done has been more concretely important for women."[18] Because only women be-come pregnant, laws denying access to abortion directly penalize them when they are forced to bear children under oppressive conditions, in circumstances that are likely to have a devastating impact on their lives. Still, in the sense that it did not accept the primacy of women's claims, *Roe v. Wade* was not a "feminist" decision, and indeed the more radical women's groups were extremely critical of it. One of their criticisms was that the de-cision was not grounded in the principle of sexual equality, that it in fact ignored the issue of equality completely and anchored its holding in the doctrines of personal liberty and privacy.[19]

Because "the right to privacy" was the legal claim identified by the litigants themselves, it is not surprising that the Supreme Court used a liberty/privacy rationale to justify the recognition of abortion rights. There was not only a relevant precedent in the 1965 *Griswold* case, but also a well-established American social tradition, recognized by the Supreme Court as constitutionally protected, of leaving decisions about reproduction in private hands. There was also a strong belief that family relationships existed in a private realm. The idea of completely privatized family responsibilities is a slightly different concept from that of individual privacy. The family is regarded as a small government in its own right, one that works out various problems of internal management without state intrusion. The state intervenes from time to time to set limits—to protect women (from wife beating, for example) or to protect children from parental abuse, but, by and large, the inner dynamics of family life are not to be interfered with directly. It has been understood by everyone that this concept of family "privatism" is an essential element in our social system. Reproduction takes place in the family, and the economic burden of child-bearing and child-raising is borne by this private institution. Although the Constitution does not mention families any more directly than it mentions abortion or contraception, there is little question that the framers of both the original document and the Fourteenth Amendment would have been in agreement, if the matter had come up, that family life should be left a private matter. Family rights are Ninth Amendment rights in the classic sense—rights that the people retain even though they are not expressly protected by a written document.

Nineteenth-century legislation outlawing both contraception and abortion was in conflict with this settled principle of governmental non-interference in family affairs. Insofar as any government had the power to intrude in domestic relations, it would have been the state government. State law is concerned with morality, regulates entry into marriage and divorce, and forces family members to live up to the responsibilities imposed on them by the common law. In early America, although abortion was not unknown, it belonged in the family setting, and was a woman's affair, not a matter for public regulation. There was

no reason for state law to interfere with or regulate the reproductive process itself, except to try to penalize reproduction that
took place outside of the context of family life. To the extent
that *Roe* held that decisions about reproduction should be private
and should not be interfered with by the government, it tapped
into this reservoir of belief in family "privatism," articulated in
an earlier case, *Prince v. Massachusetts*, as the idea that "there is
a realm of family life which the state cannot enter without substantial justification."[20] The "birth control" cases, *Griswold v.
Connecticut* and *Eisenstadt v. Baird*, speak more specifically of a
right to marital and sexual privacy, but the privacy at issue is
not simply that of the individual.[21] That this was the Court's
understanding became clear in 1976, when it affirmed a Virginia
decision upholding a sodomy law and linking rights to sexual
privacy to the marital condition.[22]

An alternative basis for the decision was that of individual
liberty— "the right to be free from all substantial arbitrary impositions and purposeless restraints"—a liberty protected by the
Due Process Clause.[23] Liberty and privacy in this context are
much alike: both involve the right to be left alone. The Court
was unclear whether the "right-to-choose" an abortion was to
be found in the liberty or the privacy doctrine, but it clearly
thought that either would support the holding.

WHERE WAS EQUALITY?

The other constitutional anchor for the abortion decision should
have been the concept of equality—equality without regard for
gender. In the 1960s abortion became a public issue as part of
the campaign for equal rights for women. Although it was not
argued from this perspective, and none of the opinions even
mentions the principle, equality is what this decision is really
about. From the first, abortion rights have been a key issue in
the woman's movement. The NOW Bill of Rights, adopted by
the National Organization for Women in 1967 at its first national
conference, included as its Section VIII "The right of women to
control their own reproductive lives by removing from the penal
codes laws limiting access to contraceptive information and devices, and by repealing penal laws governing abortion."[24] Be-

cause abortion symbolized the subordination of women, not as much to men as to a male-dominated, patriarchal social order, it was a rallying point and organizing principle for what was then called "women's liberation." Feminist writing about abortion recognized that equality was the prize at stake.[25] Rhonda Copelon Schoenbrod and Janice Goodman, lawyers who had participated in much of the early abortion rights litigation, discussed the implications of the decision shortly after it was handed down and pointed out the common concerns in *Roe* and the 1954 desegregation case:

> Jan: I see parallels between *Brown* and the abortion decision even more so than between *Brown* and *Reed* because the abortion decision goes to the guts of the women's struggle and also of society's view of women just like the right to equal and integrated education did for Blacks.[26]

Laws governing reproduction are essentially laws classifying by gender. Like racial classifications, they not only coerce non-conforming individuals, but also burden whole groups, allotting their members inferior roles to play in the social order. By defining women as child-bearers and imposing rules related to that function on all women whether or not they wish to bear children, the law treats all women in a discriminatory manner, requiring all to observe rules that are appropriate only to some. The ability to control reproduction allows those women who do not want to be defined by traditional roles to demand inclusion on an equal basis in the larger world of work and public affairs, rather than being confined to a dependent social role and a subordinate position within the family. The demand that individuals be allowed to direct their lives according to their own abilities and aspirations, rather than being allocated assigned roles as members of a class, was the same kind of broad claim to equal treatment in society made by racial minorities. Birth control practices and devices, with abortion as a back-up in case of failure, remove a disabling condition that has made equality impossible. Reproductive control allows individuals to choose their assignments in life, and for those women who choose motherhood, it promotes equality within the family itself, allowing the evolution of more egalitarian structures in which men and women plan children and share work and family responsibilities.

If equality was the true issue in the abortion cases, why did the Supreme Court fail even to mention the concept? The most obvious answer is that the litigants themselves raised the issue only marginally; some of the briefs argued that poor women and minorities were denied equal protection by state laws prohibiting abortion because they could not travel to states with permissive abortion laws or take advantage of procedures that wealthier women could use to circumvent legal restrictions.[27] The argument was that rich and poor were subjected to differential treatment. Existing equal protection doctrine did not provide a point of departure for an argument that the Constitution demands equal treatment of men and women without regard to reproductive potential or that anti-abortion legislation burdens all women because it denies them reproductive choice. The existing precedents, insofar as there were any on sexual equality, applied to situations where males and females were similarly situated, yet were treated differently because of stereotypes about women that did not take into account individual capabilities. The landmark *Reed* case, for example, overturned a state law that required the choice of males over females where there were contests between family members over appointments as executors of estates. The law was held to be discriminatory because it established an arbitrary preference in favor of males and prevented individual women with business skills from receiving appointments as executors.

Contrary to what one might expect, equal protection doctrine does not offer a broad guarantee of equality. Decisions interpreting the Equal Protection Clause have emphasized that it refers to the principle that "all men are equal before the law," and that equality before the law requires simply that all persons in similar situations be treated similarly and that no man or class be given special privileges.[28] The principle does not require that laws make no distinctions between different classes of persons and things, because legislation, as a practical matter, must make distinctions between categories, between swamps and deserts, between optometrists and ophthalmologists. Classifications must be reasonable and not purely arbitrary, but they do not have to be made with "mathematical nicety." Legislative judgments about factual differences on which classifications should be based are presumptively valid.[29]

The joker in the deck, of course, has been the phrase "all persons similarly situated." Because men and women are different, legislative classifications based on gender have not been held to offend concepts of equality, and as long as laws are reasonably related to those differences they have not been considered discriminatory. The only question that legislatures have had to ask was whether a gender classification served a rational legislative aim or (more recently) was clearly related to a substantial state purpose. *Equal protection doctrine, then, has actually been used to keep women subordinate, rather than to guarantee them equality* because it justifies separate, special treatment with no checks to see whether such treatment is burdensome, or even necessary. The concept of political equality has been difficult to reconcile with the opposing tradition of the common law, which assigns women an inferior social status. There has always been an inherent contradiction between the recognition of women as full citizens, equals in the political community, and their assignment to a dependent social role and a subordinate role within the family because of their reproductive functions. Even if social and political roles can be separated (and the Supreme Court attempted to do this in the context of racial segregation in *Plessy v. Ferguson* and ultimately met with failure), there tends to be seepage between the two spheres. As an example of this seepage, consider the opposition to women's suffrage; many critics of the Nineteenth Amendment were certain that married women would be incapable of forming independent political opinions and that their votes would inevitably reflect the political views of their husbands. It was also felt that private responsibilities in the home would create conflicts with a public role as full citizens.[30]

A recent article by Professor Sylvia Law of the New York University School of Law, entitled "Rethinking Sex and the Constitution," has located the source of much of the analytical difficulty in equal protection/gender cases in the failure to distinguish clearly between gender itself and reproductive functions. Her argument is that courts have assumed that the laws treating men and women differently because of actual physiological differences between the sexes are justifiable because they are related to "real" differences.[31] Judges have not applied equal protection analysis to this type of legislation because they assume such legislation creates no danger that differential treatment will be based on false or stereotyped assumptions about individuals. But, in fact, Professor Law maintains, "assumptions about biological differences and destiny [have] provided the prime justification for creating a separate, inferior legal status for women."[32] Statutes based on reproductive differences are exactly the laws that *should* be subjected to a sophisticated and careful scrutiny, because all such laws "implicate equality concerns."[33] Professor Law asserts that legal structures based on biological differences have been used to support male dominance and are inconsistent with constitutional ideals of equality. The appropriate function of the law is not to "enforce a general vision of what men and women are really like," but to allow them to define themselves.[34] In order to reconcile the reality of biological differences with an ideal of equality, Law proposes that a distinct test be used to measure the impact of laws that are related to reproductive biology. Any law in the reproductive area would be subjected to careful judicial scrutiny to ensure that (1) it has "no significant impact on perpetuating either the oppression of women or culturally imposed sex-role constraints on individual freedom, or (2) if the law has this impact, it is justified as the best means of serving a compelling state purpose."[35] If they were subjected to this test, laws restricting abortion would be found to deny equal protection. When the state denies access to abortion it denies women relief, now medically available, from the burdens of unwanted pregnancies. Unwanted pregnancies not only burden women (and not men) physically, but also deny females rights of self-determination, the responsibility for making moral decisions about the quality of life available to a prospective child, and opportunities for sexual expression.

Rather than breaking new ground by exploring the possible application of the Equal Protection Clause, the Supreme Court in *Roe v. Wade* adopted the more settled privacy/liberty approach. In spite of the criticisms leveled at Justice Blackmun's opinion, in 1973 and afterwards, it put forward a humane, careful, judicious compromise and probably handled the problem as well as it could have been done. It balanced the opposed and conflicting interests of child, mother and state as fairly as possible and stated the solution in terms of accepted constitutional principles. The Court concluded that the dilemma which abortion presents is not capable of solution by giving a total victory to any one side—giving the woman an absolute right to terminate pregnancies, giving the fetus a right to life that overrides the rights of all other parties or allowing the state free rein in determining the balance in this area of competing rights and values. The trimester compromise had the advantage of recognizing three of the most important interests involved, and it also gave the state some guidelines within which to design new abortion statutes, rather than leaving these limits to be worked out in a series of follow-up court cases.

Justice Blackmun's compromise took into account certain social realities that a narrower approach would have ignored. One of these was that early abortions were now medically safe, in fact safer in most cases than actual childbirth. Second, it was a fact, no matter what the Court decided, that hundreds of thousands of women a year were having illegal abortions and would continue to resort to this solution.[36] Third, many of the older state abortion laws were archaic, enacted in response to pressures and motives that no longer existed, and were poorly attuned to contemporary conditions. Some had been passed as part of earlier legislative campaigns to improve public morality. Many were overly harsh. Others, like the Texas statute, made no provisions for abortion to safeguard health, to prevent the birth of seriously deformed children or to abort conceptions that followed rape or incest. By 1973 the public was in favor of laws allowing abortion for these "hard" reasons.[37] Fourth, there was a burgeoning woman's political movement that felt strongly that equal rights were not attainable without access to effective control of reproduction. A Court decision validating anti-abortion laws with only a health/life exception would have given constitutional legitimacy to this restrictive position and made it less negotiable politically. The Court's decision, then, was essentially a clean-up operation that swept the scene clear of ancient litter, outlined the constitutional limits that new abortion law would have to respect and then dumped the subject back into the political process.[38]

There was a narrower path that the Court could have taken. All nine of the Justices agreed that the Texas law was too broad and restricted access to abortions too narrowly. The Court could simply have overturned it, outlining its defects and leaving the Texas legislature to make whatever changes it decided were necessary. Seven of the Justices agreed that the Georgia law under attack in the companion case, *Doe v. Bolton*, required procedures so complicated and burdensome to women seeking abortions that it prevented legitimate requests for abortion from being honored.[39] By rejecting these two laws but by refusing to outline the scope of the right to choose an abortion, the Court would have passed the buck back to the state legislatures, using much the same pattern adopted in the capital punishment decision, *Furman v. Georgia*, decided a year earlier.[40] But it is hard to see how some kind of "legislative" approach could have been avoided altogether; the Court would still have had to give the states some indication about the permissible limits of state regulation. The strategy adopted was designed to defuse the controversy. Once it was clear what the limits of the abortion right were, state legislative bodies could be left alone for a period of time to formulate new statutes within the framework set out by the Court. A single decision followed by a period of judicial inaction was likely to minimize public agitation; a series of cases would have kept attention rivetted to the subject.

ABORTION AND THE FAMILY BATTLE

The Supreme Court's compromise did not defuse the abortion controversy; in fact, it polarized the antagonistic parties even further. Supreme Court decisions themselves often become the focal points of political disputes. *Dred Scott* (to which this decision has frequently been compared), *Brown v. Board of Education* and the school prayer cases are a few of the more notorious examples. The Court evidently did not expect such an explosive political reaction to what it must have regarded as a moderate and carefully reasoned opinion that avoided most of the controversial issues. There is also no indication that any of the Justices saw that the decision might be understood as destructive of traditional family life.

In the political reaction that followed this decision, the fetus rather than the family became the focus of the controversy. Right-to-Life rhetoric is phrased mostly in terms of fetal life: life beginning at the moment of conception, the fetus as a form of human life and abortion as murder. The fetus is a powerful symbol. But although the controversy rages over its "right to life," the dynamics of the dispute may lie at a deeper level, in the implications that the recognition of reproductive rights has for women and families. The rhetoric of conservative politicians, blaming the instability of modern families on the rejection by women of their traditional sex roles, contains an important perception. The liberation of women from their reproductive roles does undercut the patriarchal family and loosen its coherence, and women have opportunities today which they did not have in the past to reject traditional assignments of family responsibilities. The Roman Catholic Church, that quintessentially traditional and patriarchal institution, recognized the significance of the Supreme Court's abortion decision as soon as it was handed down. Galvanized into action, the church began the organizing effort that would serve as both a model and political base for a coalition of Catholics, anti-abortionists, fundamentalist Christians and social conservatives later to be labeled the New Right.[41]

The debate however, was not structured in terms either of sexual equality or of the impact of abortion policies on the family. By defining the abortion issue in terms of the fetus and emphasizing religious and moral arguments, Right-to-Life forces pulled off a political coup and turned their opposition into a symbolic crusade. Finding themselves labeled immoral, anti-life and anti-family, pro-Choice supporters finally realized that it was a mistake to let the opposition occupy the high ground of moral legitimacy unchallenged. They began to point out that, although there are powerful religious and moral buttresses behind traditional family structure and the sex roles in it, different family configurations are possible, and are, in fact, in the process of evolving. Family arrangements based on equality of the sexes and shared responsibility for children and for work are much more compatible with the guarantees of political and legal equality in the Constitution than is the family of the common law tradition. Feminist ethicists such as Beverly Wildung Harrison also contested the claim that the pro-Choice position was selfish or immoral. In the context of the hard decisions women are compelled to make, she states, abortion, although not in itself desirable, can be a moral choice just as the conscious decision to bear a child is a moral choice.

To defend the morality of procreative choice for women is not to deny reverence toward or appreciation for many women's deep commitment to childbearing and child nurturance. It does ask that women collectively come to understand that genuine choice with respect to procreative power [not simply for the sake of choice] is a necessary condition to *any* and *all* women's human fulfillment.[42]

After *Roe* the Supreme Court stepped away from the battlefield and refused to consider another major abortion case until 1976. The state law which was challenged in *Planned Parenthood of Central Missouri v. Danforth* is a fairly typical example of state statutes passed as part of the legislative reaction to *Roe*.[43] But the main importance of the case lies in the Court's rulings on spousal and parental consent. These issues had been avoided in the earlier case. In *Danforth*, some of the dissenting Justices seemed for the first time to have become aware that an emphasis on individual rights could have a destructive impact on family unity.

Missouri's new abortion statute, passed in 1974, contained many of the same kinds of provisions that were being included in legislation in other states. Missouri was one of the states in which Right-to-Life forces had quickly captured the state legislature. The abortion statute being challenged was designed both to answer questions which the Supreme Court had left unanswered, and to restrict the impact of the ruling wherever possible. It defined "viability," demanded written consent from women about to undergo abortions, required that they have the consent of their husbands or, if minors, of their parents, prohibited the use of certain abortion techniques, made recordkeeping mandatory, and required physicians, on pain of criminal penalties, to make an effort to save the fetus.

Justice Blackmun again wrote the majority opinion, following the general direction of his *Roe* opinion, although the vote supporting his position was now 5 to 4, rather than 7 to 2. Justice John Paul Stevens had replaced Justice Douglas and both he and the Chief Justice joined the dissenters. Some seemingly neutral provisions of the statute, such as the recordkeeping requirements, were upheld. Other sections, such as requiring the husband's consent before an abortion could be performed and providing that unmarried minors receive the permission of their parents, were overturned.

The two concurring Justices and the four dissenters expressed concern about family relationships and the wisdom of giving quite as unrestricted a right to choose, even during the first trimester, to the individual woman alone. Justices Stewart and Powell, concurring, thought that immature minors should be required to consult with their parents or with an authoritative adult, perhaps a judge. The dissenters agreed with the Missouri legislature that the father had an important stake in the life of his child, which the state might protect; they also felt that parental consent requirements were well within accepted limits on the decision-making capabilities of minors.

In this case, the clash between the individual rights approach of the majority and the concern of the minority for protecting familiar family relationships is clearly revealed. The dissenters show that they believe that family interests are interconnected and that it is disruptive to the family as an institution to allow women unrestricted access even to first trimester abortions. The father as well as the mother has rights that deserve protection; minors, even those who are physically mature, need the counseling and protection of their families. These Justices would have allowed the state to use its authority to ensure that the father's authority be respected and that parents be included in the decisions about abortion made by their children. The majority recognized that there was a "family issue" but felt that, because of her physical involvement in pregnancy, the mother's interests should be given a greater degree of protection. Justice Blackmun stated that he did not believe that giving a husband or parents the right to veto an abortion would strengthen a family. If consultation did not take place voluntarily, he stated, the chances were that family ties had already been weakened.

The question left undecided by this case, one that was extremely important to the pro-family movement, was the degree of freedom that adolescents should have to decide, without family involvement, to have abortions. *Danforth* held that parents should not have an absolute veto under all conditions but did not rule out some requirement of parental consultation. It took three more decisions, *Bellotti v. Baird*, *HL v. Matheson*, and the 1983 Akron Ordinance case, to explore this question in detail in the context of several different types of statutory provisions.[44]

Abortion funding cases, decided over a period of several years, show a different dimension of public policy toward the family. By the time the first of these cases reached the Court, political reaction to the *Roe* decision was still exploding at full force. Reluctant to create a massive confrontation with the political branches and unsure of the wisdom of extending abortion rights further, the Court refused to order the public funding of abortions for indigent women. *Maher v. Roe* (1977) held that a Connecticut prohibition against the funding of non-medical abortions did not deny equal protection, even though the state continued to pay the expenses of childbirth. *Beal v. Doe* (1977) ruled that the Social Security Act did not require the states to fund non-therapeutic abortions. *Harris v. McRae* (1980) accepted Congress' decision to refuse to fund any abortions except in a narrow range of circumstances. (The exact dimensions of these exceptions were fought out every year on the floor of Congress.)[45] The Court in effect accepted the limits placed on its decision by the political branches.

By default, political decisions not to fund abortions for the poor established a policy of encouraging poor women who did not want children to establish marginal families. Many of these marginal families would probably later need public support. The increase in teenage pregnancy, the rapid rise in the number of families headed by single females and the likelihood of female-headed families falling below the poverty level might have convinced reflective legislators that a long-range pro-family program should include funding for indigent abortions. The moral and political climate of the anti-abortion backlash, however, dictated that abortion be discouraged and child-bearing be encouraged. Prenatal care and maternity would be covered as part of normal medical care, but non-medical abortions would not.

Even if it had desired to do so, the Supreme Court probably could not have forced Congress or the state legislatures to choose another policy. Dissenting Justices pointed out the social consequences of the Court's decision, Justice Thurgood Marshall, in *Beal v. Doe*, spelling out the impact that the decision would have on poor families:

The enactments challenged here brutally coerce poor women to bear children whom society will scorn for every day of their lives. Many thousands of unwanted minority and mixed-race children now spend blighted lives in foster homes, orphanages, and "reform" schools. And opposition remains strong against increasing Aid to Families with Dependent Children benefits for impoverished mothers and children, so that there is little chance for the children to grow up in a decent environment. I am appalled at the ethical bankruptcy of those who preach a "right to life" that means, under present social policies, a bare existence in utter misery for so many poor women and their children.[46]

The Court rejected the temptation to hear another abortion case until 1983, when it decided *City of Akron v. Akron Center for Reproductive Health, Inc.*, refusing again to repudiate the principles enunciated in *Roe v. Wade*.[47] Anti-abortionists had hoped that the Court would reconsider its position on abortion and that Justice Sandra Day O'Connor's vote would be enough to swing the balance the other way. The vote remained at 5 to 4, in spite of the fact that the U.S. government now submitted a brief *amicus curiae* in support of the Right-to-Life position.

After *Roe v. Wade*, first abortion and then the American family became a political battleground. The abortion issue provided a moral rallying point for "cultural fundamentalists" who were unnerved by the pace of social change. The fetus had become a symbol of larger concerns—family dissolution, morality, secularism. Abortion intersected with a number of specific social issues with which social conservatives were concerned: sex education, women's rights, teenage promiscuity and pregnancy, divorce, changing sex and family roles, the secularization of society, pornography and the loss of religious values. To all of these dissatisfactions, the abortion issue had given a focus.

4

Punishing Pregnancy: The Pregnancy Disability Decisions

> ... society has been organized to make young people want to marry, want to have children, to make the woman want to stay at home and look after them, and make the man want to work and toil to support his children so that there will be another generation.
>
> Margaret Mead, Addressing the New York Commission on Human Rights, September 1970[1]

It was difficult for the Supreme Court Justices to see an element of sexual stereotyping in their treatment of pregnancy. It took the Court a long time to recognize that any differential treatment of the sexes presented constitutional problems; the first decision finding a clear-cut gender classification to be in conflict with the Equal Protection Clause did not come until 1971. It was even more difficult for the Court to see the treatment of pregnant women as discriminatory, inasmuch as pregnancy is not the exact equivalent of gender, but a related condition. No one can deny that the ability to bear children distinguishes women from men. If men and women are different, the reasoning goes, there can be no constitutional objection to treating them differently. But what was hard to see was that some of the legal rules restricting the activities of pregnant women were not required by physiology, but resulted from a social order built on patriarchal principles, designed to protect the family as a reproductive institution. The patriarchal order was changing, and as it was transformed by social and economic forces, women began to demand legal adjustments that would allow them to participate more fully in the outer world of work and public affairs.[2]

Traditional views about women's roles contain many stereotypes; outdated stereotypes change very slowly because we see what we expect to see.[3] People who enter into situations with preconceptions about individuals and groups are likely to be more receptive to ideas and information that support their prejudices than to contradictory points of view.[4] Perhaps because attitudes dealing with such matters as family, women, children, sex and procreation are so close to the bedrock of personal psychology, they are very deeply held, even by judges. It is easier to be detached about political and legal change, which is external, than about subtle emotional attitudes toward sex roles and family structure. So it may have been inevitable that Congress, which is constantly being inundated with raw material about social conflicts, was more aware of the revolution that had taken place in women's employment and of the adjustments necessary to bring the law in this area up to date than were the more isolated Justices of the Supreme Court.

In a group of decisions handed down between 1973 and 1983, which considered claims that discrimination against pregnant workers was, in fact, gender discrimination, the Supreme Court reflected some of the confusion that exists in our society about the changing roles of women and the increasing movement of women into the workforce. The Supreme Court's treatment of pregnancy discrimination is extraordinarily interesting because it does not deal with the kind of clear-cut gender discrimination found in *Reed v. Reed* or *Frontiero v. Richardson*, but with a subtler form of sexual stereotyping that conflicts with the present realities of the position of women in the economy.[5] The legal distinctions which the Court makes in these cases often ignore the underlying facts and support traditional perspectives.

Reed v. Reed, decided in 1971, was the first major decision to overturn a law on the basis of a claim that it denied equal protection to women. In *Reed* the Court upheld a challenge to a

state statute which gave automatic preference to males over females in the choosing of executors of estates. *Frontiero v. Richardson*, decided two years later, in 1973, rejected a U.S. Air Force
regulation that gave automatic dependent allowances to the wives
of male officers, but required the husbands of female officers to
prove dependency. In both of these cases, the laws involved
were held to discriminate against females as such. Pregnancy
rules, however, covered only those females who were pregnant,
requiring them to stop work a certain number of months before
delivery and sometimes to stay at home for a stated length of
time afterwards.

Pregnancy has always been used as an excuse for sex discrimination. Because women cannot escape from their reproductive
functions, the argument goes, they are unsuited for positions
of responsibility or serious work. A good example of this type
of reasoning can be seen in an editorial in the *New York Herald*,
published in 1850:

They want to fill all the other posts which men are ambitious to occupy,
to be lawyers, doctors, captains of vessels and generals in the field.
How funny it would sound in the newspapers that Lucy Stone, pleading
a cause, took suddenly ill in the pains of parturition and perhaps gave
birth to a fine bouncing boy in court. Or that Rev. Antoinette Brown
was arrested in the pulpit in the middle of her sermon from the same
cause and presented a "pledge" to her husband and the congregation;
or that Dr. Harriot K. Hunt while attending a gentleman for a fit of
gout or fistula in ano, found it necessary to send for a doctor, there
and then, and to be delivered of a man or woman child, perhaps twins.
A similar event might happen on the floor of Congress, in a storm at
sea or in the raging tempest of battle, and then what is to become of
the woman legislator?[6]

Women who tried to assume important male roles, the editorial suggested, would inevitably have to abandon their responsibilities to answer the demands of biology. Although biology
assigns only child-bearing to females, traditional descriptions of
the family give women the primary responsibility for child care
as well. According to the accepted ideology, the raising of children is the private burden of the family unit and should take
place in the home. The family has primary legal, moral and

economic responsibility for its children, and the father's position as family breadwinner allows the mother freedom from paid employment. Unmarried women should work, but it is assumed that they will marry and leave their jobs, and that while they are single they will not need the higher wages men need to support their families. Women's work, even where it is paid, is devalued because it is seen as temporary and marginal.

State and federal courts have accepted this family ideology, for an ideology is what it is, without question, and their opinions are full of judicial statements to the effect that women are delicate beings, who, as the mothers of the race, should be kept in the home to nurture and protect the children, away from the sordid events of business and politics.[7] As recently as 1961, when women comprised 33 percent of the total civilian labor force, Justice Harlan was able to write that the state might excuse women from their responsibilities to serve on juries because "Despite the enlightened emancipation of women from the restrictions and protections of bygone years, and their entry into many parts of community life formerly considered reserved to men, woman is still regarded as the center of home and family life."[8]

Before World War II, the gap between ideology and actual fact was hidden. Relatively few women, predominantly from lower income groups, worked outside the home. In 1940 approximately 25 percent of the nation's jobholders were women. Wartime demands brought an increasing number of women into employment, and since 1947 the increase in the number of women in the labor force has been steady and substantial, increasing by 21 percent between 1947 and 1983. The Bureau of Labor Statistics reported that 52.9 percent of American women were working during February 1983 and that of the 112 million persons in the labor force 48 million (43 percent) were women.[9] As the percentage of women employed has risen, so has the number of married women who work, even though they have small children at home. This number is still growing. The workforce now includes a large number of women who are not married or who are no longer married, but who have children and are the heads of households.[10]

Even though the number of employed women has been steadily rising, many of the discriminatory practices that have always attended women's employment have remained in force. Women have usually been at a disadvantage in employment outside the home. Although the situation is now changing, for most of our history they have had difficulty obtaining jobs in competition with men, have been limited to certain types of "female" occupations by custom and were excluded from many jobs by law. They were given lower pay. In addition, they faced differential treatment because of their reproductive capacity. One of the rationales for refusing to hire women was the contention that they were temporary employees, likely to become pregnant and leave the job, abandoning the employer after the expense of training. Yet, pregnant workers were not encouraged to stay on the job; industry as well as schools and government offices often insisted on unpaid maternity leave, and a number of states limited the employment of pregnant women by statute. Mandatory maternity leave was not a short-term proposition; it might last as long as six to eight months and might indeed be terminal if seniority rights were lost, as they often were. Women returning from childbirth were reinstated in lower level jobs, at lower pay. Loss of seniority often meant loss of benefits and pension rights.[11]

Part of the rationale for discriminating against the pregnant woman was derived from the idea that she needed special protection and needed to be home after birth to care for the new child. Rules protecting pregnant women resembled earlier protective legislation, state laws requiring special conditions for working women on the assumption that they were more fragile than men or in greater need of moral guidance. These laws kept women from taking certain "unsuitable" (often higher paid) jobs or made it inconvenient for employers to hire them by requiring special treatment. Like the protective laws, pregnancy rules often worked to the detriment of women. Feminists maintain that among the major social objectives of such rules were the reinforcement of patriarchal social structures, the subordination of women to men and the elimination of job competition.[12]

Some of the justifications for compulsory maternity leave were less rational. After the baby began to "show," it was embarrassing to have pregnant women around in offices and factories where they would be visible or in schoolrooms where children could see them.[13] Some employers argued that if they were kept on the job, they might go into labor unexpectedly and cause all sorts of problems. By sending women home early in pregnancy, enforced maternity leave insulated them from insult and ridicule, as well as protecting their real interests. It is likely that these reasons were rationalizations for even deeper emotional reactions, such as the Victorian view that pregnant women were obscene to look at and should remain hidden at home. Prejudices about pregnant women have roots in even earlier times and more primitive superstitions. The idea that pregnant women should be kept at home and not mix with others is of ancient lineage. Traditional European society "harbored profound suspiciousness about the pregnant woman's power to contaminate the world about her."[14]

Pregnancy rules also reinforced the traditional assignment of male and female roles. The workplace was for men. Even though it might include a few unmarried women and younger females who had not started their families, working mostly in clerical and support positions, the world of work was male.

These widely held opinions did not always match realities. As noted earlier, even before the 1940s women worked outside of the home. Working-class women have always had to work, although they may have been doing domestic work or piecework or other types of invisible labor. Large numbers of black and immigrant women worked for wages.[15] By 1974, when the first pregnancy case was decided, it was clearly incorrect to think of women as homemakers rather than workers. The norm was no longer the all-male labor force, and the factory or office was no longer an all-male haven except for the "girls" in the front office. The old ideology was patently obsolete. By this time, working women comprised nearly 42.2 percent of all civilian workers, were typically married women with children, did not regard work as temporary and regarded pregnancies as temporary disabilities. Women who wanted children but did not intend to leave employment permanently left with the intention of returning as soon as possible.[16]

Early guidelines established by the Equal Employment Opportunities Commission (EEOC) to aid in enforcement of the Civil Rights Act of 1964 recognized these facts and directed employers to treat pregnancy as a temporary disability. The Commission perceived discrimination on the basis of pregnancy as sex discrimination, finding that the assumption that women would become pregnant and leave the labor market was in fact sex stereotyping and helped justify the unfavorable treatment of employed women.[17]

There was a factual basis for such a conclusion. Enforced maternity leave, especially for the working woman who had not intended to become pregnant, was often punitive in its impact. If she was married, the woman was probably working because her wage or salary was necessary to keep the family afloat; if not, her job was her source of income. If she was laid off as soon as she became noticeably pregnant, the likelihood of finding another job was non-existent, but unemployment benefits were unavailable because she was not "available for employment," one of the requirements for receiving unemployment compensation. Even as late as 1960, thirty-five states explicitly excluded pregnant women from eligibility for unemployment benefits, and the period of exclusion ranged from eight weeks to six months.[18] Pregnant workers were not entitled to the protection or medical help which was available to other workers under sick pay and disability plans, and, in addition, had to bear the extra expenses and medical bills connected with the new child.[19] The late 1970s brought court challenges to these rules under both the Equal Protection Clause of the Constitution and the Civil Rights Act of 1964.

THE LA FLEUR CASE: FREEDOM TO CHOOSE WHAT?

By acting to penalize the pregnant teacher for deciding to bear a child, overly restrictive maternity leave regulations can constitute a heavy burden on the exercise of the protected freedoms.[20]

As was true of many other family-related cases, *Cleveland Board of Education v. La Fleur*, the case that overturned compulsory, unpaid pregnancy leave for teachers, was developed as part of an organized litigation effort. The sponsoring organization, the Women's Law Fund (WLF), was a Cleveland, Ohio, group that split off from the Women's Equity Action League (WEAL) over this very issue, the need to challenge pregnancy discrimination. The WLF received a two-year, $140,000 grant from the Ford Foundation to take this controversy into court.[21] The target chosen for the initial attack was an Ohio school district which required pregnant teachers to take unpaid maternity leave for five months in advance of delivery and prohibited their return to work until the semester beginning after the new child had reached the age of three months. The companion case, *Cohen v. Chesterfield County School Board*, involved similar provisions in Virginia.[22] Chesterfield County required a four-month leave before the birth of the child, and required a physician's certificate before teaching could be resumed. The Virginia rule, however, did allow some exemptions from the four-month period. A number of other, similar school district policies were challenged in federal courts during this period, and almost all of the lower courts held that discrimination against pregnant women was sex discrimination.[23] Rules like these had been in force in public schools throughout the nation for years.

The Women's Law Fund attorneys developed their case, in the main, on traditional equal protection grounds.[24] But instead of treating these rules as discriminatory in the sense that they denied equal protection, the Supreme Court handled the case as a due process problem, using the decision in *Roe v. Wade* as a model.[25] The freedom which the Court saw threatened was the right to choose motherhood. According to Justice Stewart's majority opinion, overly restrictive maternity leave requirements that forced her to leave her job put too heavy a burden on a woman's decision to bear a child. State-imposed pregnancy rules thus denied her the right to choose childbirth free from unnecessary state interference. As applied to school teachers, such maternity leave requirements also denied due process by setting up as an irrebuttable presumption the rule that all pregnant women were incapable of teaching after the fifth month and were unable to return to work until the child was three months old.[26] Although the districts did have a justifiable interest in the continuity of teaching and in the fitness of teachers, these rules, the opinion explained, did not reflect the actual condition of most pregnant teachers and were not validly related to the school's legitimate handling of personnel problems.

It is interesting to speculate about the court's decision to rest this holding on due process rather than on equal protection grounds. In two important earlier decisions, the Supreme Court had used equal protection analysis to show that state laws that classified persons according to gender and then treated them unequally denied the equal protection demanded by the Constitution.[27] Even though pregnancy classifications were not overt gender classifications, since not all women were pregnant, they were clearly "sex-linked" or "sex plus" categories. The basic issue, then, that had to be answered was: if one treats pregnancy differently from other disabilities or conditions, is one (in view of the fact that *only* women can become pregnant) in effect discriminating on the basis of sex? The due process analysis allowed the Court to avoid holding that discrimination against pregnant women was gender discrimination. The decision in *La Fleur* showed that the Court was not yet ready to tackle a question that was related so closely to traditional views of women as child-bearers and homemakers.

Justice Stewart's majority opinion had the support of five Justices. Even though he rejected the pregnancy rules as encumbering the right to choose, he sympathized with the school board. In a footnote, he repeated one of the hoarier stereotypes; school boards probably have the power to set reasonable cut-off dates during the last few weeks of pregnancy, he stated, to avoid disabling conditions, or the "possibility of labor beginning while some teacher was in the classroom."[28] The majority was clearly unwilling to hold that pregnancy disability rules involved sex discrimination. There must have been a considerable amount of sympathy for Judge Clement F. Haynsworth's opinion, stated below in the Court of Appeals, in *Cohen v. Chesterfield County*, the companion case. Judge Haynsworth reasoned that sex discrimination was possible only where men and women were competing for something, and one gender won the contest because policies or legal rules placed members of that sex in a favored position. He agreed that only women could become pregnant, but he argued that this did not mean that laws treating pregnancy differently from other disabilities or conditions were per se discriminatory. Laws that required all persons to be clean-shaven would, under that analysis, discriminate against men because they could not apply to women. Pregnancy regulations were aimed at a condition, not at women themselves.[29]

Justice Powell supported the majority decision, but in his concurring opinion he attempted to instruct his colleagues about the realities of personnel problems in the schools. Powell had had extensive experience with school systems as a member of the Richmond, Virginia, school board and the Virginia State Board of Education and was aware of the real nature of the discriminatory rules. He insisted that the proper basis for the decision was equal protection and that sexual discrimination was the true issue. Most school teachers, he noted, were women, and a certain percentage of them were pregnant at any given time. To penalize these women for a condition that was so clearly sex-linked, without a clear need for the protective rules, did deny equal protection. Justice Powell pointed out that the school board's justifications were not rationally related to the rules that were imposed, and that it was probably true that the main motivation behind this type of rule was the outdated and unacceptable idea that pregnant teachers ought to be kept out of the sight of children. Clearly, in the 1970s this nineteenth-century prejudice was not an adequate basis for school policy.

Some members of the Court must have agreed with Judge Haynsworth that pregnancy rules did not deny equal protection, but the majority chose the due process approach, probably because it allowed them to overturn obviously restrictive practices without committing themselves on the question of whether pregnancy rules that disadvantaged women discriminated because of sex.

The real issue in this case is not, of course, the "right to choose" childbirth, but the right of women to decide to be both workers and mothers rather than having to choose between the roles. State laws requiring unpaid maternity leave when it is not necessary for the health of the mother or the welfare of the child place an economic penalty on the families of the women who choose childbirth, but they also reinforce traditional sex roles. The assumption which such laws embody is not that the woman has the right to choose childbirth, but that pregnant women do not belong at work and that after children are born they should stay at home to provide mothering and child care. Many families today cannot afford to choose between children and the wife's employment. They must have the wife's income for the economic welfare of the family, and they do not agree that reproduction and child care require an exclusive commitment, but believe that these activities can be combined with work.

The traditional view also accepts the underlying assumption that the family alone should be responsible for the costs of child-rearing.[30] Some European countries now reject the idea of a completely privatized responsibility for child-raising, regard pregnancy leave as normal and provide public subsidies for maternal (or paternal) leave after the child is born. The Swedish and French governments pay a family allowance to all parents with children, and also provide substantial public facilities for day care.[31] Our own program of Aid to Families with Dependent Children recognizes that there are public as well as private interests at stake in reproduction and child-raising; punitive pregnancy leave requirements, on the other hand, are founded on the assumptions that families alone would bear the costs of children, that child-rearing should be a full-time responsibility of the wife and that couples unable to bear these burdens should not have families. By 1974 there was considerable support for the alternate view that pregnant women should be covered by unemployment compensation when they were forced to leave work, that seniority rights should not be lost during pregnancy and that a general system of disability insurance, treating pregnancy as a temporary disability, should be required of all employers.[32]

Title VII, Section 703 (a) (2) of the Civil Rights Act of 1964 forbids discrimination by an employer against any individual because of race, color, religion, *sex* or national origin. By 1974, both the Equal Employment Opportunities Commission and several lower federal courts had held that any employment policy that discriminated against pregnant women *was* sex discrimination and that such policies were forbidden by the Civil Rights Act. But the Supreme Court had not yet ruled either on the constitutional question—whether the Equal Protection Clause itself forbade discrimination against pregnancy—or on the question of the correct reading of the statute—whether rules based on pregnancy were sex discrimination forbidden by the Civil Rights Act.[33]

GEDULDIG V. AIELLO: "PREGNANT WOMEN AND NON-PREGNANT PERSONS"

A case coming to the Court from California forced the Court to decide the constitutional question. The Court had avoided an equal protection ruling in *La Fleur*; in the California case it was forced to meet the issue head on.

The state of California had a state-operated disability plan that insured workers against illness and injury. The plan was supported by a 1 percent tax on wages and salaries. It covered a multitude of possible injuries, illnesses and operations (sports injuries, plastic surgery and prostatectomies were all covered) but excluded pregnancy. The state argued that it would be too costly to cover pregnancy, that pregnancy was not, after all, a disability because it frequently involved a voluntary decision and that broad coverage of pregnancy would drive up the amount that workers would have to contribute to the state plan. Several pregnant women challenged this policy. The state courts, in the meantime, had ruled that pregnancies involving illness or unusual medical problems were covered, but that normal pregnancies were not. In the case that came to the Supreme Court *sub nomine Geduldig v. Aiello*, the women workers argued that any plan that discriminated against pregnancy while covering other problems requiring medical attention did, in fact, discriminate against women and was forbidden by the Equal Protection Clause.[34]

In spite of the fact that by this time both the EEOC and most lower federal courts had agreed that discrimination against pregnancy was discrimination on the basis of gender, the Supreme Court ruled 6 to 3 to the contrary. Justice Stewart, who had written the Court's opinion in *La Fleur*, denied that sex discrimination was involved. The state had decided to cover certain types of illnesses and disabilities but to exclude others. There was no constitutional requirement that the state cover all disabilities, merely that it have a good reason, which was not discriminatory, for excluding some. Excluding pregnancy did not involve gender discrimination, Stewart stated, because there was no risk from which men were being protected and women were not.[35] The state had a legitimate interest in the fiscal integrity of its insurance plan, and the exclusion of normal pregnancies from the risks covered promoted that interest.

Justice Stewart's opinion emphasized the economic issue in the California plan and again ignored the issue of sex discrimination, mentioning it only in a footnote—which read: "The lack of identity between the excluded disability and gender as such under this insurance program becomes clear upon the most cursory analysis. The program divides potential recipients into two groups—pregnant women and nonpregnant people."[36]

For the majority, the decisive factor was the state's claim that inclusion of normal pregnancies would inflate the costs of the plan. The language of Justice Stewart's opinion emphasized financial considerations. All of the following words and phrases refer to costs: "funded entirely from the wages of participating employees," "required to contribute," "mandatory," "wholly supported by employees," "self-supporting, never drawing on general state revenues," California's commitment "not to increase the contribution rate," "affordable by all employees," "more costly" (to include pregnancy), "higher rate of employee contributions," "would not be self-supporting."[37]

It may also have occurred to Justice Stewart, although he does not mention this point, that the inclusion of normal pregnancy could be seen as having the effect of requiring workers without children to subsidize the child-bearing costs of families, a significant change from both existing government policy and general economic practice.[38]

Substantial evidence had been developed by this time that laws treating pregnancy as a special condition were frequently used in ways that discriminated against women, and the EEOC and six Courts of Appeals had held that pregnancy discrimination was a form of sex discrimination under the Civil Rights Act.[39] But it seems clear that the Court's majority still agreed with Judge Haynsworth that laws treating pregnancy as a special condition did not necessarily discriminate against women. Some

Justices may also have felt that the ERA would soon be passed and that it was preferable to have reform in this controversial area come from constitutional amendment rather than from further expansion of the Equal Protection Clause.[40]

GENERAL ELECTRIC CO. V. GILBERT: STEREOTYPES AND SIGNALS

Two years after *Geduldig* was decided, the Court ruled unfavorably on a second case involving the pregnancy disability issue.[41] Unlike *Geduldig*, the *Gilbert* case arose under the Civil Rights Act of 1964. Workers at the General Electric plant in Salem, Virginia, challenged the company's failure to provide disability payments for workers absent because of pregnancy on the grounds that their exclusion was sex discrimination within the meaning of the act. But Justice Rehnquist, writing for the Court, found that the two cases presented much the same issue and that *Geduldig* should be followed. He quoted from the earlier decision and cited the principles established there, but the main point he made was that normal pregnancy is a special condition with clearly defined characteristics, and unless pregnancy is being used as a pretext for discriminating against women, there is a reasonable basis for dealing with it as a unique physical state. He repeated Justice Stewart's classification in *Geduldig*—if persons are divided into two categories, "pregnant women and non-pregnant persons," it becomes clear that there is no discrimination on the basis of gender, because many non-pregnant persons are women. The ruling in *Geduldig* was clear: exclusion of pregnancy from a disability benefits plan providing general coverage was not gender-based discrimination.[42]

Justice Brennan's dissent pointed out some of the weaknesses of the majority's approach by comparing the conceptual framework used in the case with that used by the Court below and the EEOC. On its face, a plan excluding pregnancy looks like a normal assignment of risks on basic actuarial principles, and excluding one risk is not discriminatory as long as there is "no risk from which men are protected and women are not." However, if one begins with the proposition that pregnancy is a prime risk for women and that this prime risk is omitted from an otherwise comprehensive plan (which does cover a number of conditions like prostatectomies and circumcisions that are specific to the reproductive systems of men), the neutrality of the arrangement is less obvious. Justice Brennan thought it was relevant to point out the fact that General Electric (GE) had never had policies that protected women workers; in earlier years the company had not even included women in its insurance plan, arguing that they were only temporarily in the labor market and were expected to marry and leave the company. Viewing the matter in the context of GE's overall policies toward women, Justice Brennan doubted that exclusion of pregnancy was really a "gender-neutral" risk assignment. Nor was pregnancy a uniquely *voluntary* condition; other medical conditions (sports injuries, attempted suicides, venereal diseases, elective cosmetic surgery), all covered by the plan, involved some measure of voluntary behavior. Justice Brennan's dissent, concurred in by Justice Marshall, concluded that the District Court's ruling in favor of pregnancy coverage agreed with the overall objectives of Title VII of the Civil Rights Act.[43]

In 1977, in *Nashville Gas Co. v. Satty*, the Court tried for a third time to handle the issue of mandatory maternity leave and exclusion of pregnancy from disability coverage.[44] Nashville Gas Company required pregnant employees to take leave without sick pay; in addition, the pregnant employees lost their job seniority when they took maternity leave. This was such a harsh penalty that the Supreme Court found it difficult to uphold the plan in its entirety. It overturned the provision requiring loss of seniority, but followed the precedent in *General Electric Co. v. Gilbert* in allowing the company to exclude pregnancy from the general coverage of its disability plan. Such a plan did not involve gender-based discrimination, the Court held, because it was facially neutral, had no discriminatory effect and was not used as a pretext for discrimination.

CONGRESS REVERSES THE COURT: THE PREGNANCY DISABILITY ACT OF 1978

A storm of criticism by labor and women's groups greeted these decisions, and Congress acted quickly to reverse the Court's refusal to hold that discrimination against pregnant women was sex discrimination. In 1978, it amended the Civil Rights Act of 1964 to overturn the rulings in these cases. The act made discrimination on the basis of pregnancy, childbirth or related medical conditions illegal in all employment decisions, including hiring, promotion, and seniority rights. Pregnancy was also to be covered by health insurance and disability plans. The only condition related to pregnancy that was not fully covered was abortion; employers could exempt elective abortions from their health insurance plans, although they could not refuse to cover abortions where the life of the mother was endangered. The abortion exemption in the act was the result of heavy lobbying by anti-abortion groups, including the Roman Catholic Church, and was so strongly opposed by women's organizations that it caused some of them to argue for the defeat of the main provisions of the act. The act was passed over these objections.[45]

In passing this legislation, Congress accepted the 1972 Guidelines established by the Equal Employment Opportunities Commission as correctly embodying its intent to treat abortion, childbirth and recovery therefrom in the same manner as other temporary disabilities. The Committee Report on the bill accepted testimony before Congress as demonstrating that the assumption that women would become pregnant and leave the labor force led to the view that women were marginal workers. The new act guaranteed that women would not be forced to leave work unnecessarily because of pregnancy and required that employers include the same benefits for pregnancy and childbirth-related absences that were provided for other disabled workers. This included temporary and long-term disability insurance, sick leave and other forms of employee benefit programs.[46]

Congress thus repudiated the Stewart-Rehnquist argument in *Geduldig, Gilbert* and *Satty* that exclusion of pregnancy from a program of employee benefits did not constitute sex discrimination and reaffirmed the Brennan-Stevens position, stated in dissenting opinions, that "contemporary disability programs are not creatures of a social or cultural vacuum devoid of stereotypes and signals concerning pregnant women employees."[47]

THE REVERSE DISCRIMINATION CASE

The most recent chapter in the controversy over the relationship between pregnancy and sex discrimination was written in 1983, when the Court heard a dispute over the meaning of the Pregnancy Discrimination Act.[48] The Newport News Shipbuilding & Dry Dock Company provided hospitalization benefits for pregnancy and childbirth for both its female employees and the wives of its male workers. However, the coverage provided female employees was more extensive than that allowed the wives of male employees. EEOC guidelines indicated that such an arrangement was unlawful, and the company challenged the agency's interpretation of the act. The resolution of the dispute hinged on congressional intent. Had Congress intended only to make sure that discrimination against female workers because of pregnancy was unlawful, or did the language forbid any discrimination based on pregnancy? If Congress intended the latter, medical plans with less coverage for the wives of employees would violate the act, because they made conditions of employment for males less desirable than conditions of employment for females. The Court held that the act, read in conjunction with the Civil Rights Act, forbade reverse discrimination against male employees. Justices Powell and Rehnquist disagreed with this reading of the statute.

In this case the Supreme Court, in effect, admitted that it had erred badly in 1976, when it decided *General Electric Co. v. Gilbert*. The majority opinion quoted committee reports and debate in the House and Senate castigating the earlier decision; for example, Senator Jacob Javits (R., New York) is quoted as saying, "What we are doing is leaving the situation the way it was before the Supreme Court decided the Gilbert Case last year."[49]

It had taken a long time to convince a majority on the Supreme Court that disparate legal treatment of men and women, seemingly justified by biological differences between the sexes, often reinforced traditional social roles and reflected stereotypes about women that no longer reflected the outside world. Some of the Court's reluctance to extend equal protection doctrine unequivocally to gender issues probably reflected the view that this change should come through the proposed Equal Rights Amendment rather than through judicial decision-making. The Justices may also have realized, subconsciously, that the treatment of pregnancy as a temporary disability, even in the context of employment practices, rather than as a condition that inexorably defined the female role, removed another key support to the structure of the traditional family. Pregnancy leave rules force women to return home and assume responsibility for child-raising; refusal to cover pregnancy under health insurance schemes makes working conditions for women less attractive.

Although there is no evidence that the structure of family life has changed radically in the last century except perhaps in size and number of children, it is clear that the *behavior* of family members and attitudes toward family functions have changed a great deal.[50] The behavior of women, especially as it relates to two areas—divorce and employment outside the home—has had a profound impact on the family.[51] The massive change in the number of women employed that has taken place in less than half a century has inevitably had serious consequences for a social unit, such as the family, which has always been extremely sensitive to economic and social change. The upward trend in figures for both divorce and employment indicates dissatisfaction among both men and women with the traditional assignment of roles and the hierarchical command structure within the patriarchal family. Of course, the two trends are related. The possibility of economic survival and independence makes divorce possible for women and justifiable for men. The economic independence of females may also stimulate dissension between wives and husbands, although the evidence for this is not clearly established.[52] Some studies suggest that the divorce rate for women rises with a rise in income, and others that it is closely related to family size and that couples with small families are more likely to divorce than those with large families.[53] Patterns of marriage, divorce, reproduction and employment are all interrelated. It is also clear that the changed relationship between women and employment was well established long before reborn feminists began to assert it as a political right and that it came in response to economic pressures on families rather than to ideological agitation.

The Supreme Court has, as usual, been exposed to these changes indirectly, as a part of its duty to decide legal questions. The same social problems and pressures that concern legislatures also reach courts—although in their disguise as discrete disputes over the interpretation of legislation or the constitutionality of statutory provisions, the underlying policy issues are often hidden, even from the Justices. In the pregnancy cases, the majority Justices seemed not to see the significance of the problems before them, handling them as sterile exercises in doctrinal reasoning in spite of the educational efforts made by the Courts of Appeals and the EEOC, which should have revealed their importance. The significance of the cases lay not in the fact that mandatory pregnancy leave restricted a "right to choose" or set up irrebuttable presumptions. The medical insurance cases were not simply exercises in classification. The Court was being asked to reassess public policies that reflected an older consensus about the relationship of women and work, policies that accepted and built on a rationale of different roles for men and women, against a new set of social facts. The new facts showed women employed at almost the same rate as men, although still burdened by government rules and employer attitudes that kept them in a position of inequality, as well as by the fact that they were still saddled with the primary responsibility for child-raising. In the new context, equal protection was no longer seen as equality within the sphere assigned to one's gender, but had become a demand for equality of opportunity and equal treatment whatever role one decided to assume. We are now seeing the spillover of the quest for equality at work into the family itself. This result might have been expected and could very well have beneficial long-term effects, helping the family reorganize itself in a new direction—one that recognizes the importance of women's economic contributions, reduces the pressure on males to be sole, responsible breadwinners and allows divorced and divorcing females and single women with families to support their children.

5

Teenage Pregnancy and
Adolescent Sexuality

The teenage pregnancy problem is intertwined with a number of important issues including: the morality of premarital sex, abortion, illegitimate births and the lack of economic well-being and the need for public assistance of many of these teenage families.
Committee Report on S.1090, "Adolescent Family Life" bill.[1]

Three recent Supreme Court decisions, one decided in 1977 and two in 1981, deal with issues of teenage pregnancy and adolescent sexuality.[2] Two of the decisions build on the contraception and abortion cases, and the third presents a problem of reverse gender discrimination. In *Carey v. Population Services* a divided Supreme Court overturned a New York law forbidding the sale of contraceptives to minors. The plurality agreed that it was irrational to make pregnancy a punishment for fornication and that there was constitutional protection for the right to choose *not* to have a child, whereas the dissenters were willing to defer to a legislative judgment which assumed that keeping contraceptives out of the hands of teenagers would discourage sexual promiscuity. In *Michael M. v. Sonoma County Court* five Justices upheld a statutory rape statute even though it contained a doubtful gender classification. The important governmental objective attributed to the legislature (the objective that supposedly justified a distinction based on gender) was that the punishment of males for illegal sexual activity was a useful method of deterring teenage pregnancy. *HL v. Matheson* presented a challenge to an abortion notification law. The legal problem presented was whether such a law interfered with a female minor's right to choose an abortion. Here the practical consequence intended by the legislators was preventing pregnant minors from aborting their offspring without conferring first with their parents. The law was upheld, again by a divided Court.

In all three of the areas examined by the Court traditional relationships were in jeopardy, the country, like the Justices themselves, was divided about the proper direction for policy to take and the issues under consideration had become subjects for political debate. The divisions on the Court showed individual Justices responding in different patterns. Justices Brennan and Marshall reacted favorably to claims of individual rights, Justice Rehnquist and Chief Justice Burger would have preferred that the court defer to state legislative judgments in all three cases and the five remaining Justices formed shifting alliances with one position or the other.

Teenage pregnancy became a public and political issue sometime during the 1970s. In 1976 Planned Parenthood of America published a research report entitled *Eleven Million Teenagers: What Can Be Done About the Epidemic of Adolescent Pregnancies in the United States* which dramatically described the size and extent of the problem.[3] Adolescent sexuality and child-bearing were not only creating troublesome social conditions, but they also seemed to supply a focus for the debate over the changing nature of the family. As the Committee Report on Senator Denton's Adolescent Family Life Bill, quoted above, indicated, teenage pregnancy is related to many other family concerns with social implications—morality, illegitimacy, sexual freedom and promiscuity of adolescents, abortion and family control of children. The issue also intersects with political concerns about the cost of public welfare, the well-being of racial minorities and federal intrusion into family life.[4]

The immorality of the young and the newer generation's loss of the virtues of yesteryear have always been popular subjects for nostalgic lamentation. But by 1976 concern over the corruption of the young was not entirely an exercise in nostalgia; the increase in teenage pregnancy was a fact, a fact with a number of serious social implications.

Scholars writing about the family point out several factors that seem to be behind the increase in teenage pregnancy. Premarital sexual activity is not an exclusively contemporary problem. A historian who has made a study of historical trends, using what figures are available, has found evidence that one of the distinctive developments of social life over the last two centuries has been the increase in sexual activity before marriage.[5] Figures collected from public documents in Europe and England show an increase in illegitimate births and premarital pregnancies, slowly rising from 1750 on, even with advances in contraception.[6] One of the best explanations for this trend is increased sexual activity—an increase due, it is surmised, to changes in the economic system which deemphasize community values and standards of behavior and emphasize individual and personal goals and satisfactions. Out-of-wedlock conception dropped between 1850 and 1940, probably because of increased use of contraception, but even so there is a long-term upward trend in illegitimate births, which rose sharply everywhere after World War II.[7] Changes became striking after 1960, largely because of a greater willingness of young women to have intercourse before marriage. Illegitimate births among teenagers have soared, because adolescents are irregular in their use of contraception.[8]

Peer pressure, with the behavior of older teenagers influencing younger and younger children, makes the problem worse, as do other environmental factors, including the waning of parental authority, the development of a youth culture encouraged for commercial reasons, the commercialization of sex and its exploitation in the media, and even the seductive qualities of popular music.[9] Many adults are convinced that sex education programs in the schools and the availability of contraception and abortion all encourage sexual experimentation among young people.[10]

Not only have teenage pregnancy and adolescent sexual activity become more prevalent, but they have also become more visible. The unmarried teenager no longer drops out of school and marries, or moves away from home for a few months and then puts the baby up for adoption.[11] If many pregnant teenagers have abortions, many also decide to keep and raise their babies without marrying. Because of the increasing reluctance of young people to marry, the rate of marriage has dropped 4 percent for whites and 45 percent for blacks since 1970. The United States has one of the highest rates of teenage child-bearing in the world, although the rate of increase has declined slightly during the past two decades. A million teenagers a year become pregnant, and over 600,000 give birth. One-third of these births are to unmarried mothers, although probably 54 percent are conceived out-of-wedlock.[12] Figures for a single year, reported in the Committee Report on Senator Denton's Adolescent Family Life Bill, indicated that in 1978 an estimated 1 million teenagers became pregnant, 600,000 births occurred and there were 300,000 abortions and 100,000 miscarriages.[13] In 1978, half of the babies born to women nineteen years of age or less were illegitimate. Most were not put up for adoption; about 94 percent of the women elected to keep their children, and these children came into the world with poor prospects for a successful life.[14] This enormous increase in teenage pregnancies and births presents a whole range of public problems, for many of these young mothers are not equipped either for motherhood or for economic survival. They are likely to add to the welfare burden, and the children will often suffer from deprivation and neglect.[15]

Liberals and conservatives approach this cluster of problems in different ways. Each group wants to reverse the trend or reduce the social consequences of the trend, but liberals have generally believed that if the trend cannot be reversed, at least its adverse consequences can be diminished by positive programs, governmental as well as private, which target the teenage population. Groups such as Planned Parenthood of America think that the best way to approach this trend and its problems is with realistic sex education, family planning programs that reach teenagers, access to abortion or prenatal care and various kinds of support programs for the young mother. Senior researchers at the Urban Institute in Washington, D.C., have even suggested that a cost-effective plan for reducing teenage childbearing would be to offer a $2,000 reward to any girl on welfare who reached age twenty without having babies.[16] Although liberals have not written off the family, they think it needs governmental help in handling adolescent behavior. From the political perspective of people with these views, the Supreme Court decisions overturning state laws that prohibited contraceptive use and abortion were necessary and constructive changes in the law. Because they contributed to the stability of family life by allowing people to plan children or prevent the births of unwanted children, these decisions were not perceived as "anti-family."

Conservative groups, on the other hand, are likely to think that the answer to many family problems can be found in a return to traditional values. They urge chastity and sexual abstinence as a means of preventing unwanted pregnancies and recommend the restriction of access to contraception and abortion. They want government to "send a message" to young people that it is wrong to get pregnant outside of marriage, and to make it impossible for a pregnant girl "to jump in a van and go down to get an abortion." They advocate the teaching of morality in the home and at school and suggest various methods of getting the family re-involved in exercising its traditional controls on adolescent sexuality. They also advocate the adoption of state and federal laws protecting the family with tax breaks and other provisions.[17] They do not want government to leave family formation to informal forces, but emphasize the strengthening of those traditional controls, social and legal, that discouraged promiscuity in earlier times. Senator Denton's bill proposing the appropriation of money for research into the causes and consequences of adolescent promiscuity and the provision of support services to young families suggested measures that would make the "right" kind of positive contribution to the stability of family life. The bill emphasized parental consultation, adoption counseling, prenatal and postnatal health care, family counseling, consumer and homemaking education. From the conservative point of view, the Supreme Court's contraception and abortion decisions undermined family relationships by giving women freedom from their reproductive roles, undercut the authority of the father and encouraged sexual promiscuity by removing the fear of unwanted pregnancies and loosening even further the ties between sex and reproduction.[18] The Justices probably had not initially considered either the contraception or the abortion decision as anti-family; indeed, they may have thought that both were "family planning" decisions. But there was a new political climate by the end of the decade, and the Court was beginning to feel subtle and not so subtle pressures to retreat from its stand on reproductive rights.

THREE CASES: CONTRACEPTION, STATUTORY RAPE AND ABORTION NOTIFICATION

Carey v. Population Services International illustrates the difficulties the Justices were having in mapping out a constructive approach, within constitutional guidelines, to disputes raising family issues.[19] The decision overturned a New York anti-contraceptive statute, but it did so by a divided vote and was unclear in its method of handling the issues involved.

In 1972 New York passed a law limiting the sale of contraceptives in the state. The statute had three main provisions: it made it a crime to sell contraceptives to minors under sixteen; it forbade the selling of contraceptives by anyone but licensed pharmacists; and it forbade the advertising or display of contraceptives. New York argued that one of the main objectives of the law was the deterrence of sexual activity by the young; by making contraceptives unavailable, the law would increase the hazards of such activity and thereby discourage persons from engaging in it. By forbidding contraceptive sales to young people the law would make a clear statement about public disapproval of premarital sex.

By majority vote, the Justices found that the law interfered excessively with the rights of people (including young people) to make personal decisions about sex and reproduction without the interference of the state, extending the principle that there is a constitutional right to "freedom of choice whether or not to bear a child." But only four Justices, Brennan, Marshall, Stewart and Blackmun, supported this position in full. The concurring Justices, White, Powell and Stevens, found the law imperfect for differing reasons: White because the state had not demonstrated that the law actually had the intended deterrent effect,

Powell because it was too broad and kept contraceptives away from minor, married females and because it prohibited parents from giving contraceptives to their own children, and Stevens because the law was so irrational that it denied due process. Justice Rehnquist's dissenting opinion argued for deference to the state legislature and asserted that the law was a legitimate exercise of the police power. The Chief Justice dissented without opinion.

This decision and the opinions written to explain it illustrate several things about the Justices' approach to "family" issues. First of all, the liberal position, here supported by four Justices, was basically an "individual rights" position, grounded on the rights to liberty and privacy. This group of Justices, at least in this case, found that contraception related to the "right" to choose to beget or not to beget children, a right recognized by the decisions in *Griswold v. Connecticut, Roe v. Wade* and *Eisenstadt v. Baird*.[20] Insofar as this law keeps contraceptives from people, it interferes with their rights to make private decisions dealing with procreation, marriage, child-rearing and similar matters that should be left free from governmental interference. The right of the individual to make such decisions is part of the liberty of a free man (or woman). The precedents followed in this decision are the birth control and abortion cases, but there are subtle differences between those cases and this case. The "choice" which is to be made here is not primarily a family planning decision. The right, if there is a right at stake, might more accurately be described as the right of a teenager to have sex without fearing pregnancy. Justice White and Justice Stevens are much closer to the mark in speaking about the claimed right as a "right to put contraceptives to their intended use."[21]

For the state to abridge a fundamental right, it must be able to show a compelling state interest. New York contended that the act was defensible as a regulation of the morality of minors. The Court refused to accept that such regulation was acceptable simply because the state's power is greater over minors than over adults. New York had also claimed that one of the main objectives of the law was the discouraging of teenage sexual activity; but the state had not supported its contention that teenage sexual activity increases when contraceptives are available.

By basing the decision on a "right to choose," the Supreme Court handled the important underlying issue of discouraging teenage sexual activity, which New York claimed was one of the main objectives of the law, very gingerly. Justice Brennan stated that "there is substantial reason for doubt whether limiting access to contraceptives will in fact substantially discourage early sexual behavior."[22] The state had not offered any proof that it would. The appellants and *amici* on the other side, however, cited a "considerable body of evidence and opinion indicating that there is no such deterrent effect." The opinion took judicial notice of the fact that teenage pregnancy was a problem, but stated that it was not basing its decision on social science data. The Court did not, however, completely reject the legislature's traditional view that the availability of contraceptives encouraged promiscuous sexual behavior and that if methods of birth control were not available, fear of pregnancy would discourage teenagers from engaging in sex. It merely held that New York had not borne the burden of proof in establishing its case.

Although Justice Powell's concurrence contended that the law was defective because it withdrew access to contraceptives from persons who should be legally authorized to use them (married minors, parents who wanted their children to have contraceptives, adults ordering from mail order firms), he also expressed the opinion that New York would be justified in passing a law that required some form of parental consultation before adolescents were given or sold contraceptives. The state might not ban contraceptive sales, but it would act constitutionally if it passed a law bringing adolescent sexuality back under parental control. Justice Powell did not, however, suggest a practical means of implementing his suggestion.

Only Justice Stevens dealt with what were clearly the underlying social realities and looked at the practical effects of the legislation. The state did have an interest in the sexual activity of young people, he wrote. But common sense indicates that many young people will engage in sexual activity regardless of what the New York legislature does about contraceptives. The state's prohibition of contraceptive sales is largely symbolic, but the effect of this symbolic act is counterproductive and irrational.

"It is as though a state decided to dramatize its disapproval of motorcycles by forbidding the use of safety helmets."[23] This kind of irrational, "government-mandated harm" is a deprivation of due process of law.

The gist of Justice Rehnquist's dissent was that the Court should defer to the legislature; his opinion came close to being a modern "Noodle's Oration," as he used extravagant rhetoric to contend that the heroes of Bunker Hill and Gettysburg would turn over in their graves if they knew that the Constitution they had helped to produce and preserve was being used to protect the right to peddle contraceptives at truck stops.[24]

Michael M. v. Sonoma County Court upheld a statutory rape statute that applied only to males.[25] Again, as in *Carey*, the legislation was based on one of the traditional methods of dealing with unacceptable sexual activity, penalizing the disfavored acts. The California law at issue made it an unlawful act for any male to engage in sexual intercourse with a female under the age of eighteen years who was not his wife. The Supreme Court accepted the gender classification in the statute in spite of the fact that it was based on a number of clear stereotypes, as well as being the kind of protective statute that seemingly protects women, but might, in fact, involve rather subtle forms of sex discrimination. Teenage women are protected from the hazards of sexual experimentation; their male counterparts are not.[26]

In spite of the majority opinion's refusal to investigate legislative motivation, it is apparent that California's statutory rape law, first passed in 1850, was not originally designed to "prevent teenage pregnancy" but to protect the virtue and chastity of young women.[27] The law thus reflected a nineteenth-century stereotype about the nature of women and female behavior. In the popularly accepted opinion of the time, woman was by nature not only chaste but also the repository of virtue, morality and sensibility. Unlike men, females were deemed to be passive and disinterested in sex. They were also sexually vulnerable, because men were predatory, aggressive, passionate and sensual. Some scholars suggest that women both gained and lost by this characterization, because it increased their status, allowed them to develop identity and self-esteem and gave them a powerful weapon in the war between the sexes.[28] Legal protection of virtue and chastity was consistent with the acceptance of this stereotype, whatever its uses.

In his book *Women and the Law* (1969), Leo Kanowitz has pointed out that many of the provisions of the criminal law distinguish sharply between males and females in situations where they appear to be similarly situated.[29] The prime motivation for much of this legislation appears to be acceptance of the idea of a double standard of morality, the view that society can tolerate much more freedom for the male in sexual matters than it can for the female. Two consequences flow from the acceptance of such a double standard. First, it implies less capacity on the part of the female to control and direct her own life. Second, it justifies the idea that the male can be penalized as the aggressor, the assailant, the trespasser, whether or not the conduct is mutually consensual. Statutory rape statutes presume that females under a certain age are incapable of meaningful consent to sexual relations; this legal fiction makes it logical, consistent and rational to punish the male. Some of the statutes, but not all, apply only when the female was "previously chaste," and others presume chastity in all females below a certain age. Here the underlying premise is that young, chaste females should be off-limits to male aggression, probably in part because their marriageability would be damaged by leaving them unprotected, as would the father's authority over females under his control. Crimes of "seduction" and "enticement" may have been grounded in the same underlying motives.[30]

Although such statutes appear to discriminate against males, to a large degree they also reinforce ideas of female inferiority. The belief that young females are sexually "off-limits" may also underlie some of the extreme discomfort that is felt about the pregnant teenager, whose predicament is often greeted with hostility and moral outrage. A feminist lawyer has summed up this complex of attitudes:

Possibly one of the greatest displays of misogyny is directed toward the pregnant teen-ager. Her condition brings out all the hatreds of the [usually married, old, male] determiners of her fate. These men include school principals, school administrators, judges, doctors, state legislators, and psychologists. They combine, having previously denied her information about access to birth control, to make her feel shame and guilt—about having sex, and about being a fertile female [a fertile male is not so punished].[31]

Emotion-laden stereotypes about females and about pregnancy lie behind these attitudes: discomfort at visual evidence of sexuality, moral disapproval of the female as a "seductress," atavistic fears of pregnant women, envy of the unknown sex partner. All of these feelings may be projected onto the unhappy girl, and it seems possible that similar feelings contribute to the emotional climate surrounding the public problems that teenage pregnancy presents.[32]

In its argument in court, the state of California justified its statutory rape legislation, including the gender classification, as necessary to prevent illegitimate teenage pregnancies, and the Supreme Court of California upheld the statute on this basis. The U.S. Supreme Court affirmed. Justice Rehnquist's opinion in *Michael M. v. Sonoma County Court* was joined by Justices Stewart and Powell and Chief Justice Burger. The Court agreed that the prevention of illegitimate teenage pregnancy was one of the purposes of the statute, and that the statute did not discriminate on the basis of gender. The Court found that males and adolescent females are not similarly situated as far as the consequences of sexual intercourse are concerned and that a "gender-neutral" statute would present serious enforcement problems for the state. The majority was clearly disturbed that teenage pregnancy had increased to such alarming proportions and believed that the state was justified in taking any measures it considered useful in checking and controlling the problems presented by the rising numbers of abortions and illegitimate births.

Justice Blackmun voted to support the state law, although he wrote a separate opinion. Blackmun has generally disagreed with the conservative bloc's handling of abortion and contraceptive cases, believing that those Justices have not appreciated the fact that the level of teenage pregnancy constitutes a major social crisis. In his view, the restriction of access to abortion and contraception is generally contraindicated by the increase in illegitimacy. Because the Court now recognized teenage pregnancy as a major problem, Blackmun concurred and agreed that the California law was "a sufficiently reasoned and constitutional effort to control the problem at its inception."[33]

Justice Stevens, in dissent, was the only Justice to explore the assumptions and stereotyped attitudes behind both the state law and the majority opinion. First, he noted the assumption that in sexual relations the male is always the aggressor. A second proposition accepted by the Court that is probably untrue is the assumption that the female bears most or all of the risks in sexual intercourse. (The words "consequences," "risks" and "injuries" are used a number of times in the opinion, and Justice Stevens calls intercourse "risk-taking conduct.") A third assumption that is probably unwarranted is the proposition that the male should be held responsible and the female protected from the consequences of intercourse.[34]

The remaining dissenters objected to the unnecessary use of a classification based on sex, arguing that the state had not substantiated its need for a statute that penalized only males. The law contained an overt gender classification but did not justify it by demonstrating a substantial relationship between the classification and the objective of the law.[35] There is no evidence that a strategy that singles out males is a valid approach to the problem of reducing the sexual activity of adolescent females. The dissenters thought that a gender-neutral statute would work just as well, a statute written to penalize any *person*, male or female, engaging in sexual conduct with an underage person. Many states have rewritten their laws in this fashion.[36]

Justice Stevens' dissent was based on a different perception of the nature of the problem and its practical implications. Stevens agreed that the problem area was teenage sexual activity and that a law directed at teenage sex, even one that prohibited it outright, would clearly be constitutional whether or not it was effective. But the law in question had serious flaws. It was unfairly directed at males only, and males are not the only participants in the "risk-taking activity"; indeed, they share some of the risks, although the law assumes there are no risks for males. In a later comment on this case in a law review, Professor Arnold H. Loewy agreed, calling the statute a blatantly sexist statutory rape statute, rejected by thirty-seven other state legislatures. He commented that "Michael M. . . . illustrates that it is extremely easy to trip over a sexual stereotype without ever recognizing it."[37] Justice Stevens found that it was irrational to penalize 50 percent of the criminals and to let the other 50 percent off, scot-free. The law was based on stereotypes and traditional attitudes toward male-female relationships; more importantly, there was no evidence that "a statutory prohibition will significantly affect the volume of that activity or provide a meaningful solution to the problems created by it."[38] Justice Brennan's dissenting opinion also pointed to this fact, citing California figures showing that only an average of 61 juvenile males and 352 adult males were arrested for statutory rape each year between 1975 and 1978, whereas there were almost 50,000 pregnancies among California girls between the ages of thirteen and seventeen in a single year, 1976.[39] The Court chose to ignore these revealing figures and to defer to the legislature's judgment that statutory rape laws could and did deter male actions. That it also ignored the fact that the prevention of teenage pregnancy might not even have been one of the California legislature's motives when it first passed this statute only adds to the puzzling quality of the decision.

In both *Carey* and *Michael M.*, the Court dealt with state legislation that used traditional techniques for reinforcing social controls on illicit sexual activity. The New York legislation was premised on the idea that access to birth control devices encouraged promiscuity, and that without contraceptives the female's natural fear of pregnancy would cause her to reject sexual advances. California had prescribed criminal penalties in order to deter the undesirable conduct. All of which goes to prove, in Professor Loewy's words, that it is extremely easy to trip over a sexual stereotype without even recognizing it.

Neither *Carey* nor *Michael M.* discussed the role of the family in relation to adolescent sexual activity. Questions about the rights of husbands and fathers and about whether parents could veto abortions for minors had been raised in 1976 in *Planned Parenthood of Central Missouri v. Danforth*.[40] In this case the Supreme Court held that the state could not give either husband or parents an absolute veto over a woman's abortion decision.

This decision left unanswered a number of extremely controversial questions about parental responsibility for the welfare of minors. After a series of decisions ending in 1979, the *Bellotti* decisions, the Court concluded that mature minors had a qualified right to make their own choices about whether or not to bear children.[41] But the idea that a child could have an abortion without consulting her parents or that a minor could arrange to have an abortion on her own was in conflict with a long tradition that required parental consent for all forms of medical treatment for minor children.[42] The *Bellotti* decisions dealt with the rights of mature minors and the methods by which abortions could be authorized over the objections of their parents. In *HL v. Matheson*, the Court tackled the even touchier question of the rights of other minors who were not as mature.

In 1974, Utah had passed a general abortion statute that had the overall purpose of restricting the availability of abortion, one of the many such statutes enacted after the decision in *Roe v. Wade*. The statute explored a number of different means by which access to abortion could be discouraged without actually denying the constitutionally recognized right to "choose" an abortion. Among other provisions, the Utah statute required written consent before a patient could have an abortion, required abortion counseling and required physicians to notify the parents of unmarried minors or the husbands of married minors before performing abortions.[43] In this case, the section of the statute requiring notification of the parents of unmarried minors was challenged. *HL v. Matheson* did not fall exactly under the rule of the *Bellotti* case because H.L. (the young woman) had not tried to establish, in District Court, the fact that she was a mature minor and because the statute did not require parental consent to an abortion, but required only that parents be notified. The narrow question presented by the case was whether a statute that required that the parents of all minors be notified of impending abortions, but provided no special exemption for mature minors, was valid. Although the legal problem seems complicated, the underlying issue was clear enough: would the Court accept, in principle, the power of states to require parental notification before performing abortions on minors?

The conflicting interests in this case were also clear. On one hand there was a whole list of "family values," which the Utah statute presumably was trying to protect: family integrity, parental control of children, parental responsibility for helping minors make important decisions and the family's role in teaching morality and in protecting adolescents. There was also a number of underlying assumptions about parent-child relationships: the assumption that the family would support its members, that the child's interests would be protected and understood and that there would be no basic conflict between the child's interests and those of the parents. In requiring notification the state was mandating parent-child consultation and was ensuring that an abortion decision would be a family decision and not just the decision of the child.

Later, dissenting to a decision upholding the statute, Justice Marshall pointed out some problems with the assumptions behind the legislation. There is no guarantee he said, that the child's interest and the family interest will be the same. Some families will be punitive, and others will pressure the minor not to have an abortion even if it is in her best interest to do so. In requiring notice to parents, the state is thus intentionally creating a disincentive to abortion; subtle and not so subtle pressures inside particular families may mean that a notification statute becomes, in reality, a requirement of parental consent.[44]

In deciding this issue, the Supreme Court split into three groups. The majority decision rested in part on a technicality. It held that H.L. had not established that she was an emancipated minor, so that she had no standing to challenge the possibility that the statute could be applied to mature minors. Insofar as the statute applied to immature minors, it was constitutional. Five Justices, in effect, supported this decision. Justice Stevens, concurring, thought that the Court should have decided the question it avoided here: whether such a statute could be applied to mature minors. Three dissenters, Justices Blackmun, Marshall and Brennan, held that the statute interfered too greatly with a minor woman's right to a free choice on the abortion question.

The dissenting opinion raised another question: did this statute truly support the traditional American concept of the family, or was it rather an intrusion by the state into what should be considered a private domain? There are a number of subpropositions behind this question. The belief that families are private governments that should remain as free as possible from outside interference is part of the accepted family ideology. When the American family is working well, it makes collective private decisions, minor children respect parental authority, and the family unit protects and fosters children and acts in their best interests. When it is not working properly, the state cannot establish, by fiat, what the family unit has been unable to preserve. When the family does not act in the best interests of the child, its actions are unjustified and the state can intervene. The family remains private until it is disfunctional, and it is only then that public authorities can be called in to take up the slack. By requiring parental notification, the Utah statute required that parents be involved in abortion decisions in all situations, including those in which interfamily communication had broken down and those where there were conflicts of interest between parents and the child. The Utah statute put legal limits on a minor's ability to make her own decisions on abortion, assuming that the parents' contribution would always be in the best interests of the child, an assumption that is not always true.[45] In the name of supporting family authority, it also extended state regulation into the decision-making process of the family itself.

These three cases do not really turn on rights at all, but on broader questions of social policy, related to changing family structure, sex roles, the conditions under which reproduction should take place and government responsibility for supporting mothers and children in need. In these cases, the Court never had a choice between clear, rational, agreed-upon family policies and the claims to freedom from governmental interference put forward by individuals. There is no political consensus about how to control teenage sex and child-bearing, or even any agreement that it can be controlled. The Court was asked to choose between traditional policies of doubtful efficacy and individuals' claims that these policies were irrational or discriminatory. In one case, *Carey*, the Court rejected state legislation which clearly would have made the social problem worse. In *Michael M.*, the Court rejected an individual claim that seemed specious, yet the conflicting state policy was of doubtful practical effect. In the third case, the Court decided on a narrow basis that the state could use its regulatory power to enforce traditional family controls over adolescents.

One of the most interesting things revealed by these cases was the unwillingness of the Justices, generally, to face facts. Only Justice Stevens, in *Carey*, pointed out that the law was irrelevant, or at best a symbolic gesture. In *Michael M.*, Stevens again pointed out that assuming laws against sexual activity were effective, laws that exempted half of the human race from liability were half as effective as laws that covered both sexes. In *HL v. Matheson*, Justice Marshall was the realist, pointing out that, although families ought to have the best interests of their children at heart, objective scrutiny of how families work reveals that they sometimes have other agenda. The Court's unwillingness to look realistically at social facts is at least partly responsible for the confusion in these cases. But in addition, in all three cases, the Court demonstrated considerable reluctance to undermine traditional legal disincentives to sexual activity outside of marriage and sexual experimentation by teenagers. Here again, as in the illegitimacy and pregnancy cases, the older rules were structurally important in maintaining the family unit, as was the proposition that sex and reproduction could not be separated and should take place in a family setting.

The division on the Court in these cases is similar to the kind of division found on other constitutional issues. Two Justices are at each end of the political spectrum. But "conservative" Justices Burger and Rehnquist are "interventionist"—they support legislative attempts to regulate the family "for its own good." The two "liberal" Justices are oriented in favor of individual rights, taking positions in favor of individual freedom from government controls. To some extent they accept that part of the family tradition that suggests it is a private social institution and should remain free from governmental regulation. The five centrist Justices do not consistently vote with one or the other of the extreme positions, but "float" back and forth, their decisions often seeming to depend on the particular facts in each case. In this group Justice Stevens stands out as appearing to be more clearly aware of the importance of the social facts behind the legal issues, and as exhibiting a willingness to take judicial notice of the actual impact of governmental policies.

In part, the Supreme Court's lack of certainty about the direction which the law relating to families should take is representative of the divisions in society as a whole over family policy. The Court's decisions in these three cases reflect the general lack of consensus over the best way to handle a specific set of problems, those generated by teenage sexual activity.

AFTER 1980: A NEW DIRECTION FOR FAMILY POLICY?

President Reagan's electoral victory in 1980 brought a new direction to governmental policies related to adolescent pregnancy. In the opinion of many of the voters who had backed Reagan, public policy, including that of the federal government, has been deeply involved in family breakdown. According to this view, if governmental policies cannot be designed to reinforce families and support traditional family values and structures, they should not, at least, be allowed to have a destructive impact on family life. Throughout his first term, the President backed a constitutional amendment and legislation, sponsored by "pro-family" forces, that would have outlawed abortion. These efforts were not successful. If they had been, there would have been serious repercussions for adolescents, because it is estimated that about one-third of the 1.5 million abortions performed each year are performed on teenagers.[46] Although it opposed abortion, the administration also sought cuts in programs intended to deter unwanted pregnancies and provide pregnant women alternatives to abortion. The President was successful in cutting one of the most important of these programs, the family planning program financed under Title X of the Public Health Service Act of 1970, a program that funds clinics run by hospitals, health departments, Planned Parenthood affiliates and other social service agencies.[47] Conservative groups have always been critical of the federal government's involvement in family planning, contending that its programs are successful only in encouraging sexual promiscuity, especially among adolescents, and in promoting abortion. The administration did not have the votes in Congress to abolish these programs altogether, but it did succeed in cutting back funding and in adding restrictions that prohibited abortion counseling. Although all of these measures were labeled "pro-family," it is hard to believe that they add up to a rational attack on the problems created by teenage pregnancy.

Some conservative Senators, however, tried to find more positive methods of addressing problems connected with adolescent sexual activity, introducing bills they hoped would help the nation return to tried and tested methods of dealing with family-related problems. A Family Protection Act sponsored by Senators Roger W. Jepson (R., Iowa) and Paul Laxalt (R., Nev.) offered proposals that would:

a. create a legal presumption in favor of parental supervision of a child's moral and religious formation;

b. allow corporal punishment;

c. prohibit funding of contraception or abortion without parental notification;

d. support state power over juvenile delinquency, child, spousal abuse;

e. prohibit legal services for abortion, busing, divorce, homosexual rights;

f. prohibit funding of groups advocating homosexual rights;

g. authorize military pay to dependents;

h. give various tax breaks to families for care of the elderly;

i. support prayer in public schools, parental influence in the schools, and traditional sex roles.[48]

This bill was not passed, but it expressed the views on family policy of many of the conservative Republicans. Senator Jeremiah Denton (R., Alabama) introduced an "Adolescent Family Life" bill in April 1981 which proposed "chastity" as a solution to the problem of adolescent sexuality.[49] The advocacy of chastity, in so many words, was later removed from the bill, but the Adolescent Family Life Program, as enacted, set up demonstration projects designed to encourage teenagers to postpone sexual activity. Senator Denton's program was also designed to encourage pregnant girls to put their babies up for adoption, and it forbade the suggestion of abortion as an available option. The legislation is now under constitutional attack because it allows religious groups to apply for demonstration grants, because it has funded "family life" programs in parochial schools and because its anti-abortion views supposedly reflect a sectarian religious perspective.

The cutting back of federal social programs that were objectionable to the New Right happily coincided with the Reagan administration's budget-cutting priorities. If a coherent family policy has emerged from the Reagan period, it is one that is negative, deregulatory, exhibits fiscal restraint and favors a return of family-support functions to non-governmental institutions. However, there have been some interventionist measures, some attempts to use law directly to promote New Right policies positively, especially by conservative "pro-family" people in key administrative positions. Margaret Heckler, Secretary of Health and Human Services, supported an administrative rule that required parental notification whenever minors asked to be supplied with contraceptives under programs funded by the government.[50] This ruling, the so-called squeal rule, was later rejected by decisions in two U.S. Courts of Appeal.[51] The appointment of a leading conservative, C. Everett Koop, to the Surgeon General's post resulted in various anti-abortion moves as well as a plan to ensure full medical treatment for newly born infants with severe birth defects—the "Baby Doe" rule.[52] This rule, which would require expensive hospital care for many infants unlikely to survive, seems to be inconsistent with the demand for an overall decrease in funding for child care programs.

These levels of political controversy have been reflected only faintly in the Supreme Court's decisions, but the divisions on the Court over family policy are related to the fact that the country is extremely divided over the handling of many of these family problems. The fragmentation on the Court is also related to the lack of a clear theoretical basis for the Court's family decisions. The *Carey* case and the recent *Akron* abortion case found the Court relying on precedent, unwilling to retreat from its earlier rulings that established a constitutional right to choose whether or not to conceive and bear children.[53] Both the *Akron* case and *HL v. Matheson* indicate that the Court is not willing to move much further than its present position on abortion. *Michael M.* and *HL v. Matheson* decided in 1981 show that the Court still accepts rather traditional ideas about the relation of law to family functioning and that it is unlikely to overturn legislation that is not radically out of line with established precedents or clearly at odds with new social conditions.

6

Who Should Socialize the Children?

School reformers argued the precedence of state responsibility over traditional parental responsibility for education. Hiram Barney, Ohio's school commissioner in 1854, wrote that "for educational purposes, the State may with propriety be regarded as one great School District, and the population as constituting but one family, charged with the parental duty of educating all its youth." The Wisconsin Teachers' Association declared in 1865 that "children are the property of the state," an argument often heard in favor of more state activity in common schooling.

Carl F. Kaestle[1]

For an example of a decision that can be better explained by family ideology than it can by principles of constitutional law, we might consider *Wisconsin v. Yoder*, a free exercise decision handed down in 1972.[2] The central tenet of the family ideology that applies here is: parents have a right to control the education and socialization of their children. On first reading, this case appears to be a simple dispute between the Amish community and the Wisconsin educational system. Seen from this limited perspective, the decision is equitable, and the balance struck seems to be a just resolution of the conflict between the two parties. But on further inspection it becomes clear that there is more to the case than meets the eye. A whole list of contemporary educational concerns underlies this decision: public versus private schools, secular versus religious education, the importance of compulsory public education, the adequacy of the public schools, the role of parental choice in state educational policy and probably others.

To understand the Court's decision, it is necessary to start, not with the *Yoder* case itself, but with two family-school-religion cases decided in the 1920s, *Meyer v. Nebraska*[3] and *Pierce v. Society of Sisters*.[4] There had been earlier school-related cases, but these had raised questions about racial segregation and the separate but equal doctrine.[5] *Meyer* and *Pierce* were early tests of legislation imposing state policies on local educational systems. The opinions in both of these cases contain strong statements by the Court about the rights and responsibilities of parents in the education and socialization of their children. The decision in *Meyer v. Nebraska* (1923) upheld the right of a teacher to teach German in the face of a state law prohibiting the teaching of foreign languages to young children. The decision in *Pierce v. Society of Sisters* two years later upheld the right of private schools to conduct their businesses and held that a state law requiring that all children go to public schools deprived private educational institutions of their property rights without due process. The Court found that the legislation in both cases was arbitrary, depriving the parties of liberty and property without good reasons: both of these decisions were "substantive" due process decisions.

In spite of the narrow focus of the actual holdings (that the state could not forbid foreign language teaching or private schooling), the *dicta* in the cases make it clear that the fundamental right given constitutional protection was the traditional "natural right" of families to make educational choices for their children unless the state had a compelling public reason for restricting this liberty. Although questions of religious freedom are also present in these cases because some of the schools involved were parochial schools, it is apparent that the right the Court was interested in protecting was the right of parents to exercise some control over the education of their children in the face of the increasing power of the public school system. The

Court was thus ruling against complete state domination of the educational process.

There were "state interests" behind both of these laws. By passing the legislation challenged in the first case, *Meyer*, state legislators had decided that the state educational system should be used to promote "Americanism." By forbidding the teaching of foreign languages, or teaching *in* foreign languages, the state law would speed up the process by which the children of immigrants were assimilated and made into good Americans. In 1919, when the law was enacted, many Lutheran churches still used German in their services, and German-language instruction was important, in part, because it allowed the children of German-speaking Lutherans to participate in religious services with their parents and to pray with them at home. Nebraska's law applied to both public and church schools, and the case arose when a teacher at the Zion Evangelical Lutheran Congregation was convicted for teaching Bible stories in German to a child of ten.

The oral argument in the *Meyer* case emphasized the parent's right to control the education of his children. Arthur Francis Mullen, the attorney for Meyer, contended that there was constitutional protection for this area of liberty.

[The] right of a man to communicate with his family and the right of a man to give religious instruction to his children; the right to be free in his home; the right to maintain private educational institutions, and in these matters to be let alone—surely these are privileges and immunities protected by the Constitution of the United States.[6]

The Supreme Court agreed that it was the natural duty of parents to give their children suitable education, and found that the right to choose the kind of education they should have was a liberty protected by the Fourteenth Amendment, locating this protection in the Due Process Clause. Legislation such as this law prohibiting foreign language teaching might be reasonable in wartime or in emergency situations, but there was no adequate reason to accept it in a time of peace or tranquility.[7]

The motivation behind the Oregon law requiring all children to attend public schools was largely nationalistic and anti-Catholic. Many citizens in the 1920s feared that Roman Catholic parochial schools would undermine democracy by educating groups whose primary allegiance would be to the Vatican rather than to America.[8] Proposed by a statewide popular initiative procedure, the Oregon law, by requiring state education for everyone, was designed to ensure that the proper patriotic sentiments would be instilled. In spite of the fact that the decision was based on the property rights of private schools, the opinion in *Pierce* also articulated the traditional view that parents should have a choice in matters related to the upbringing and education of their children and that laws interfering with these family rights were unconstitutional.[9]

Both cases emphasized the parents' role in their children's educational decisions and put some limits on state educational systems. In the early twentieth century public confidence in the ability of the state to socialize children was strong. But there had to be limits to what states could impose in the way of curriculum requirements: they could not forbid the teaching of ordinary educational subjects, such as foreign languages, in the schools. Neither could states give the public schools a monopoly on education; a place had to be left for religious and private education. *Meyer* was important because it set limits to indoctrination. *Pierce* was significant because it provided an alternative to public education for people, principally Roman Catholics, whose religious views were in conflict with what was taught in the common schools; if they disagreed with programs selected by the Protestant majority, they could set up and attend their own educational institutions. The so-called Pierce compromise was an attempt to avoid majority-minority confrontations on public school curricula and practices by allowing the objectors to opt out.[10] The problem with this approach, however, was that not all parents could afford private schooling; the right to escape, for some, was dependent on their ability to pay private school fees or the willingness of church schools to provide scholarships. Because the states are prohibited from contributing any financial support to private religious schools, the compromise has a Catch-22 quality. A decision that came almost twenty-five years later, *Everson v. Board of Education*, offered a means of avoiding this dilemma by allowing the state legislature to help parents directly, rather than subsidizing the sectarian schools themselves.[11]

Although *Meyer* and *Pierce* indirectly involved the issues of religious liberty, the decisions in these cases do not support claims by religious sects to exemption from compulsory education laws that require formal schooling of some kind. Under the Pierce compromise, religious dissenters can set up their own schools, but they cannot argue that religious liberty excuses them from general state laws requiring education or setting standards governing the quality of that education. Justice James C. McReynolds expressly rejected that idea in the *Meyer* case, writing that

The power of the state to compel attendance at some school and to make reasonable regulations for all schools including a requirement that they shall give instruction in English, is not questioned. Nor has challenge been made of the State's power to prescribe a curriculum for institutions which it supports. Those matters are not within the present controversy.[12]

Neither case suggested that the state could not require education for all children below a certain age, prescribe reasonable curricula, regulate the qualifications of teachers or require minimum standards of health and safety. Catholics and Lutherans, for example, were left free to establish their own schools and to prescribe their own curricula free from unnecessary state interference, but there was no argument that these sects were exempt from compulsory education laws.

WISCONSIN v. YODER, 1972

Yoder is ostensibly a free exercise case. The general constitutional principle invoked there was the First Amendment's prohibition against laws interfering with the free exercise of religion, a provision made binding on the states by the Fourteenth Amendment. In interpreting this clause, the Supreme Court has made a distinction between religious belief itself and practices based on religious beliefs. The state cannot regulate or compel religious belief. But although the protection of belief itself is complete, religious practice stemming from that belief may sometimes be regulated. Government may act to protect the public against social harms thought to flow from religiously motivated behavior—laws forbidding polygamy, commercial sales on Sunday, child labor and laws requiring vaccination have all been upheld on this principle.[13] But if in some situations the activities of particular religious sects are contrary to public policy and must give way to the public interest, there are also occasions when religious practice is protected and the state obliged to find alternative ways of reaching its goals that interfere less directly with religion. In the language of constitutional theory, there are times when even "a compelling state interest" may not outweigh the protection of belief, and government may be required to choose "the least restrictive alternative." In conflicts between religious practices and the general public welfare, the Court's function is that of weighing the needs of the state against the intrusion of its regulations on religious belief.

In the *Yoder* case, the opposing interests to be balanced against each other were state compulsory education laws and the religious beliefs and practices of the Old Order Amish. Old Order Amish communities in Wisconsin provided their own schools through the eighth grade but did not provide facilities for the first two years of high school. They claimed exemption from state laws requiring schooling until the age of sixteen; the religious community did not want children of that age enrolled in the public high schools and exposed to the secular influences and competing life styles to be found there. The Amish have a long history of resistance to compulsory public education, and Amish communities have often pulled up stakes and moved from one state to another to avoid being forced to conform to state education requirements.

The criminal conviction and small fine imposed on Amish parents for failure to send their children to school would normally not have been the occasion for a lengthy appeal through the state and federal courts. But a civil rights organization, the National Committee for Amish Religious Freedom (NCARF), formed several years earlier to give the Amish moral and financial support, saw in this case another opportunity to test the application of compulsory school attendance legislation to religious objectors generally.[14] In the past, courts have invariably rejected such claims, even by sects that had a heritage of historical and religious uniqueness. In the 1950s, Orthodox Jews, Muslims and members of the "Ancient and Divine Order of Melchisadech" all failed to convince state courts that their religious claims merited exemption from state compulsory education laws. NCARF had failed in its earlier attempt to bring the conflict between the Amish and state authorities to the Supreme Court. *Certiorari* had been denied in *Garber v. Kansas* (1967), a case that the state had won in the Kansas Supreme Court.[15] In 1971, contrary to what might have been expected from past experience, the Justices not only granted *certiorari* to review a Wisconsin Supreme Court decision upholding the Amish claim to exemption, but also affirmed the state court's decision. It agreed with the state supreme court that compulsory education past the age of sixteen would introduce Amish children to secular high school values, create conflict with Amish religious beliefs and might lead to the destruction of the religious community.

Earlier court decisions on all levels had consistently protected public education from the separatist tendencies of religious sects. But a new wind blowing in the 1970s was creating a climate that was increasingly hostile to public education. Whereas earlier courts had looked only deeply enough to ascertain whether there was a legitimate secular purpose behind state school laws, as there undoubtedly was, new doubts about public education caused the Justices to look more closely at the other side of the equation, to see what kind of alternative educational system the Amish community provided.

The Amish cause was not hurt by the fact, revealed clearly in the Chief Justice's opinion, that the Justices admired the Amish way of life, finding it praiseworthy in many respects. It was religiously oriented and unworldly, rejecting such elements of modern life as telephones, automobiles, radios and television. The Amish were law-abiding and industrious, self-sufficient and God-fearing. Their children were given a sense of community, taught cooperation and indoctrinated in the religious values of the sect. Amish communities have no juvenile delinquency, no crime rates, and do not accept welfare benefits. Chief Justice

Burger noted that the Amishman resembled Jefferson's ideal, the sturdy yeoman farmer. By forcing Amish juveniles into the public school system, the Court would endanger an ancient way of life and also substitute a flawed educational system for one that was proven and practical.[16]

In the decision, the Court was at pains to point out that this case did not involve a choice between religious belief and education, because even after they left the classroom the Amish children would be educated in a manner that would equip them to function well in the adult life of their community. During the trial of the case in the Wisconsin County Court, civil rights organizations supporting the Amish cause were careful to describe in detail the kind of "alternate" education that Amish families offered their adolescents—practical, vocational training in farming and domestic economy.[17] The point was made clearly in the record that this type of education at home and on the farm was not necessarily inferior to public schooling. Although the state does have a compelling interest in seeing that all young people are adequately prepared for life, the Court accepted the argument that the vocational training offered on Amish farms would, in fact, be an adequate substitute, for most of the Amish children, for one or two additional years of formal education.

The essence of the constitutional argument in the case ran as follows: education is a very important function of the state and the state has a high responsibility for the education of its citizens, but this interest in education does not automatically outweigh fundamental liberty interests. The importance of education must be balanced against other values. In the Wisconsin case the two important values arrayed against educational policy were the rights of religious liberty and the rights of parents to make decisions about their children. These values are closely intertwined. The Court found that the correct balance favored the religious claims because there was minimal impact on education (only a few children were involved and their education was not seriously hampered), but the effect of the compulsory education laws on the religious community would be destructive. Freedom of religion, therefore, outweighed state educational concerns.

Although the weighing process engaged in by the Court seems unexceptionable, existing precedents did not necessarily dictate the result. The principal "free exercise" precedent relied on by the Court was *Sherbert v. Verner*, a 1963 decision concerned with the claim of a Seventh Day Adventist to unemployment benefits.[18] Adell H. Sherbert, the appellant, had been discharged by a South Carolina mill because she would not work on the Sabbath designated by her sect (Saturday). She filed for unemployment compensation benefits under South Carolina law, but was found not to qualify because she was "unavailable" for six-day-a-week jobs, and therefore, according to South Carolina, her lack of employment stemmed from her own free choice. The Court agreed with her argument that this policy was discriminatory, holding that, although the state law did not *directly* interfere with her religious belief, by excluding all "sabbatarians" from unemployment coverage, it "penalized" individuals for following the dictates of their faith. Earlier cases had held that government might not burden religious belief directly (by expelling students from school for refusing to salute the flag, for example), but this decision expanded the concept to include indirect burdens created where individuals, by choosing to follow the religious practices dictated by their faith, made themselves ineligible for state benefits.

The Yoder situation was by no means an exact parallel. Yoder was penalized directly for failing to perform a duty created by the state—to send his children to school. But he was penalized, not for a particular religious belief or practice, but for a generalized belief that public schools would make his children unfit for the Amish community's way of life. In previous cases, even where laws punished or forbade actions derived from religious beliefs, state regulations had usually been upheld. Previously decided cases directly in point included older cases such as *Reynolds v. United States* (punishment of polygamy) and *Jacobson v. Massachusetts* (fine for refusing to be vaccinated), *Prince v. Massachusetts* (penalizing a parent for letting her child sell religious literature), as well as *Braunfeld v. Brown* (fines for opening a business on Sunday).[19] Another problem in finding a controlling precedent was that it was not clear in this case whose rights were at stake. As is also true in many other "family" cases, the Amish children as well as their parents had important rights, and the rights were interrelated. As Justice Douglas was to point out in dissent, the children had rights to an education which were not explored in this litigation. Although *Yoder* can be seen as a free exercise case on the *Sherbert v. Verner* model, the Court could just as plausibly have used the alternative line of cases as precedent and held that there was a limited intrusion on religious freedom but a strong state secular interest in requiring educational opportunity for all children.

If this case were truly a free exercise case, one would expect to see a more extended discussion of free exercise doctrine. But the central focus of most of Chief Justice Burger's analysis is on parental rights and the parent-child relationship. Although religion is involved—because the Amish community is religious—the case is much more closely related to state cases involving parental decision-making in the child's interest (medical treatment, sterilization, voluntary commitment to institutions).[20] In some of those cases, the course of action the parent chose was also dictated by religious beliefs. But the emphasis in the majority opinion was not on the rights of children, but on the traditional rights of parents to determine what education their children should receive. The opinion was built largely on the *Meyer* and *Pierce* precedents—not on the actual holdings in those cases, but rather on the *dicta*, the general statements about parental rights to control the education of children, especially when the choice of education is strongly related to religious belief. Nine times in the majority opinion the Chief Justice asserted that the religious training of children was the traditional function of the family:

Yet even this paramount responsibility [public education] was, in Pierce, made to yield to the rights of parents to provide an equivalent education in a privately operated system.

[The Court held there that the Oregon statute] unreasonably interfered with the interests of the parents in directing the rearing of their offspring, including their education in church-operated schools.

[As that case suggests, the] values of parental direction of the religious upbringing and education of their children have a high value in our society.

[The Free Exercise Clause protects] the traditional interest of parents with respect to the religious upbringing of their children. . . .

[Recognition of the State's claim] would call into question concepts of parental control over the religious upbringing and education of their minor children. . . .

... intrusion by a State into family decisions in the area of religious training would give rise to grave questions of religious freedom.

[This case involves] fundamental interests of parents—as contrasted with that of the State, to guide the religious future and education of their children. The history and culture of Western civilization reflect a strong tradition of parental concern for the nurture and upbringing of their children. The primary role of the parents in the upbringing of their children is now established beyond debate as an enduring American tradition.

[And quoting Pierce, the State] unreasonably interferes with the liberty of parents and guardians to direct the upbringing and education of children under their control. . . . The child is not the mere creature of the State; those who nurture him and direct his destiny have the right, coupled with the high duty, to recognize and prepare him for additional obligations. . . .

Pierce stands as a charter of the rights of parents to direct the religious upbringing of their children.[21]

Although both decisions were cited extensively to support parental rights, they did not really involve identical issues and both were related to the political controversies of their own times. *Meyer* was concerned with a state law forbidding the teaching of foreign languages and was related to the anti-German sentiments abroad in the country after World War I. Here was no real challenge to the rights of parents to choose a suitable education for their children, but rather a question about limits on the power of legislatures to control curricula in the public schools. The Oregon law challenged in *Pierce* sought to eliminate private and religious schools entirely and to give the state a monopoly in education. This law would have precluded *all* private choice in educational matters. The Wisconsin law, in contrast, simply required some acceptable form of education for children until they reached the age of sixteen. The Amish were not prohibited from arranging private religious schooling for their children or from working out a compromise with state educational officials that fulfilled the general objectives of the state law.

The decision is a balancing decision, then, that ostensibly weighs the requirement of education for all children until the age of sixteen against a claim of interference with religious belief and the free exercise of religion. Seen in these terms, the decision is persuasive because its effect on universal public education is slight whereas a requirement that Amish children be educated in public schools would be devastating for the Amish sect. But the rhetoric of the opinion points in another direction, emphasizing the traditional rights of parents to supervise the education and religious training of their children. The constitutional problem addressed by the case derives from the impact that the socialization of Amish children by the public schools would have on the religious community and, derivatively, on the religious beliefs of individuals in the community—a problem for which there was no clear precedent (except perhaps the Mormon cases, which were decided the other way). A collective right, rather than an individual right, is being asserted here. The Amish community almost becomes a symbol of the family, a family "writ large."

A concurring opinion by Justice White quotes *Brown v. Board of Education*, the most important educational case of the half-century, to the effect that "education is perhaps the most important function of state and local governments" and "compulsory school attendance laws and the great expenditures on education both demonstrate our recognition of the importance of education to our democratic society." Education is "the principal instrument in awakening the child to cultural values, in preparing him for later professional training, and in helping him to adjust normally to his environment."[22] Even if the balance was correctly struck in favor of the Amish, the concurring Justices were concerned because the precedent set by this case allowed parents to use religious belief as an excuse for denying their children educational opportunities. They wanted to make it clear that the Court was not supporting the principle that idiosyncratic religious views could be used to block a child's right to an education, and they wanted to make sure that this precedent was confined to its facts so that it could not be used more broadly to undercut public education.

Another value, this one pushed to one side in the majority's balancing but discussed in Justice Douglas' dissenting opinion, is the separate interest of children in educational decisions affecting them. Traditional legal rules treat the family as a unit and accept the parent's decisions as properly representative of the child's needs. The rights to religious freedom and educational choice that are discussed in the opinion of the Court are those of the Amish parents who have been fined for refusing to send their children to school. But the children, fourteen and fifteen years of age, presumably have views both about religion and about education that may or may not be identical with those of their parents. The Court does not discuss the independent interests of the children; their rights are assumed to be identical with those of their families and the religious community. In some recent cases, courts have begun to assess the child's interests separately, recognizing that parents and children may have divergent interests in many types of situations—about custody and medical decisions, among others. *Tinker v. Des Moines*, one of the other major educational pronouncements of the Supreme Court, established the principle that children have First Amendment rights that they "do not leave at the schoolhouse door."[23] Presumably they also have some rights to be consulted about educational decisions affecting their whole lives.[24]

Family cases more frequently than not involve overlapping rights. If the children have a right to be educated and to be consulted about the kind of education they want and need, the parents have rights, too—the right to pass along their values to their children, the right to have some role in forming the educational programs of state-run schools. In recent years, especially, parents with objections to the content of public education have come to believe that they are powerless to make their wishes effective.

THE WANING OF THE "PUBLIC SCHOOL LEGEND"

Politics as well as ideology helps explain the *Yoder* decision. One way of understanding the emphasis of Chief Justice Burger's opinion is as a reflection of conservative political concern about the impact of public education on the family. According to this view, the public school system is not only failing to educate but is also undermining family authority and accepted moral values. Having taken children away from their families, the schools are now indoctrinating them with alien principles, with a philosophy of "secular humanism" and a hedonistic morality.[25] Desegregation has been partly to blame for the massive changes in a system of public education that had been in place since the Civil War, a system that had been widely accepted as an Americanizing, democratizing force. Integration, school consolidations and busing have weakened local control; the school prayer and Bible reading cases, decided in 1962 and 1963, respectively, imposed unpopular national policies on local school districts. In a number of these situations, the Supreme Court itself has been condemned as the agent responsible for taking control of the educational process away from local school boards representing the wishes of the parents, and for accelerating the centralizing, bureaucratizing, secularizing trends already evident in public education. In a very real sense, the *Yoder* decision was a response to the building pressure for alternate avenues of education, and it has been cited in later challenges to state laws imposing minimum standards on private schools as endorsing a constitutional right "of the parent to choose a private religious school for his child."[26]

One of the original selling points for a system of free, tax-supported common schools had been that they would complement parental authority, teach middle-class values and assimilate immigrants and the poor into the belief system of the majority. Schools were expected not only to train children for citizenship in a Republic, but also to teach generally accepted moral values and the Protestant virtues of obedience, industry, self-restraint and respect for property.[27]

People in different classes with different political perspectives or different educational philosophies could agree on a list of purposes for common schooling; moral education to produce obedient children, reduce crime, and discourage vice; citizenship training to protect republican government; literacy for effective economic and political participation; and cultural education for assimilation and unity.[28]

This general agreement on the mission of the public schools has broken down, and conservatives are now attacking the schools as enemies of middle-class values. Some professional educators have begun to call for "educational deregulation" and disengagement of the state from "excessive educational control."[29] Both the family and the schools have become planks in the political platforms of the New Right.

Enrollment in non-Catholic, non-public schools increased during the 1961–1971 period, even though there was an overall decline in private school enrollment because Catholic enrollments themselves were decreasing.[30] Not only the Amish, but also members of other religious sects were anxious to withdraw their children from the public schools in order to supply them with an alternate, church-related education, designed to reinforce rather than undermine family and religious values. For the first time, these defectors were predominantly Protestant. Total enrollment in non-public schools declined about 28 percent between 1965 and 1975, but enrollment in so-called Christian or fundamentalist schools climbed by as much as 118 percent. The movement of the fundamentalists out of the public schools was in part due to dissatisfaction with desegregation and dislike of busing, but there were additional complaints that academic offerings were declining, discipline was poor or non-existent, and anti-religious, secular attitudes were dominant. In the opinion of these parents, the public schools were no longer serving the purpose of socializing children to accept middle-class values, instilling patriotic and moral precepts and the Protestant work ethic. Parents were also upset because the schools were not teaching fundamentals, and the educational bureaucracy in charge of school programs seemed to be less and less responsive to parental wishes or popular control.[31] Some of the anti-school rhetoric was devastating. Tim LaHaye, a prominent fundamentalist religious leader and former president of the Moral Majority in California, wrote:

The public school system, once the most successful of its kind in the world [when it was based on traditional moral values], has, during the past sixty years, become the third most destructive force in America, at least where the family is concerned. For families with junior-high, high school or college-age young people, it is even more harmful than the government. For them, the public school, purportedly their friend, has become a deadly enemy. Nothing creates more discord between parents and children than the humanistic philosophy taught in our nation's public schools.[32]

As their enrollments grew, fundamentalist religious schools began to use litigation to mount serious constitutional challenges to existing state educational policies, especially to compulsory education laws and statutory provisions governing the regulation and accreditation of private educational institutions. The new schools not only wanted exemption from general state school regulations, but also favored tax exemptions, and educational vouchers or scholarships that would give parents a real alternative to public education. Parents of those students remaining in the public schools began to take political action to make changes in the schools themselves, putting pressure on legislatures and school boards to change curricula and add or remove particular programs. There were demands that some form of religious observance be put back into the schoolroom—moments of meditation or silent prayer, if nothing else; there were also proposals that course offerings be modified to satisfy conservative complaints. Sex education courses were especially objectionable.[33] The movement to require the teaching of "creationism" along with the Darwinian theory of evolution was another manifestation of this trend. Parent organizations also objected to particular textbooks and to the inclusion of "unsuitable" books in school libraries. During the 1970s, there was a great deal of political ferment about these issues, and a sprinkling of cases raising constitutional problems began to reach the Supreme Court. The Justices approached these problems with a basic commitment to the public school legend, although they disagreed about the proper balance between community control, state educational policy and student rights.

TWO MODELS OF THE PUBLIC SCHOOL

The public school ideology has always contained potentially conflicting ingredients. From the first, the school was seen as an extension of the family, a complementary institution that would remedy failures in child training by the family itself, especially by groups in society like the poor or new immigrants who ignored their educational responsibilities. The school was thus *parens patriae*, a substitute parent, to whom real parents delegated the task of education and the responsibility for discipline and training. The quotation at the beginning of this chapter from an Ohio school commissioner who states that the school district could be visualized as "one family, charged with the parental duty of educating all its youth," illustrates this point of view. Like family life, the school environment was a special protected area with its own rules, and student-teacher relationships were similar to parent-child relationships.

On the other hand, the school was designed to serve the state, to be a training ground for citizens. Not only did future citizens learn American history and democratic principles, but they also acquired the literacy, skills and information necessary to perform their prospective political duties. The principles governing political participation were not always exactly congruent with those governing relationships within the family. Insofar as the schools were training grounds for citizenship, they needed to teach equality, democracy, freedom of thought and expression, respect for rights as well as for rules. Relationships in this "political model" contained some inherent conflicts with those in a hierarchical "family model" that emphasized respect for authority and disciplined obedience to orders—not the most useful characteristics for independent citizens in a free-wheeling democracy.

There were also seeds of conflict in the issue of locating control of the public schools. The imposition of a state school system itself implied some loss of local choice and control. Locally elected school boards were designed to bridge this gap between the wishes of families and localities and the content of an educational system increasingly dominated by professional educators and regulated by the state. The idea of local control is a necessary part of the "family model,' and the elected school board and Parent Teachers Associations are the conduits through which local opinions about education are transmitted to the schools.

This concept of two models, or two visions of the public schools, is useful in understanding the dynamics of the Supreme Court decisions in school cases. Traces of these two models of the public schools surface in a number of the Supreme Court's education cases, and the Justices tend to divide along liberal/conservative lines as well as according to their attitudes toward the nature of the public school functions. Two cases, decided in 1969 and 1975 respectively, *Tinker v. Des Moines* and *Goss v. Lopez*, extended the protection of constitutional rights into the class-room, *Tinker* holding that students had some rights to free expression and *Goss* that school disciplinary proceedings must respect rudimentary due process requirements.[34] The *Tinker* case, of course, illustrates the possibilities of conflict between the state's programs of indoctrination and those of the family. But after these two cases, the momentum seemed too slow, the interest in student rights diminished and in *Ingraham v. Wright* the Court held that the use of corporal punishment in schools did not violate protections against cruel and unusual punishment.[35] After 1977, the Burger Court seemed more concerned about reinforc-ing the ability of school authorities to maintain order than it did about further protecting student rights.

The opinions in a 1982 case, *Board of Education of Island Trees Union Free School District v. Pico*, illustrate the degree to which different Justices accept different models of the public schools.[36] There is a good deal of agreement on some matters. All of the Justices acknowledged that the public schools had ugly problems with disorder, violence and crime.[37] Justices on both sides of this split decision also agreed that in the administration of the public schools there was "a legitimate and substantial interest in promoting respect for authority and traditional values, be they social, moral or political."[38] Public schools were vitally important in "the preparation of individuals for participation as citizens," and as vehicles for "inculcating fundamental values necessary to the maintenance of the American political system."[39] But there was divergence about what "preparation for citizenship" meant and about the ranking of various "fundamental values."

The lawsuit in the case was initiated by high school seniors who objected to the actions of their local school board members in removing books from the school library. Influenced by a po-litically conservative organization of parents who were con-cerned about educational legislation in New York (PONYU—Parents of New York United), school board members took a list prepared by the organization to the school libraries in their dis-trict and directed that any listed books be removed. Nine books, which the board characterized as "anti-American, anti-Christian, anti-Semitic, and just plain filthy," were removed from the li-brary shelves.

Although the case was narrowly decided on technical, procedural grounds, five Justices agreed on the general principle that such removals were unconstitutional when they were for the purpose of censoring ideas.[40] The Brennan opinion, supported only by two other Justices, emphasized the importance of access to ideas, concluding that "Our Constitution does not permit the official suppression of ideas."[41] Students preparing for "active and effective participation in the pluralistic, often contentious society in which they will soon be adult members" need to receive information and ideas, and the First Amendment protects their right to have what they need. This group of Justices obviously saw school as a microcosm of the political world, a place where students should begin the process of learning to make independent assessments of their own.

The dissents were especially interesting because they not only recognized that the function of schools was the indoctrination of children, but also asserted that if that function were to be performed properly, school boards representing the views of parents and the community must be allowed to influence the content of courses and to choose teaching materials. In Chief Justice Burger's language,

How are "fundamental values" to be inculcated except by having school boards make content-based decisions about the appropriateness of retaining materials in the school library and curriculum. In order to fulfill its function, an elected school board MUST express its views on the subjects which are taught to its students. In doing so those elected officials express the views of their community; they may err, of course, and the voters may remove them. It is a startling erosion of the very idea of democratic government to have this Court arrogate to itself the power the plurality asserts today.[42]

The Chief Justice's opinion and the other dissents inveighed against the interference in local school policies by federal courts (and by students), and rejected Justice Brennan's articulation of a "right of access to ideas." They ridiculed the charge that there was any suppression of ideas in this case; rather, there was a legitimate exercise of choice by the school board not to place books containing vulgarity and profanity on the shelves of school libraries.

Justice Rehnquist's dissent disclosed that behind these disagreements there was a difference of vision among the Justices about the nature of the educational function of the public schools. He noted that the government plays different roles when it acts as sovereign and when it functions as educator.[43] As educator, the state "is engaged in inculcating social values and knowledge in relatively impressionable young people." This vision corresponds to the family model described above, because families instruct in morality, mold young minds, develop character, guide and correct, and choose methods of instruction. Families also protect children from information they are not yet ready to handle. But after noting that there was a difference between the state's function as educator and its other roles, Justice Rehnquist let the matter drop and did not examine the implications of the distinction.

Justice Brennan's opinion conforms more closely to the political model. Brennan understood the proper function of schooling to be the development of judgment and independence, gradual exposure to the variety of experience. The ultimate objective of the educational process, according to this view, is to transform the child into the autonomous political person required by the democratic system. This transformation is not made by suppressing ideas but by teaching judgment. School boards should supply information, not censor it; schools should not indoctrinate but should teach students how to handle the multitude of competing ideas in the world outside the school. Vulgarity and profanity are part of experience and cannot simply be ignored. In addition to preparing students for political responsibilities, the schools should also teach respect for constitutional principles—one of which is the "fundamental value of freedom of speech and inquiry."

The idea that schools have a responsibility to teach constitutional principles, and that this is done, in part, by example, by respecting individual rights in the school environment, re-emerged in another context three years later. In *New Jersey v. TLO*, a search and seizure case, the Court held that there was a less demanding standard for searches of students at school than there was for searches made in the context of a criminal investigation.[44] The Court was again split into liberal and conservative factions, with the liberals in favor of strict protection of personal privacy and the conservatives more concerned about school discipline. Although the decision had the beneficial result of bringing school searches under the protection of the Fourth Amendment, it authorized teachers and principals to make limited, reasonable searches without establishing probable cause or without securing warrants.

The incident from which this case arose was the search of a girl's purse by an assistant principal. The girl had been seen smoking in the bathroom and was ordered to report to the principal's office. When she denied smoking, in fact denied that she smoked at all, the principal took her purse and examined it. He found both cigarettes and evidence that she was selling marijuana. The case itself was an appeal from a state Juvenile Court finding that the girl was delinquent. Although major doctrinal issues involved the applicability of the Fourth Amendment to school searches and the constitutional standard required for searches made in the school environment, the split on the Court again revealed competing visions of the nature and function of the public school experience. A six-Justice majority accepted the idea of the school as a special place, with special rules—more like those in a family—where students are subjected to discipline for their own good and where authority is used to develop character. Teachers and principals, they stated, resemble parents, who would not be obliged to obtain warrants or follow the rules governing probable cause because such a requirement would make discipline impossible. The Justices voting with the majority did not think that students could be afforded a full array of constitutional protections in school, in part because of the impact of such requirements on the educational process and in part because they were not necessary. Although this model seemed to accept the notion that the school acted *in loco parentis* and that school authorities fulfilled a parental role, Justice White's plurality opinion explicitly rejected that doctrine. Instead, he adapted the rule used in "stop and frisk" cases to school searches. The reasonableness of any search should be determined by a twofold inquiry: "first, one must consider 'whether the . . . action was justified at its inception'; second, one must determine whether the search as actually conducted 'was reasonably related in scope to the circumstances which justified the interference in the first place.' "[45] Translated from these opaque phrases, the test seems to require that the Court decide in each situation whether it thinks the search was justified by the circumstances and whether the scope of the search was broader than necessary, hardly a precise or definite yardstick.

The opinions in *New Jersey v. TLO* deal, on the doctrinal level, with familiar search and seizure principles but echo the Justices' more personal feelings about public schools. All members of the Court deplored the violence that had invaded the protected school environment. Justice Blackmun's opinion reminisced about school discipline in his own school days, citing the need for a prompt response to bad boys with pea shooters and water pistols— hardly a typical problem in today's school.[46] Justice Powell wrote about the camaraderie of the schoolhouse, where students "spend the school hours in close association with each other" . . . "and often know each other and their teachers well." "Of necessity teachers have a degree of familiarity with, and authority over their students that is unparalleled except perhaps in the relationship between parent and child."[47] He found less of an "expectation of privacy" in such surroundings and less need for formal constitutional protections. Justice Powell's opinion quotes extensively from his earlier opinion for the Court in another school case, *Ingraham v. Wright*.[48]

The dissenters, on the other hand, emphasized that constitutional protections applied to school authorities as well as to arbitrary actions by other agents of the state. Justice Stevens also suggested that the school taught respect for constitutional rights when it respected the students' own rights to privacy. He quoted Justice Louis D. Brandeis' opinion in *Olmstead v. U.S.* which noted that "Government is the potent, the omnipresent teacher . . . it teaches the whole people by its example. . . . If the Government becomes a lawbreaker, it breeds contempt for law; it invites every man to become a law unto himself."

All three of these cases, *Yoder*, *Island Trees* and *New Jersey v. TLO*, are concerned with the socialization of children, and they tell us that the Supreme Court accepts the following propositions. Schools have taken over much of the educational function, but parental decisions are still important, especially where they involve religious beliefs and where they relate to the values that are to be transmitted to children by the educational apparatus. This far the Justices agree, but there seems to be some underlying division over how much liberty there can be in the classroom and over whether the school's function in inculcating fundamental values includes teaching, by example, the importance of constitutional restraints. The disagreements seem almost to flow from different perceptions of the nature of the public schools.

The *Yoder* case is a pivotal case because it embodies many of the central issues in the contemporary political debate over the family. The Amish family arrangements described in *Yoder* may well have symbolized for the Supreme Court the strengths of a traditional family which could enforce discipline and teach morality and respect for authority while it nurtured and educated its young. This view of the family has great nostalgic appeal and deep roots in the American tradition. The Court's resolution of the conflict between the Amish and the state of Wisconsin, rather than representing merely the protection of an ancient non-conformist religious group from homogenizing forces, may also have symbolized the deep yearnings that many conservatives have for a return to the ideal of family-church-community centered education.

But for most people, this type of family control of education has not been a fact of life for a hundred years—not since state governments began to make education a public responsibility. The public school long ago replaced the home as the primary educator as well as a competing source of socialization and value inculcation. The assumption of this responsibility by the state does not mean, however, that the family has been entirely displaced. Both wings of the Court probably agreed with this idea, although in *Pico* the majority was worried about the possible "bookburning" tendencies of citizen pressure groups and tried to work out a distinction that would protect the educational process from excessive zeal on the part of conservative reformers. The Court will certainly be asked, in the next few years, to examine other parts of the traditional relationship between parents, schools, religious education and children. The pressure for alternatives to public education will also bring up questions about the amount of aid to religious schools which is compatible with existing interpretations of the Establishment Clause.

The new trend may be toward some form of state aid to parents who want alternatives to the public schools. At least one recent decision points that way. In *Mueller v. Allen*, the Court upheld a state income tax deduction for educational expenses, indicating that the majority may be leaning in the direction of approving aid that benefits parents directly, rather than going to the schools.[49] Justice Rehnquist's opinion for the Court built on the propositions advanced in *Meyer* and *Pierce* and emphasized in *Yoder*: parents should have control over educational decisions affecting their children, and alternatives to compulsory public education must be found for parents with dissenting views.

What Is a Family?

Policies and legislation involving services to families have in the past been punitive toward family forms that differ from the traditional.

Betty E. Cogswell and Marvin B. Sussman[1]

How far is government entitled to go in defining what a "family" actually is? And to what extent do constitutional protections of liberty and privacy insulate the family from governmental intrusions?

In an essay in *The Supreme Court Review*, Professor Robert A. Burt has speculated that the Supreme Court's bias in favor of "families" is selective in that the Court approves of certain kinds of families but disapproves of others. The paternalistic, authoritarian family of the Amish community is approved, but other kinds of families, welfare families, non-marital families and informal groupings and communal arrangements that perform some of the functions of families do not receive the same kind of judicial imprimatur.[2]

The Court has touched on questions of the formation of families and their different configurations in connection with a variety of different issues: zoning, public welfare, laws regulating entrance into the marriage relationship and the claims of non-marital families to protection from hostile regulation.

The key "family" case of the decade, *Moore v. City of East Cleveland, Ohio*, was a zoning case.[3] It raised important questions about the constitutional basis of family rights, and also asked what kind of family the Supreme Court was willing to give constitutional protection. In this case the Court held directly that the Constitution protects the "sanctity of the family," and discussed the range of choices in family living style which were among the liberties protected by the Due Process Clause of the Fourteenth Amendment.[4] Earlier cases had established that a great many liberty interests were rooted in the family—the right to choose marriage partners, to marry, divorce, have children or not to have children, and to decide how children are to be raised and what they are to be taught. But is family living itself a basic civil right protected in a substantive sense by the Due Process Clause? To what extent does the Constitution protect the right to live in a family? And, most important of all, what is a family?

The Moore case reached beyond fundamental decisions or choices, such as the right to marry or the right to choose to have children, in order to discuss the nature of the actual composition of the family unit. It raised an important new constitutional question: Can the state dictate or discourage particular configurations of family living, or are these matters among the choices which, barring some actual threat to the health or safety of the community, should be left to private determination? This issue had been barely touched on in earlier cases. Polygamy as a form of marriage had been definitely ruled out in 1878 in *Reynolds v. U.S.*[5] In *Loving v. Virginia*, decided in 1967, interracial marriages, once seen as a legitimate matter for state prohibition, were held to be matters of individual choice.[6] State prohibitions based on age, degree of relationship or health were presumably still valid, as were requirements of blood tests, marriage licenses and some form of ceremonial solemnization of the new relationship.[7] But once a new family has been formed it acquires a protected legal status.

Moore involved a city housing code in East Cleveland, Ohio, which zoned part of the city for single-family homes, defined single-family homes for this purpose in terms of degrees of relationship and limited the number of relatives who might live together simultaneously. In trying to limit the number of relatives who might crowd into one house, the ordinance defined family very narrowly. The "family" could include the head of the household and spouse and any of their parents. Unmarried children with no children were allowable. But if these children had families themselves, only one such family could live with the original household. Mrs. Moore's family did not fit these specifications because, whereas one son and grandson were within the ordinance's strictures, a second grandson from a different son's family exceeded the allowance under the ordinance.

Mrs. Moore challenged the ordinance under the Due Process and Equal Protection clauses of the Fourteenth Amendment. The Supreme Court, in a 5 to 4 decision, agreed, holding that this intrusive regulation of the family was so arbitrary and unfair and so foreign to American history and tradition that it violated the substance of due process. Justice Powell's opinion for the plurality (Justice Stevens concurred in the judgment alone) made several basic points. First, a regulation which intruded so drastically on family prerogatives absolved the Court from its usual obligation to defer to the legislature. Second, basic decisions on family matters were protected by the Due Process Clause, and state laws superseding them could only be sustained if they advanced important governmental interests. Here the ordinance was not well designed to promote the interest claimed by the city. Therefore, it must fall.

In making his case for freedom of choice in family matters, both Justice Powell in the plurality opinion and Justice Brennan in a concurrence, praised the extended family and described the importance of such family units in American history and culture. The plurality opinion thus added family living to the list of values protected by "substantive due process." These families of uncles, aunts, cousins, parents, children and other kinfolk had supported and helped each other and shared household and child-raising responsibilities. Cleveland's ordinance rejected an important traditional value in American life. Justice Brennan's opinion described the importance of extended families for the immigrant and minority experience, and pointed out that extended families were still a common form of family organization. Justice Marshall joined in this opinion.

The writing in Justice Powell's plurality opinion and in Justice Brennan's concurring opinion was very nostalgic and romantic. Just as Chief Justice Burger's opinion in the *Yoder* case reflected an underlying longing and yearning for the simple, community-based educational systems of the past, so the opinions here suggest that some members of the Court visualize the extended family as the basic social welfare agency of happier and simpler times, when families clung together, took care of their aged relatives and provided each other with the security and support which the nuclear family of today often lacks. Modern sociological investigation indicates that this view of the extended family as the basic traditional form and of the nuclear family as a later development is an oversimplification, is probably not historically valid and does not describe existing family relationships accurately.[8] For the first time, however, a Supreme Court opinion mentioned some of the changes taking place in American families. In the footnotes to his opinion, Justice Powell cited sociological studies and census data on changing family patterns, as well as a law review article (written, in part, by a former law clerk) on the "Constitutional Protection for Personal Lifestyles."[9]

In the *Moore* decision, the Court indicated that local governments would not be allowed to define "family" too narrowly: "Ours is by no means a tradition limited to the nuclear family. The tradition of uncles, aunts, cousins, and especially grandparents sharing a household along with parents and children has roots equally venerable and equally deserving of constitutional protection."[10]

Not all the permutations of family living, however, qualify for constitutional protection. Deviations from the accepted family forms of the middle class found in the families of the poor have often been seen by legislatures to be products of shiftlessness and lack of moral standards rather than as the adjustments poor families are forced to make by the social, economic and legal problems they face because of their poverty.[11] Common law marriage, non-marital living arrangements, desertion, large extended families occupying the same quarters, unmarried mothers heading families—all of these seemed more typical of lower than of upper or middle-class living patterns. Although Congress and state legislatures have recognized the importance of protecting needy children when these marginal families fail to provide for them, legislatures have not always stopped at supplying aid, but have felt justified in using regulations to try to regularize the living arrangements of welfare families. Until recently, the Supreme Court has not seen any constitutional problem with this intrusive regulation.

One of the first things to note about family law is that there is a difference between the family law of the poor and the traditional legal rules that govern the relationships of families that are not dependent on public assistance.[12] Ever since the passage of the Elizabethan Poor Laws, when society first began to assume responsibility for the indigent, that assumption of responsibility has been accompanied by regulation, on the theory that "he who pays the bill can attach conditions related or unrelated to the purposes of the grant."[13] Whereas one set of rules governs such matters as husband-wife relationships, marriage and divorce, the ownership of property, custody of children, parental rights and family-child relationships for non-dependent families, another set of regulations, enacted by legislatures and administered by welfare agencies, governs the same kind of relationships in families receiving public assistance. The traditional privacy of the home, and the freedom to govern family relationships in that protected environment free from government intrusion, has not applied to welfare families. The basic rationale for state regulation is fiscal and economic—the taxpayer has a right to keep costs down. This motive, however, has often become entangled with others; political considerations, moralistic and punitive impulses, have combined with the overriding public interest in fiscal responsibility to justify differential treatment of the families of the poor.[14]

Before the late 1960s and the welfare rights litigation campaigns sponsored by various organizations in that period, these differences in the treatment of family rights for the poor and the non-poor were not seen as having constitutional dimensions.[15] But beginning with *King v. Smith* in 1968, some of these regulations were challenged.[16] *King v. Smith* involved an Alabama law, similar to laws that existed in other states, which treated a male who visited the home and had sexual relations with a welfare recipient as a "substitute father" for eligibility purposes. Here, in spite of the fact that there had been no formal ceremonial marriage, that there was not even a common law marital arrangement and that there was no evidence that the substitute father was the natural father of the children, the state treated him as legal husband and father with support obligations. When such a situation existed, the state withdrew public assistance from the mother and the family. This law was challenged as denying equal protection under the Constitution. The Supreme Court did not reach the constitutional issue but did overturn the regulation as incompatible with the purposes of the Social Security Act.

Other cases brought during the same period resulted in the imposition of other constitutional checks on welfare regulations. State residency laws were found to burden a constitutional right to travel, and the constitutional requirement of due process of law was held to cover welfare terminations, at least to the extent of requiring some type of prior hearing.[17] Even though a sprinkling of decisions gave some constitutional protections to welfare families, the Supreme Court continued to accept the standard view that the families of the poor might be treated differently from other families; by accepting the public dole, they had forfeited some of the rights to liberty and privacy which were part of the standard family ideology. *Dandridge v. Williams*, decided in 1970, allowed a state to put a cap on support payments to individual families, in effect imposing a penalty on excessive procreation by the poor.[18] *Wyman v. James*, 1971, upheld as reasonable a state regulation requiring welfare recipients to accept "home visits" by welfare workers, even though these unwelcome inspections had been challenged as a breach of the traditional privacy of the home.[19]

Restrictive policies in public assistance programs reflected state concerns about morality, illegitimacy and the responsibility for child care of families receiving welfare payments. Congress has also used benefit programs to influence the private ways in which families live, often penalizing configurations that congressmen deem undesirable. The 1971 Amendments to the Food Stamp Act of 1964 were designed to eliminate food stamp abuse by employable workers living together in unrelated family groups. For food stamp purposes, after 1971, a household was defined as a group of related individuals living and cooking together. The legislative history of the amendments seemed to indicate that Congress was expressly trying to exclude "hippies" and "hippie communes" from participating in the food stamp program. A similar limitation on eligibility excluded persons eighteen or over who were claimed as dependents for tax purposes by someone not a member of the household receiving food stamps. Presumably, this amendment was designed to keep food stamps from being used by non-indigents and college students. The actual effect of both sets of amendments, however, was to exclude non-related old and poor people who were neither hippies nor students, and who were living together and pooling resources in order to survive.

The Supreme Court rejected both amendments.[20] There was some evidence in the debtate over the amendments that Congress had been concerned about communal living and had wanted to ensure that "flower children" would not abuse the food stamp program by pooling their resources and living in idleness on the public dole. The Court decided that these anti-hippie amendments denied equal protection because they created an irrational classification by designating "non-related" household groupings as ineligible stamp recipients. A bare political desire to harm an unpopular group was not sufficient to constitute a legitimate governmental interest. An amendment challenged in *United States Department of Agriculture v. Murray*, one of the cases, was also held to be unconstitutional because it created an irrebuttable presumption (that a child being used as a tax deduction was actually being supported by the parent using the deduction) and therefore denied due process of law. The Court did not say that legislatures must treat all of the new family arrangements as the equivalents of traditional families, but its rulings meant that these variant types of families could not be discriminated against without legitimate reasons.

In both cases the parties contesting the congressional restrictions were clearly in need, and the deprivation of food stamps worked severe hardship on them. In *United States Department of Agriculture v. Moreno*, one appellee was a fifty-six-year-old diabetic who shared child care responsibilities with a mother of three in return for nursing care and help with living expenses. She was denied food stamps. Another family, caring for an indigent girl, could not use her stamps because she was unrelated. A third appellee shared an apartment so that her daughter could go to a school for the deaf; she was denied food stamps because the woman whose apartment she shared was also on public assistance.

Even though the rulings in this group of cases resulted in equality of treatment for some kinds of deviant family forms, it is more likely that the individual decisions were dictated by the Court's concern for the suffering created by the discriminatory or arbitrary regulations, rather than by any desire to protect the rights of individuals to live in whatever private arrangements suited their particular needs.

A forthright attempt to reinforce approved models of family organization by rewarding traditional families with additional public funding was, however, found to violate the Equal Protection Clause. In 1971, New Jersey enacted a statute designed to "preserve and strengthen family life." The state provided grants to supplement the incomes of the types of families which the legislature wanted to support and encourage. Desirable families were those that consisted of "a household composed of two adults of the opposite sex ceremonially married to each other, who have at least one minor child by both, the natural child of one and adopted by the other, or a child adopted by both."[21] The District Court had sustained this legislation as being rationally related to a proper legislative purpose. It had found that the state's objective was to strengthen legitimate families. It had accepted the state legislature's conclusion that legitimate families were more likely to instill proper social norms in their children, and, therefore, it was in the state's interest to encourage that type of family. The District Court agreed that a plan directed at married families only was reasonable; if non-marital families had been allowed to benefit from the legislation, the state might have been perceived as encouraging conduct that violated its laws against fornication and adultery. The trial court did not believe that the legislation was designed to punish illegitimate children, or that it was directed at children at all. It was aimed at families as units. The program actually encouraged legitimatization of children because families could make themselves eligible for additional support payments by marrying.

The Supreme Court rejected the District Court's interpretation of the statute. Announcing its decision in a *per curiam* opinion, the Court overturned the legislation on the grounds that it denied equal protection to illegitimate children, citing *Levy v. Louisiana* (1968) and *Aetna Casualty and Surety Co.* (1972) as precedents. There were certain strategic considerations behind this approach. By deciding the way it did, the majority avoided holding that a state legislature might designate one form of family as a preferred form, rewarding "good" families while penalizing others. The Court thus failed to establish a precedent that would have allowed state legislatures to favor one particular family form at the expense of another.

Much of the state's interest in encouraging stable, intact families and in regularizing the family relationships of the poor arises from its concern for the public purse. Unmarried women with children and families headed by women who have been widowed, divorced or deserted are likely to need and claim public assistance. About 45 percent of the children cared for by a single mother live in poverty, and, as of 1982, about 8.4 million women were heads of households. Both the national and state governments contribute to social welfare programs; approximately $12 billion a year is spent directly on AFDC, another $10 billion on food stamps and billions more on Medicaid and housing programs.[22] This enormous burden on the public treasury would be eased if men who father children without assuming financial responsibility for them could be induced to pay child support. Many fathers—married, unmarried and divorced—who do not live with their children are under either voluntary agreements or court orders to make monthly payments or supply other forms of financial assistance, but only about 65 percent of the child support owed is actually paid.[23] States have tried different schemes for enforcing the support obligations of absent parents, but most of these plans have failed to produce satisfactory results. Existing enforcement methods threaten the delinquent father with jail and sometimes sentence him to jail, but there are so many problems with this procedure that state legislatures are continually casting about for better approaches.

An original scheme adopted by the Wisconsin legislature in 1973 was designed to discourage non-supporting fathers from starting new families when they were failing to help existing children. Instead of threatening these parents with jail, the legislature came up with a new kind of sanction. It forbade "non-custodial" parents who had minor children whom they were under court order to support from remarrying. No marriage license could lawfully be issued in Wisconsin to any person covered by the statute, except on court order; any marriage contracted by these persons was void; and persons acquiring licenses in violation of the statute were subject to criminal penalties. The ban on remarriage could be lifted, but only after the offending parent had convinced a state court that he (or she) was now meeting the support obligation and that the children were not and were not likely thereafter to become public charges. The statute was worded so that it would cover both males and females, although its principal target was the non-supporting, non-custodial father.

The Supreme Court was asked to decide on the constitutionality of this statute in a class action challenge under the Equal Protection and Due Process clauses of the Fourteenth Amendment. In *Zablocki v. Redhail* the Court held that the statute was unconstitutional.[24] The majority opinion, written by Justice Thurgood Marshall, handled the case as a classification problem under the Equal Protection Clause. The classification set up by the state, on which the remarriage ban was imposed, covered "any Wisconsin resident having minor issue not in his custody . . . which he is under obligation to support by any court order or judgment." Parents of children who were not in this situation were not covered by the statute. There were no restrictions on "custodial" parents. There were no restrictions on parents who were not meeting child support obligations but were not under court orders to do so.

The Court held that past decisions established the principle that the right to marry was "of fundamental importance" (citing family rights decisions from *Maynard v. Hill* in 1888 to *Moore v.*

City of East Cleveland in 1977).[25] Because the legislative classification in the Wisconsin statute significantly interfered with "the exercise of that right," the Court was required to subject it to "critical examination." After careful examination, Justice Marshall found that, although the state's interest in enforcing support orders was important, the statutory scheme was defective. It had a number of problems. If reproductive choice was constitutionally protected, but the right to marry was not, the Constitution, in effect, protected the right to have illegitimate children. The Court found that "if appellee's right to procreate means anything at all, it must imply some right to enter the only relationship in which the State of Wisconsin allows sexual relations legally to take place."[26] The other basic flaw in the scheme was that it did not simply burden a constitutional right, but it absolutely prevented some people, the indigent, from marrying. Indigent, unemployed fathers will never be able to obtain the necessary court orders; either they will lack the financial means to meet their support obligations or they will not be able to prove that their children will not become public charges.[27] The impact of the classification, then, fell differently on the rich and the poor. As Justice Stevens explained in his concurring opinion, "the rich may marry, the poor may not."[28] This restriction on indigent fathers would not help support existing children. It might even work against the children's interests by preventing a man from improving his economic condition through marriage. Nor would it keep the poor from having more children; the net result of preventing marriage "is simply more illegitimate children."[29]

Zablocki v. Redhail was a significant decision because, as Justice Powell pointed out in a concurring opinion, it could open up to constitutional scrutiny all state restrictions on entry into marriage. If marriage was a fundamental right, then prohibitions against bigamous, incestuous or underage marriages could be challenged. Requirements that marriages be heterosexual, or that they be preceded by health checks, such as blood tests, were vulnerable on the grounds that they interfered unconstitutionally with a fundamental freedom.

Perhaps a more interesting dimension to the decision was its recognition that conditions of poverty could affect the ability to exercise constitutional rights. In other cases, the Court has been reluctant to weigh the effects of poverty on the ability to exercise fundamental rights. In the abortion funding cases, for example, the Court held that the right to choose an abortion was not burdened by indigency, the fact that poverty might prevent access to abortion services. *Maher v. Roe* held that a Connecticut regulation prohibiting the funding of abortions that were not medically necessary put no burden on the right to choose. "The indigency that may make it difficult—and in some cases, perhaps, impossible—for some women to have abortions is neither created nor in any way affected by the Connecticut regulation."[30] If one applies the argument used by the Court in those cases to the Wisconsin law, one might argue that the statute does not burden the right to marry because anyone who is willing to support his existing children is free to marry. The fact that he cannot afford to support the children is irrelevant; the condition of poverty is one that exists independently of the state regulation and is not a burden imposed by the state.

In all of the decisions discussed above except the food stamp cases, claims to rights stemming from family status were based on blood or marital relationships. Although few cases raising questions about the legal and constitutional status of variant family forms have been decided at the Supreme Court level, state courts have been struggling with legal problems raised by the increasing experimentation with alternate life styles. The family is nothing if not adaptable. There is a rich profusion of family configurations and novel relationships on the contemporary social scene: persons not married but living together, with or without children, people living together for convenience and companionship, foster homes, communes, group homes, homosexual or lesbian "marriages." Relationships between children and their parents are no longer based simply on biological ties; divorce and remarriage have produced complicated constellations of step-parents, step-children and half-brothers and sisters. New kinds of legal problems have been raised by artificial insemination, surrogate mothers and test-tube babies. Most of these new family relationships have some but not all of the characteristics of traditional families, or fulfill some but not all family functions.

An attempt to list the social needs that families fulfill would probably include the following: provision of secure relationships for sexual activity and procreation, provision of an environment suitable for child-rearing, creation of small, self-sufficient economic units, supplying of psychological and emotional support, and provision of care in sickness and old age. Many of the alternate family forms perform more than one of these functions, yet the law has been slow to characterize them as families. People living in these relationships are beginning to ask for the status, privileges and protections that the law affords more traditional families.[31] There is a plausible argument for accepting, regularizing and extending legal protection to many of these family configurations in order to promote stability and to allow state regulation.

Foster families, artificial families created by the state, have been especially plagued with identity problems. Designed to provide a family environment for children who have been abused or rejected, or who cannot be raised by their own parents, the foster family performs family functions but is not recognized as the equivalent of a natural family. Because foster care is, in theory, temporary and envisions the return of children to their homes as soon as their biological parents can provide for them, the foster family has been put in an ambiguous situation, full of contradictory cross-pressures. It is set up by the state on a contractual basis, and the foster parents are paid for their services. On the other hand, designed to replace parents even though on a temporary basis, it often becomes permanent; it offers not only food and shelter but love and emotional support as well. However, because children who become too attached to their foster parents may find it difficult to return to their natural families, the state discourages the formation of ties that are too close, and in some instances has had a policy of moving children from place to place to prevent the development of close associations. The conflict between the child's need for permanency and the goal of eventual reunification with its biological parents has been hard to resolve.[32] Psychologists and foster parents themselves have exerted pressure to solve this policy dilemma by forcing the state to recognize that where "psychological parenting" has become a reality, both foster families and foster children should be accorded legal protection on the same terms as natural families. Nevertheless, the Supreme Court has not been willing to take this step, or to give the foster child-parent relationship constitutional protection.[33] The biological connection is the one that is constitutionally preferred.

In the Court's ideology, "family" implies a biological relationship between children and parents.[34] Blood ties, even in the absence of marriage, deserve careful protection. By comparing several of the cases dealing with the rights of unwed fathers to the leading decision on foster families, *Smith v. Organization of Foster Families for Equality and Reform*, this judicial preference becomes clear. In *Foster Families*, a 1977 decision, Justice Brennan argued that the family protected by various earlier decisions of the Court was a family based on biological and marital relationships. "The usual understanding of 'family' implies biological relationships, and most decisions treating the relationship between parent and child have stressed that element."[35] Although the kind of familial relationship developed in foster homes cannot be dismissed as unimportant, he wrote, it is a different kind of relationship than that of the natural family. A foster family is created by the state and is basically a contractual relationship in which the foster parents agree to take care of the child and, in states like New York, also agree to relinquish the relationship when directed to do so by welfare authorities. The Court was unwilling to hold that foster families enjoyed fundamental "liberty" rights to raise and care for their foster children, even when they had established strong parent-child relationships. Emotional bonds, however strong, could not override the biological tie with the natural parents. The Court saw the foster child-foster parent connection as a contractual relationship from which constitutional rights could not flow. The natural family, on the other hand, had its foundation in "intrinsic human rights."[36]

A number of cases examining the claims of unwed fathers to the "care and companionship" of their children demonstrate the importance the Court accords biological relationships. Although the Court has not been willing to protect a "mere" biological relationship unless the father has taken some responsibility for or shown an interest in his child, the biological tie was recognized as important in *Stanley v. Illinois*, and was established as a constitutionally protected interest in three adoption cases, *Caban v. Mohammad, Quilloin v. Walcott* and *Lehr v. Robertson*.[37] Caban, who had helped care for his non-marital children, was permitted to block their adoption by their mother's husband. Quilloin was not allowed to legitimate a child to prevent its adoption, but only because he had neglected to take this action earlier. Lehr was not allowed to block the adoption of a daughter he had never seen because he had not taken available steps to establish a relationship with her. The *Lehr* case occasioned a vigorous dispute among the Justices, as had the earlier cases, about the difference between a "mere biological relationship and an actual relationship of parental responsibility." Dissenting Justices White, Marshall and Blackmun stressed the importance of the biological relationship. The *nature* of the relationship gives it constitutional protection, they asserted. "The 'biological connection' itself is a relationship that creates a protected interest."[38]

Although the Court has allowed some extension of the concept of family to include biological relationships unsolemnized by marriage, it has resisted the idea of recognizing non-marital living arrangements as protected family groups and has refused to protect such groups from exclusionary zoning. Communities have often been hostile toward family-type groupings that do not conform to preferred neighborhood patterns. Zoning, first adopted as a legal device to protect the homogeneous single-family suburb from the city, has been adapted and elaborated in a number of ingenious ways to protect property values and conservative styles of living, and to keep neighborhoods homogeneous.[39] The U.S. Supreme Court has stayed largely out of zoning disputes, but its one landmark decision, *Village of Euclid v. Ambler Realty Co.* (1926),[40] has been described as an expected reaction by a conservative bench that "regarded the intrusion of industry *and apartments* into single family zones as cousin to a public nuisance, similar to the intrusion of a tuberculosis sanitarium."[41] Zoning ordinances are used in subtle ways to fence people out. Racial zoning is unconstitutional, but it is still possible to control the character of neighborhoods by regulating lot size, number and type of buildings, and to limit occupancy of homes to members of single families related by blood, marriage or adoption.

The village of Belle Terre on Long Island had passed a zoning ordinance restricting to two the number of persons unrelated to one another who might occupy one-family dwellings. The owners of a house and three students who were part of a student household of six renting the house and studying at the State University at Stonybrook challenged the ordinance on various constitutional grounds. In *Village of Belle Terre v. Boraas*, the Supreme Court upheld the ordinance as a valid zoning regulation, denying that it impinged in any way on fundamental rights.[42] The ordinance did not deny equal protection because it was reasonable and not arbitrary and involved an area of social legislation where stricter standards of review were not required.

Both Justices Brennan and Marshall dissented. Marshall's dissent, which went to the constitutional issues, pointed out that this type of zoning ordinance was frequently used to discriminate against "undesirable" groups. Instead of upholding the ordinance, he would have held that it discriminated on the basis of "a personal lifestyle choice as to household companions," because it limited to two the number of unrelated persons, bound by professional interest, love, friendship, religious or political affiliation or mere economic interest, who could occupy a single-family home. Justice Marshall thought that inasmuch as fundamental rights of association and privacy were involved here, the Equal Protection Clause required the courts to subject this classification to strict scrutiny. The basic rights which he found to be violated by the ordinance were the right to establish a home, to satisfy intellectual and emotional needs, and to choose to live with family, friends, professional associates or any others. The zoning ordinance applied restrictions not because of any real threat to the community, but because of the community's disapproval of the life styles of the people involved. Any number of persons could live together, causing problems for the schools and the neighbors, creating parking congestion and noise, and so on, as long as they were related by blood or marriage. But more than two unrelated people wanting to live together for reasons of personal congeniality were prohibited from doing so by law.

The majority decision, explained in an opinion written by Justice Douglas, rejected this reasoning and accepted the regulation as a straightforward zoning regulation that denied no fundamental rights. Cities may legitimately use their zoning powers to protect the blessings of quiet seclusion and clean air and to make certain neighborhoods "sanctuaries for people." Justice Douglas used emotional language to describe suburban residential zoning: "A quiet place where yards are wide, people few, and motor vehicles restricted are legitimate guidelines in a land-use project addressed to family needs."[43] This paean to peace and quiet must have reflected some of the Justice's strongly held preferences and reminds one strongly of his attack, back in 1952, in *Public Utilities Commission v. Pollak*, on the invasion of his privacy by recorded music and advertising on city buses. Parenthetically, one might recall that Justice Felix Frankfurter, who felt equally strongly about his privacy, took himself out of that case because he recognized his own lack of objectivity.[44]

The zoning ordinance here was probably designed to protect property values by keeping landlords from renting to college students with irregular habits and a disregard for middle-class neighborhood values. This type of zoning ordinance also restricts group homes—homes in which a number of unrelated adults have decided to share a house for practical reasons as well as for companionship. Such ordinances may be less restrictive than the Long Island model, frequently adopting the "rule of five"; no more than five unrelated individuals may share the quarters. One assumption behind this type of zoning law was that groups of unrelated persons living together would be immoral and would be unsuitable neighbors for families with young children.[45]

The *Moore* case, discussed earlier, was decided three years after *Boraas*. It was also a zoning case, but it was distinguished as being factually different because the city zoning regulations reached down into the composition of the natural family and prohibited relatives from living with one another—slicing deeply, as Justice Powell stated it, into the family itself. Although city ordinances might restrict the occupancy of homes by unrelated people, basic rights to family liberty and privacy were invaded when zoning laws kept kinfolk from living in the same house.[46]

A majority of the Supreme Court found that Mrs. Moore's living arrangements were well within the accepted range of family patterns; the college students' claims were not assimilable to any established family form. The Court has also been reluctant to extend family status to other types of "voluntary" families or to give constitutional protection to non-traditional life styles or to include rights to sexual experimentation within a protected right to personal privacy. Although non-marital living arrangements are now increasingly common and although there is a constitutionally protected area of reproductive choice, even where unmarried persons are involved, the Court has so far avoided questions of this sort by refusing to grant *certiorari* or by affirming the decisions of lower courts without opinion.

An example of this type of avoidance can be found in *Hollenbaugh v. Carnegie Free Library*, denied a hearing in 1978.[47] The Hollenbaugh case grew out of a situation in which a couple, the man married and the woman unmarried, had a child and began living together. The Board of Trustees of their employer, the Carnegie Free Library of Connellsville, Pennsylvania, objected to this arrangement and asked them to live apart. When they refused, they were both discharged. The employees asked for reinstatement in their jobs and money damages, arguing that they were being deprived of their civil rights under 42 U.S.C. sec. 1983. The lower courts rejected their claim, and the Supreme Court denied *certiorari*. Justices Marshall and Brennan dissented from the denial of the writ. The dissenting Justices thought that administrative interference with the private life styles of individuals was an unwarranted intrusion on personal privacy. If the constitutional protection of unconventional relationships was broad enough to cover the access of juveniles and unmarried couples to contraceptives and abortions, and a mode of living as unique as that of the Old Amish community in Wisconsin was protected, there was no reason to exclude the private living arrangements of this couple. To do so would also interfere with their ability to raise their child together. The state should have been required to demonstrate a substantial reason for interfering with the lives of these individuals, and the lower courts should have applied a test more stringent than that of minimum rationality.

The dissenters raised questions that are now being considered in some of the state courts. Claimants in these courts are arguing that living units that are permanent, perform family functions, maintain a family style of living and pose no threat to stable residential neighborhoods should not be discriminated against merely because they do not meet legal or biological definitions of families.[48] Sooner or later, in spite of its reluctance to accept these cases, the Supreme Court of the United States will be forced to consider their claims to constitutional protection.

8

The Darker Side of the Family

The testimony of his supervising Juvenile Officer indicated that Eddings had been raised without proper guidance. His parents were divorced when he was 5 years old, and until he was 14 Eddings lived with his mother without rules or supervision. There was the suggestion that Eddings' mother was an alcoholic and possibly a prostitute. By the time Eddings was 14 he no longer could be controlled and his mother sent him to live with his father. But neither could the father control the boy. Attempts to reason and talk gave way to physical punishment. The Juvenile Officer testified that Eddings was frightened and bitter, that his father overreacted and used excessive physical punishment: "Mr. Eddings found the only thing that he thought was effectful with the boy was actual punishment, or physical violence—hitting with a strap or something like this."

Eddings v. Oklahoma (1982)[1]

The defendant in *Eddings v. Oklahoma* was sixteen years old when he committed the murder for which he received the sentence of death. Counsel argued on appeal that Eddings' youth and his unhappy, destructive home life should have been considered as a mitigating circumstance by the trial court when imposing the sentence. The Supreme Court agreed that the death penalty should not have been imposed, apparently accepting the view consistently held by many Americans that deviant behavior stems from bad homes; the idea that defective conditions in the home environment create criminals and cause crime has long been accepted by the public as an established fact and supplies one of the rationales for allowing the state to remove children from their families.[2] Removal from inadequate families not only protects the child, but also ensures that the children will be properly socialized.

In other situations the Court takes a rosier, more positive view of family relationships, but a good bit of its legal reasoning is uncritically based on accepted axioms. Three cases, *Smith v. Organization of Foster Families for Equality and Reform* (1977), *Parham v. JR* (1979) and *Santosky v. Kramer* (1982), recapitulate much of our classical legal thinking as it relates to children.[3] The *dicta*, the statements of principle rather than the holdings in these three cases, give us a good resumé of the Supreme Court's ideology as it applies to parent-child relationships. These are old familiar principles, anchored in the common law and in traditional family law from the time of Blackstone. Some misgivings arise, as one reads these cases, about the wisdom of deriving rules to govern modern family relationships from principles designed to fit eighteenth-century families. Political and constitutional principles may be timeless—freedom of speech, equality, the protection of the home from unreasonable searches and seizures, the right of the people to govern themselves—but somehow it seems incongruous to reach back two centuries for eternal verities that are supposed to apply to that infinitely adaptable, constantly changing social organism, the family. But for what it is worth, these are the family principles that the Supreme Court believes the Constitution protects.

There are a number of basic propositions. As we have seen in the adoption cases, the biological relationship is of primary importance. Biology and marriage create families.[4] Parents have constitutionally protected rights to conceive children and raise them.[5] The family formed by marriage is a unit, not a collection of legally autonomous individuals. "Our jurisprudence historically has reflected Western civilization concepts of the family as a unit with broad parental authority over minor children."[6] Parents speak for the unit and make decisions that are beyond the competence of immature members. "For centuries it has been a canon of the common law that parents speak for their minor children."[7] "Most children, even in adolescence, simply are not able to make sound judgments concerning many decisions."[8] One of the family's primary functions is the care and nurture of children and their socialization—their preparation for future obligations.[9] Family living involves daily association and instruction and the meeting of emotional needs.[10] Children have some independent liberty interests, but in general parents are responsible for representing their interests outside of the family. The interests of parents and children may sometimes conflict, but the law accepts the proposition that "natural bonds of affection lead parents to act in the best interests of their children."[11] History and human experience teach that parents "generally do act in the child's best interests.[12] Undeniably, there are instances of abuse and neglect, but the fact that some parents fail to meet their responsibilities does not justify state interference with the family. "The fundamental liberty interest of parents does not evaporate because they have not been model parents or have temporarily lost custody," and government should not interfere to separate children from their families or to countermand parental authority, except in cases of clear abuse.[13]

The family is a self-sufficient, private unit, and in earlier times coped with such problems as sickness and mental illness without public assistance. Parent-child conflicts were handled within the family unit, with the help of the community, the church and the family doctor.[14] But increasingly parents have called on the state for aid. Where there is significant parental abuse or dereliction of duty, the state does have the responsibility to step in and check parents, although it should not interfere merely to protect the child's own views of what is in its best interests. The child's preference should not be allowed to defeat parental authority.[15]

Although most of these statements seem to be truisms, if they are examined carefully we find that they not only misrepresent realities, but they also have important ramifications for family policy. The modern family, often headed by a single woman or split by divorce, is not always the tightly knit unit that the ideology presupposes. We are increasingly becoming aware of the problems of family violence and child abuse, that the notion of family unity and harmony is often little more than a legal fiction. Family violence is not new. Leonard de Mause's book, *The History of Childhood*, describes the frightening history of the extensive and lethal forms of violence used by parents against children.[16] In spite of concern about the amount of mayhem in the family unit today, it is possible that families may actually be less violent than in previous times.[17] Even by Blackstone's time, the law had put limits on the means that could be used to control wives and children, although the state largely ignored the problem of child abuse unless it resulted in death or disability.[18]

Traditionally, children have had few legal protections. Under the common law, the child was completely subject to the control of the family, more particularly to the will of the father. Under the common law the father could discipline his children, manage their property, take their earnings and decide on a proper education for them. These powers were justified by the responsibility to support, protect and educate which the father was obligated to assume. Interestingly enough, the law had relatively little to say about mother-child relationships as such. The mother was entitled to reverence and respect, but the unique contributions of motherhood are governed by custom and tradition rather than by legal principles.[19] Under the common law the parents' rights over the child were inviolable; now, although many parental duties have been assumed by the state, in many areas minors may have fewer legal safeguards than in the past.[20] The protection offered by a permanent, indissoluble marriage has disappeared. The property-like notion of paramount parental rights in children lingers on. In today's world it may prevent adoption, thus denying children the right to grow up in a stable, loving family.

If biology and the marriage ceremony create families, how should the law treat biological families that are not ceremonially married and various kinds of marital arrangements that do not involve children? The duty of instruction and socialization of children has been largely abdicated to or preempted by the state. Daily association and instruction may be shared with day care facilities, baby sitters, schools and peer groups. The balance of power between children, parents and state constantly shifts with the social climate, yet "the principle that underlies virtually all legal matters concerning the child is that his parents are best suited to protect his interests."[21]

At the present time when a family fails, the state, usually following a court proceeding in which neglect or abuse is established, may remove the child from its home and place it with foster parents, send it to an institution, or terminate parental rights and put it up for adoption. The state as substitute parent may not be intentionally abusive, but it can also be neglectful or careless or inadequate. Welfare services for children are often underfunded, juvenile workers overloaded with cases, and children's homes and mental hospitals poorly run and inadequately supervised.[22] Foster care, the practice of using paid, subsidized, temporary homes instead of state institutions, can also fail to serve the child's best interests when it loses its primary function as a temporary care facility and becomes a semi-permanent holding operation.[23] When the state cannot find permanent adoptive homes, when parents will not release their children for adoption or when state policy forbids the foster parents from adopting, children may find themselves shuttled through a succession of foster care homes. Removed from inadequate homes but unable to find the psychological and physical security of a permanent family, these children may find that they are left in limbo until they come of age and can become independent.

Organizations championing the cause of children's rights have used litigation as one method of drawing attention to children's issues, especially the need to have the children's own interests consulted in institutionalization, adoption, and custody cases, and to receive adequate treatment in state institutions. Isolated cases, beginning with *In re Gault* in 1967, established some basic principles governing children's rights. Juvenile justice systems cannot entirely ignore the formal requirements of procedural due process simply because the offenders are under age. Minors as well as adults have some First Amendment rights; students do not "shed their constitutional rights to freedom of speech or expression at the schoolhouse gate." Schools may not disregard the requirements of procedural fairness in expulsion proceedings. The protection against double jeopardy applies to minors. Teenagers also have reproductive rights and are not completely subservient either to the state or to their parents in making a choice whether or not to bear children.[24]

It is in these reproductive choice cases that one most clearly sees the different kinds of conflict over constitutional rights that can arise where children's rights are involved. Many of these conflicts are not bilateral but involve three or four sets of interests, often overlapping, one of which is the interest of the minor child. In *Planned Parenthood of Central Missouri v. Danforth* the state, by legislation, tried to make a female minor's access to abortion contingent on her parents' consent.[25] The Missouri legislation was based on the familiar requirement of parental consent to medical treatment for minor children. The Supreme Court, however, rejected the idea that the rights of minors could be completely subordinated to the authority and judgment of the parents. In *Bellotti v. Baird*, decided in 1979, the Court insisted that states distinguish between those minors who were competent and mature and able to make their own decisions and those immature minors who needed parental control and guidance.[26] Although after *Roe v. Wade* the state itself might not veto any woman's abortion choice completely, neither could it transfer this power to her parents.[27] In cases of conflict between a minor and her parents, it would be valid to allow a court to decide whether or not the minor was mature enough to make her own decisions, but not to require subordination of her interests to the family's wishes. Immature minors could be subjected to procedures that required them to notify or consult their parents, but any course of action was supposed to be determined with the best interests of the minor in mind.[28] The reproductive rights cases provide interesting contrasts to the *Yoder* case, in which the Court assumed that the parental decision would parallel that of the child and did not require any procedural protection for whatever separate rights and interests the child might have.

Foster care and custody cases are in some ways similar to the cases discussed above. The conflict is ostensibly between the state and the foster parents, or between the natural parents, the foster parents and the state. The child, the interested party in all of these battles, is a bystander whose rights are assumed to be represented by others, but who may be accorded no independent legal basis for asserting his or her own rights. These cases are cast in terms of the familiar two-party adversary situation, but in reality are three- or four-cornered contests.

Smith v. Organization of Foster Families for Equality and Reform reflects some of the problems involved in trying to decide problems like this in terms of traditional constitutional principles. The case, a class action suit, was one of a number of test cases involving the American Civil Liberties Union Civil Rights Project.

At issue were conflicts of interests involving four different kinds of parties: foster families, children who had been placed in foster homes, the state and the natural parents of the children. Foster care situations often include all of these parties simultaneously. In this case, three sets of foster parents were contesting the state's efforts to remove their foster children and send them back to their natural parents or to other foster homes. New York law in such cases favors the return of children to their natural families whenever possible, but provides various kinds of procedures by which foster families who object to the loss of children to whom they have become attached can have a hearing. The complaint of the foster families in this case was that the procedures provided for them by state law denied them due process.

In order to support a due process claim, it is necessary for the claimant to show that he or she has lost some liberty or property without adequate protection. Although foster parents must assume duties of care for children under their control that correspond to those of natural families, they do not acquire parental rights to legal custody.[29] Children end up in foster homes for a variety of reasons, often because some emergency has made it impossible for their parents to care for them. The foster home is supposedly a temporary expedient, and it is assumed that the children will be returned to their real families as soon as conditions improve, or that they will be given to permanent adoptive parents. However, as noted earlier, foster families often form close emotional ties with their fosterlings and contest attempts to reassign them to other families or to return them to parents whom they have not seen for many years. The foster parents in these cases argued that they had established real family and emotional ties with their foster children and that they had a liberty interest in protecting the integrity of their foster families, which was the equivalent of the family rights natural families would be able to claim in similar situations.

In order to support this claim, the Supreme Court would have had to accept the argument that the emotional ties that develop between foster parents and foster children often make the foster parents the "psychological parents" of the child even though there is no biological relationship. Theories about "psychological parenting" have been propounded in recent writings by psychologists, notably in a volume by Joseph Goldstein, Anna Freud and Albert J. Solnit entitled *Beyond the Best Interests of the Child*, published in 1973.[30] Although there is no doubt that close ties between foster parents and their charges do develop and are in some cases much closer than the ties between children and their natural parents, the step which the Court was being asked to take here was revolutionary. It was being asked to hold, as a matter of law, that these foster parent-child relationships were within the protected area of fundamental liberty protected by the Due Process Clause of the Fourteenth Amendment against state abridgment.

The Court was unwilling to take this step as a matter of constitutional adjudication. It found important distinctions between foster families and natural families. The family rights of natural families are "intrinsic human rights"; those of foster families are based on contractual relations with the state that were assumed voluntarily.

Although the Court was not willing to hold that foster families which have become "psychological families" have the same rights as natural families, it was willing to *assume* that this was the case for purposes of examining the procedures New York had provided for contesting the removal of children from foster care. It reversed the decision of the District Court, which had held that these procedures were not sufficiently protective to satisfy due process. The District Court had ruled that due process required an automatic hearing by an officer who had not been involved in the decision to remove the child, in which all parties (including the children) were represented. The Supreme Court was unwilling to require such formal procedures. New York's scheme was held to be constitutionally adequate because it did provide mechanisms by which the interests of all parties could be demonstrated, and hearings were available whenever they were demanded by foster families. The Court held that the child's interest in remaining with the foster family was represented indirectly by the foster parent, who could request an administrative hearing to protest the removal of the child. If a close relationship between foster family and child had been established, the foster parents would claim their rights to such a hearing and would state the child's interest at that time. Failure to insist on a hearing would be an indication that a true family bond had not been formed, and therefore, by definition, no family rights existed which could be denied.

The Court's due process analysis, proceeding along the lines set out a year earlier in *Mathews v. Eldridge* (1976), requires the Justices to consider three factors: first, "the private interest that will be affected by the official action: second, the risk of erroneous deprivation of such interest through the procedures used, and the probable value, if any, of additional or substitute procedural safeguards; and finally, the government's interest, including . . . fiscal and administrative burdens. . . ."[31] Using this analysis, Justice Brennan found that the private interest affected by official actions was the asserted family right of the foster family, and because the foster family had access to a full hearing on request, there was no risk of erroneous deprivation. Although there was no threat to private rights, the state would be burdened by an automatic hearing requirement that came into play whenever a foster home placement was changed. The Court struck the balance here in favor of the state, holding that New York's procedures were adequate to protect whatever liberty interests appellees had.

This analysis points up the inadequacy of using a simple individual rights approach to family cases in which there is a network of overlapping interests. The Court's precedents establish a number of family-related rights: children have the right to grow up in a family and have protected relationships with their parents; the parents have protected rights to the care and association of their children. The whole concept of foster home care is built on the family pattern, the creation of an artificial family to replace damaged or broken natural families. If the foster family does its assigned job well, parent-child ties are created that cannot be ignored by labeling this a contractual relationship; one does not create love and trust by contract. In this sense, the foster family-child relationship might be compared to the marital relationship, where there is an element of contract but also a great deal more.

Where children have been removed from their homes by the state, the natural family may also have an interest, and natural parents are allowed to intervene in these cases.[32] The natural parent is not only interested in the child's care and safety, but may also be hoping for its eventual return. The child's interest is not clearly represented by any of these parties. These cases are in some ways similar to custody suits, when the child is caught in a conflict between parents; here the child is involved in a three-way battle, in which the state, as represented by the child welfare authorities, also has a stake. In a contest in which there are such overlapping and conflicting interests, a due process hearing, with all parties separately represented, is one way to ensure that the child's distinct interests are protected. This type of adversary hearing may not be necessary in all cases and will undoubtedly be costly. There should be some way, however, to ensure that secure, happy relationships between children and their foster parents, situations in which "psychological parenting" exists, should not be unnecessarily disturbed.[33] There are some parallels with abortion cases, in the sense that there is neither a static situation nor a clear choice between conflicting claims of right, but an evolving, overlapping, linked set of relationships, interwoven with important questions of public policy. This is not a simple question of procedural due process.

In a three-way battle over custody of the child among parents, foster parents and the state, the struggle may disrupt the child's life and the outcome may be unhappy, but at least there are people who want to keep the child. In cases where natural parents want to institutionalize disturbed children, there may be a clear conflict between parents and child, and it may not be in the child's best interests to be separated from his or her family. In *Parham v. JR* the Supreme Court decided another case where the triangular relationship between children, parents and the state was clearly exposed.[34] The essential issue in that case was:

how far does the Constitution safeguard the child's own right to liberty when the child's parents decide that he or she is mentally ill and uncontrollable and seek placement in a state institution? Voluntary institutionalization of children has only recently begun to be challenged in the courts.[35] Reformers in this area of the law assert that the best protection for the child against unnecessary separation from his or her family when the family itself wants commitment is a full due process hearing, for all but short-term, temporary placements.[36]

In this class action suit, children being treated in a Georgia mental hospital challenged the state's procedures for committing children under the age of eighteen. They objected to the fact that temporary admissions could be made on an application for hospitalization signed by the parent or guardian without any kind of formal hearing procedure. Although the state had provided some checks on parental decisions in such cases, the suit submitted that the procedures were inadequate to protect the rights of children from such a formidable restriction of their liberties and denial of their rights to parenting and care.

Chief Justice Burger, who wrote the majority opinion, argued that even though Georgia's procedures allowed the parents to commit a child without a formal pre-commitment hearing, they provided adequate protection of his or her rights. Certain protections were built into the system. The seven mental hospitals in the state which treated children had differing procedures, but all provided checks to make sure that the children admitted were actually mentally ill and that hospitalization would benefit them. Most of the admissions were cases referred by community mental health centers. Admissions decisions were made by trained mental health personnel. And regular post-admission reviews of cases were held as a matter of course.

The Court found another check in the bond between parents and child. The law in most states still has a healthy, built-in bias in favor of natural parents and will accept their "natural rights" unless they are proved to be unfit.[37] It also accepts the unstated assumption that parenting is such a natural function that only exceptional parents will fail to perform it.[38] The Supreme Court recognized these bonds of natural affection and good-will as a restraining force that would keep parents from seeking solutions that would not benefit their children. It was unwilling to assume that any parents would try to "dump" or "railroad" a child; the "traditional presumption that the parent acts in the best interests of the child should apply."[39] Although the majority recognized that parents and children may have separate interests, it stated that these interests are intertwined and it was not willing to regard the children and parents as adversaries. Most children are not able to make sound decisions about medical care, and parents must make these decisions for them. Most parents will act in the best interests of the child. The child's interest, however great, cannot be seen as entirely separate from that of his or her family, but is linked with that of the parents. This is traditional family doctrine, accepted by the law since Blackstone and Kent.[40]

On the basis of these assumptions, the Court found that the procedures that protected the child against wrongful commitment did not have to be iron-clad and did not have to be cast in the adversary mode. The checks by state medical personnel which were a substantial part of the commitment process were sufficient to protect the child. Trial-type pre-commitment hearings might actually work against the child's best interests by preventing parents from seeking medical treatment. They would also tie up mental health personnel, who would be diverted from their medical duties.

A different view of the situation is found in the dissent. Justices Brennan, Marshall and Stevens first examined the trauma and tragedy of unnecessary commitments of children to mental institutions. They referred to documented accounts of the abysmal conditions in many of these institutions. And they were less ready to accept the idea that parents are always unwilling to use institutionalization as a method of handling intractable family situations and destructive and uncontrollable children. Because the deprivation of liberty is so great and the possibility of permanent damage to the child is so awesome, the dissenters believed that due process required more stringent post-commitment hearings to make sure that a mistake had not been made in admitting the child. In addition, they believed that pre-commitment hearings should be required when foster parents or social workers, acting in the name of the state, tried to hospitalize children.

It is easier to see the real issues in this case if one looks at the problems involved rather than the legal principles and traditional ideology associated with parent-child relations. The problem identified in the class action suit is that families do sometimes institutionalize children who are not mentally ill or who should be treated on an out-patient basis. They do this not because of lack of natural parent-child bonding, but because they are desperate and cannot cope with the disruption which a disturbed and unruly child inflicts on the entire family.[41] Although one sympathizes with the parents' ordeal, such children clearly do have separate interests, and the parents' solution—hospitalization—may not help them; it may be that they would be better off at home with their families, in some kind of a community treatment program. The state supplies aid to the parents by taking such children off their hands and uses administrative procedures that are designed to protect the rights of children against unnecessary institutionalization. If any of the shortcomings common to bureaucracies are present—inertia, understaffing, poor procedures, divisions of responsibility or incompetent personnel—the checks may not work.

The problem which this case poses is how methods can be devised to supply an independent check on the actions of both parents and state in the child's interests. The majority was satisfied that "Georgia's medical fact-finding processes were an acceptable way of checking these decisions." The appellees and the dissenting Justices thought that due process required formal adversary hearings.

The District Court had understood that it was faced with an essentially political, rather than constitutional, problem. The rhetoric about family-child relations is misleading, and the due process solution is inappropriate. The District Court judge rejected the argument that administrative review by the hospital staff was sufficient to protect the child's liberty interest. But then, as Chief Justice Burger complained in his opinion, the District Court "shifted its focus drastically from what was clearly a procedural due process analysis to what appears to be a substantive due process analysis" and condemned the state for not supplying additional resources for "non-hospital treatment" and "non-institutional mental health care."[42] Troubled families need alternatives to hospitalization. Full-scale adversary hearings would not supply these alternatives; they would merely divert money needed for different kinds of family support services into the hearing process itself. As the District Court saw the problem, parents would not seek to institutionalize as many problem children if the state provided more in the way of facilities for outpatient and community services. There was thus a causal relationship between the state's "intransigence" in failing to provide necessary facilities and the state's inability to provide any "flexible due process" to the appellees.

In spite of the law's axiomatic acceptance of the principle that parents act in the best interests of their children, many children end up in mental hospitals and foster care because they have been abused or neglected at home. Although parents may show very little interest in the child once it has been removed from the family, foster care and institutionalization do not require the severance of formal ties with the natural family. Formal termination of parental rights severs the legal connection between parent and child and is a step social workers are reluctant to request, a step that may cause great anguish to parents and may have deep psychological significance for the child. The procedures used in state termination statutes have come under increasing constitutional scrutiny.[43]

Two termination of parental rights cases decided in 1981 and 1982 raised due process questions about the procedures to be used in depriving parents of a legal relationship with their children. In *Lassiter v. Department of Social Services of Durham County, North Carolina*[44] the Department initiated a proceeding to terminate the parental rights of a woman serving a twenty-five to forty-year sentence for second degree murder. Abby Gail Lassiter had not been a model mother; even before her confinement to prison, her child, William L., had been removed from her custody on grounds of neglect and failure to receive medical treatment. The mother was brought to court from prison to present her case. In the termination hearing, before a District Court judge, she was not represented by counsel. She did not request assigned counsel at this time, and the judge decided that a lawyer was not necessary to protect her rights. But later she attacked the Court's termination order as denying her both her right to counsel and due process of law. In the appellate review of the case, the conflicting interests were represented as being, on one side, the mother's "desire for and right to 'the companionship, care, custody and management' " of her children and, on the other, the state's responsibility for removing children from unfit parents and finding them permanent homes.

The Supreme Court's opinion recognized the importance of the mother's right to the custody of her child, but refused to hold that the state was constitutionally required to appoint counsel to help her assert that right. Although the majority recognized that counsel would have been helpful in Lassiter's case and might be necessary to a fair hearing in some situations, it was unwilling to hold that counsel must always be appointed in termination proceedings. The rationale for this position was that counsel was absolutely required only in proceedings where defendants might lose their liberty. Otherwise, the trial judge might decide, on a case-to-case basis, whether appointment of counsel for an indigent was essential.[45]

In *Little v. Streeter*, another due process decision handed down the same day, the Court held that an indigent prisoner who had been accused of fathering a child was entitled to free blood tests as part of a proceeding to determine paternity.[46] Thus, although an indigent female prisoner was not entitled to counsel in a parental termination proceeding, due process demanded that a male prisoner be given access to blood test evidence at state expense to challenge an assignment of paternal responsibilities. Although the Court decided *Lassiter* as it did in order to avoid creating a precedent for the extension of the right to assigned counsel to a new category of cases, these two decisions are not really compatible. Both cases are indigency cases, more closely related to *Boddie v. Connecticut* than to claims to representation in criminal cases.[47] In deciding as it did, the Court, in effect, said that a man's personal interest in defending himself against paternity charges is constitutionally more important than a woman's interest in retaining a legal relationship with her child. Although Ms. Lassiter was clearly an imperfect parent, the Court's other family cases should have dictated that it gave a heavier weight to her *interest* in that relationship. The facts of the case had convinced the Justices that she had "few sparks of interest" in her son. The Court seems to have equated her "constitutional interest" in retaining her parental rights with the amount of actual interest (care, concern) she had demonstrated in maintaining contact with her child.[48]

Lassiter v. North Carolina provides an interesting parallel with another parental rights termination case which was decided a year later. *Lassiter* involved a right to counsel claim; *Santosky v. Kramer* challenged the standard of proof required in termination proceedings. In this case parents accused of child abuse contested a state proceeding that had been brought to terminate their parental rights so that children who had been in foster homes for more than four years could be put up for adoption.[49] New York law allowed the courts to use a "fair preponderance of the evidence" rule to determine unfitness, a finding of fact that was necessary before parental rights could be ended. In this context, the Supreme Court rejected the New York termination procedures, holding that parental rights were so important, and their denial such a drastic step, that due process required a higher standard of proof.

The test applied in this case, the same due process test used in *Foster Families* and *Lassiter*, involved a balancing of three factors: the private interests (the Santoskys' parental rights), the chance of error and the burden on the state of using a different procedure.[50] Weighing these factors, the Court found that parental rights were very important, the chance of error by applying a defective standard of proof was substantial and the state's interest in the lesser burden of proof was relatively slight. Therefore, due process required the more substantial burden of proof.

But whereas this holding protects the parents' interest in retaining a legal relationship to their children and keeping the family together, relatively little attention is paid to the matter of the children's separate interests, which are subsumed under the parents' interests. The Court expressly denies, in fact, that the factfinding process which is mandated has any obligation to determine the child's requirements.

The factfinding does not purport—and is not intended—to balance the child's interest in a normal family home against the parents' interest in raising the child. Nor does it purport to determine whether the natural parents or the foster parent would provide the better home. Rather the factfinding hearing pits the state directly against the parents. The State alleges that the natural parents are at fault. . . . But until the State proves parental unfitness, the child and his parents share a vital interest in preventing erroneous termination of their natural relationship.[51]

In a case involving serious allegations of neglect and abuse, however, the assumption that the parents' and the child's interests are identical is a legal fiction. The proceeding is bilateral. The state is accusing the parents of being unfit and is punishing them for their inadequacy by seeking to remove the child or children. The interests of the children are not represented except by the assumption that the ultimate purpose of the procedure is to protect them. If the parents are found to be unfit, the state will allow the children to be adopted. Whatever relationship the foster parents have established with the children is irrelevant.

At first inspection, these decisions seem wildly inconsistent. They can be reconciled in terms of formal due process doctrine, however, because factual differences give the Court a basis for applying a different rule in each case. Under our law, parental rights are deserving of great protection, so hearings depriving parents of these rights must educe "clear and convincing" evidence (or even higher standards in some states) of abuse or neglect before the parental rights can be terminated. This is the holding in *Santosky v. Kramer*. Foster families do not have the same protected status as natural families, however, so they are not entitled to the same degree of procedural fastidiousness when children are removed from their midst, even if the children have come to regard them as their "real" parents. This was the ruling in *Smith v. Organization of Foster Families*. Under the traditional ideology, it is assumed that natural parents will act in the best interest of the child, so it is not necessary to surround voluntary commitments *by parents* of children to institutions with all the safeguards of full-scale due process hearings. The Court decided this way in *Parham v. JR*. Even though the right to raise a child is a fundamental right of the natural parent, no automatic right to counsel in termination hearings exists, because no deprivation of physical liberty is involved; an indigent's right to appointed counsel attaches when lesser incursions on liberty take place only if the proceeding would otherwise be unfair. The Court decided *Lassiter v. Department of Social Services* on this theory. But, in contrast, a proceeding to establish paternity would be unfair if a putative father who was indigent were not allowed access to blood test evidence; the state may not make this evidence available only to those who are able to pay.

But due process analysis by itself is sterile when it assigns false weights, or when it does not identify many of the real rights and interests at stake in these contests. The basic formula for testing due process, set forth in *Mathews v. Eldridge*, designates three elements to be evaluated: the private interests, the government's interests and the risk that the procedures being used will lead to "erroneous decisions."

The private interests in these cases are not always correctly represented when the contests are seen as bi-polar, as involving only the interests of parents and state. In many of these cases the real parties are the children, and their interests may not be represented either by their parents or by the state welfare bureaucracy. In some cases independent representation of the children's separate interests by counsel is the answer, but in other instances undue complication of the hearing process itself may increase procedural costs and prolong the period in which the child's adoption or permanent placement is kept hanging.[52] Perfection of procedural rights may not always be the answer to the protection of children.

Formal due process analysis thus may obscure the real interests involved in these disputes. The Court's work in these cases is confused, in part, by its acceptance of basic assumptions of the traditional balance of power between children, parents and state, the assumption that the parents are always best suited to protect the child and by echoes of the older tradition of inviolable parental rights over children.

All five of these cases deal with children's rights issues that have been widely discussed as matters needing reform. Studies such as that made by the Carnegie Council on Children concluded that the best protection for the child lies in social programs that support and aid the natural family and legal procedures that protect the family from premature invasion and dissolution by the state apparatus.[53] Legislatures must provide the kind of support programs that will enable natural families to perform their duties of child-raising more easily. Unless the child is actually physically or psychologically endangered in the family setting, the law should be structured so that parental rights are difficult to terminate, even when it is the families themselves who want to surrender disturbed or handicapped children. But it is also recommended that in all proceedings where children are involved, the child's interest should be represented by counsel and that there should be full due process hearings, foster homes should be given family rights where strong attachments have developed and foster families willing to adopt children should be subsidized.[54]

Measured against this set of recommendations, the Court's work has been uneven. Although its decisions are based on the constitutional requirements of due process, there is no reason why due process should require results that prevent the sound development of family law. In terms of the recommendations of the Carnegie Council, the decisions might have gone somewhat differently. In *Foster Families*, even if the Court correctly refused to protect the family rights of foster families, the proper resolution of these issues required representation of the children's interests by some neutral party. The perfection of procedures does not always solve problems, however, and the Court should have recognized, in *Parham v. JR*, that the District Court judge was correct in stating that no amount of fiddling with hearing procedures can create justice, when what is needed is an increase in state spending for alternatives to hospitalization of problem children. The two termination cases show conflicting valuations of the rights of natural parents. It is hard to tell from the appellate record whether the state had intervened unnecessarily in taking the Santosky children from their family, but the Court made it more difficult to terminate their parental rights than was the case with Ms. Lassiter. The Streeter decision can best be understood in the context of decisions holding unwed fathers responsible for the support of extramarital children, rather than as an isolated due process problem.

Formal due process analysis may thus obscure the family interests involved in disputes. The Court's work in these cases is confused, in part, by its acceptance as basic assumptions the traditional balance of power between children, parents and the state, and, in part, by its inability to reconcile those assumptions with rules of decision designed to prevent "due processitis" from unnecessarily hampering the administration of state-sponsored programs to aid troubled families. The newness of the Court's venture into family law may also contribute to its less than sure touch in this area.

9

Constitutional Law and the Family

Issues involving the family . . . are among the most difficult that courts have to face, involving as they often do serious problems of policy disguised as questions of constitutional law.

Justice Potter Stewart, *Parham v. JR*, 1979.

There always comes a point where the stereotype and the facts that cannot be ignored, definitely part company.

Walter Lippmann[1]

The Supreme Court, like other governmental institutions has been uncertain about the direction family policy should take. Recent books about the family bear titles such as "The Futility of Family Policy," "The War Over the Family" and "The Battle for the Family," reflecting the polarization that has taken place in society generally on family issues.[2] There is no question that there is a transitional quality about many aspects of family life; many of the older certainties are eroding, and new patterns of living in families have emerged, as have new pressures and problems.

In spite of the fact that they come to the Court in no particular order, are not selected according to any set plan and are not the result of an organized litigation campaign designed to make coherent, overall changes in public policy, the family-related cases that the Supreme Court decides touch on most of the major areas of controversy: control of reproduction, gender and sex roles, teenage pregnancy, child care, education and support, new types of living arrangements, the instabilities that result from divorce, institutional care for incompetent family members and the relationship of professional family services to the natural unit.

The language of the opinions in these cases, which are constitutionalized under a variety of different principles—equal protection, due process, freedom of religion and freedom of association, the right to privacy and some others—exposes a whole system of belief related to family values. Due process and equal protection, the concepts that provide the basis for the constitutional challenges in most of these cases, supply the Justices with extremely general and flexible standards. The proper application of either standard requires that the Court recognize the existence or non-existence of plausible legislative purposes, of fair procedures and of non-discriminatory and comparable classifications, and also that it base its decisions on some kind of realistic understanding of what is going on in society. Judges are not supposed to be sociologists or to decide on the basis of social science data rather than in terms of legal principles, but they cannot make adequate legal decisions if they are not in touch with the flow of events in the world outside of the courts. Legal rules do not exist in a vacuum and cannot be applied without some appreciation of the impact they will have on specific situations. Litigation does a good job of bringing historical and adjudicative facts (the facts that are germane to a particular lawsuit) before the courts, but its record of informing courts and judges about social facts is less satisfying.[3]

The increasing involvement of courts in questions of social policy has made it important that judges have at least a rudimentary idea of what is taking place in society at large. No longer is it defensible for a Justice of the Supreme Court to say, as Oliver Wendell Holmes, Jr., once did, that "I don't read the papers or otherwise feel the pulse of the machine. I merely speculate."[4] Of course, even if Holmes did not read the papers, he was a very critical, realistic and clear-sighted observer of society and by no means oblivious to the importance of social change in constitutional adjudication. The point of all this is that it is very easy to accept assumptions about the facts for what the facts really are, and that this type of thinking is more of a problem in areas involving deeply held beliefs than it is in fields where perceptions of existing facts are not distorted by stereotyped thinking. As Holmes said in an essay on law and social reform, "But reason means truth and those who are not governed by it take the chances that some day the sunken fact will rip the bottom out of their boat."[5]

Social facts do make a difference and affect the way constitutional doctrine should be applied. And changes in the underlying factual situation can operate to invalidate legislation that was constitutional when it was first proposed and enacted. Equal protection cases provide many good examples of this proposition. It is not entirely surprising that so many challenges to laws that have arisen because of shifting social facts and changing public attitudes have come to the Supreme Court under the Equal Protection Clause. Because a decision about equal protection involves classification, whether equal things are being equally treated may depend on whether the perceived differences between the things being classified are based on fact. A case such as *Hoyt v. Florida* demonstrates the way changes in the underlying factual situation can operate to invalidate legislation.[6] The Court decided that case, upholding a Florida law permitting automatic excuses from jury service for women, on the basis of the assumption that most women need to be at home with the children and that it is beneficial to women to provide them with automatic exemptions rather than having them file written claims for exemption. As long as that assumption was founded on fact, there was a rational basis for treating men and women differently. But once it was no longer true that most women were actually staying at home with their families then the legislation was less defensible as a protection of motherhood and the home. Other values, such as women's political rights and the state's responsibility for providing representative juries, now outweighed this interest.

Another example of the different results which equal protection analysis can produce when applied to different readings of the factual situation can be found in the situation in *Michael M. v. Sonoma County Court.* The equal protection test, "middle-tier" version, requires that the Court examine a state law to see if its use of a gender classification is "substantially related" to an "important governmental interest."[7] But it makes a considerable difference whether the governmental interest is the "protection of chastity" or "the prevention of teenage pregnancy." Presumably the former, which may very well have been the original object of this legislation when first enacted, would be difficult to defend. The latter purpose clearly presents a situation that the government needs to address. But there is room for extreme skepticism about the substantiality of the relationship between a statutory rape statute and any kind of practical program to prevent teenage pregnancy. Gender classification decisions have been especially difficult for the Court to handle well; attitudes toward the roles of women in the family and in employment have changed very rapidly in the last fifty years. The Court has been able to understand claims of sex discrimination when there are clear-cut, straight-out gender classifications like those in *Reed v. Reed* and *Craig v. Boren,* in which the rationale for different treatment was not supported by real differences between men and women. But it has been less perceptive about the subtler forms of gender bias to be found in statutes that create more indirect, sex-related classifications, such as pregnancy or veterans' preference. If gender itself were declared a suspect classification, as several members of the Supreme Court have urged, the Justices would be less likely to stumble where the sexual classification itself seems valid, but the whole underlying system is clearly biased. Laurence Tribe provides us with a useful way of approaching these cases when he declares that the Court must be careful to look out for legislation that reinforces sex-based stereotypes, and that it should not allow legislatures to prevent or discourage departures from traditional sex roles by "freezing biology into social destiny."[8] Sylvia Law advances another suggestion: that reproductive capability and not gender is the key distinction, so that laws relating to reproductive biology should be subjected to strict scrutiny to see whether they impose discriminatory burdens on women.[9]

Illegitimacy is another area in which shifting social facts have undermined the utility of legal rules. Although the designation of extramarital children as illegitimate may once have served to protect legitimate families and to ensure the orderly inheritance of property, in a period of soaring illegitimacy rates the classification becomes discriminatory, and hence constitutionally defective, because it keeps non-marital children from receiving support, government payments or parental care on the same basis as legitimate children. The Court has recognized the unfairness of penalizing children for the sins of their parents, but it has been unwilling to forbid legislatures every use of legitimacy classifications. The cases in this area show the enduring quality of legal stereotypes, for traces of *filius nullius* and the outdated concept of the illegitimate child as somehow a less deserving person[10] still crop up both in acts of Congress and in state legislation. The Court has also been reluctant to overturn legislation that penalizes the unmarried mother or father of an illegitimate child, reasoning that, unlike that of the child itself, this status is the result of conscious choice. But what such an approach fails to recognize is that the status is more often the response to social conditions and economic deprivations that make formal marriage undesirable or unattainable than a preference for nontraditional life styles.[11] Can illegitimacy really be used as a classifying device without recognizing the racial, economic and sexual biases that are part of it?

Cases involving new kinds of living arrangements have also been difficult, for the Justices often accept an unrecognized preference for a model of the traditional family which is more of an ideological figment of the judicial or legislative imagination than an accurate picture of an American family that did or does actually exist. It is not surprising that such a preference underlies decisions because it is embedded in precedent.

Equal protection decisions are not the only category of cases in which stereotypes may affect judicial opinions. As far as due process is concerned, here, too, the Court often proceeds on a fictional level. In *La Fleur*, the original pregnancy disability case, the Court decided that the school rule requiring mandatory maternity leave was unconstitutional because it burdened the woman's right to choose to bear a child (following *Griswold v. Connecticut, Roe v. Wade*), a liberty protected by the Due Process

Clause of the Constitution. This seems an oddly archaic way of identifying a typical example of a class of pregnancy rules originally designed to push pregnant women out of the workplace and encourage married women with children to remain in the home. What is burdened is not the right to choose childbirth (assuming there was a choice), but the right of pregnant women to earn a living.

Our views of problems involving reproduction and sexual relations are loaded with stereotypes, some reflecting current reality, others oddly out of date. To illustrate just how many assumptions and stereotypes can be involved in single decisions, it is possible to list those present in the three cases dealing with contraceptives, statutory rape and abortion notification. In *Carey v. Population Services*, the state law was based on the assumption that parental control of children and their sexual activities was undermined by the availability of contraceptives and that restrictions on the availability of contraceptives would prevent at least some adolescent sexual activity. There were even older assumptions behind these: that the state had the authority, under its police power, to control morality, that the law should protect the chastity of unmarried women and girls, that the law should and could promote good morals, and that all of these purposes would be served by limiting the sales of contraceptives. There was also the assumption that promiscuity was dangerous to adolescents.

Some of these assumptions are not true. It is at least extremely unlikely that by decreasing the availability of contraceptives, the state can deter adolescent sexual activity, especially in light of the fact that many adolescents are reluctant to use contraception at all. Such a law is also unlikely to increase the control of parents over their children. But in this case the Court did not attempt to make a realistic evaluation of the legislative act; its decision was based instead on the idea that there was a right to choose to have children, or not to have children, which should be free from state interference. If a right was involved in this case, clearly it was better described as a "right to put contraceptives to their intended use, notwithstanding the combined objection of both parents and the State."[12] The real issue in this case, as only Justice Stevens was willing to point out, was whether a state legislature was free to pass a completely irrational law, which had absolutely no chance of successfully promoting a completely mistaken policy—a problem of substantive due process.

Michael M. v. Sonoma County Court is also full of underlying assumptions, many of which are false and some of which perpetuate stereotypes about male and female behavior that are outmoded: males are more aggressive than females in sexual situations; females are always subject to greater risks than males when they engage in sexual activity; women are childish, incapable of making their own decisions, in need of protection; the law should protect young females and may do so by punishing males; criminal statutes directed at males equalize male and female risk-taking and create a disincentive to male sexual activity. Both the idea of a double standard of morality and a picture of women as weak and inferior rest on these assumptions. The fact that the state statute challenged in this case had its roots in older legislation that at one time clearly expressed the legislature's belief that it had an obligation to protect the chastity of females should have made it particularly vulnerable. So should the fact that the same type of statute could be cast in a gender-neutral form that avoided questions of sex discrimination. So also should the social facts, described by the dissenters, showing that statutes of this type had little effect on the targeted activity—teenage pregnancy.

HL v. Matheson is basically a case dealing with the authority of parents over their minor children, and the decision of the Court was clearly derived from its acceptance of the following propositions: that parents have the right to control the actions of their minors, that families act in the best interests of their children and have better judgment than minor children, that abortion decisions affecting a child should not be made by the child alone (even with the assistance of doctors or public health officials) and that the law should give the parents a chance to counteract, if not veto outright, a minor's resolution to have an abortion. The Court did not take into account certain uncongenial probabilities on the other side, including the likelihood that the teenager's pregnancy in itself indicated a breakdown in family control and harmony, that the decision to bear a child would make important, perhaps critical, differences in the teenager's life and that the family might not always act in her interests but in terms of its own mythologies and needs.[13]

These cases also portray an idealized vision of the family itself. First, the underlying idea of the family which the Justices seem to entertain, the family in the Court's own precedents, is a stereotype, a mythological construct. It is difficult to see where all the elements of this family come from; some, such as the patriarchal, patrilineal components are derived from the Bible and the common law, but the transactions and relationships important to the law—inheritance, marriage and divorce, control of property, ability to contract—do not give us all the dimensions of that family which emerges from the Court's decisions. The most likely source of the image of family life depicted in the opinions is the personal family experience of the Justices themselves, the stable, conservative, middle-class family life of the country during the times of their own childhood. In the opinions of the Court, we see the family as a "haven in a heartless world," the sanctuary to which the tired father returns after work, a private institution designed for domestic affection and tranquility. It is also a warm, caring, kin-related group, which includes the extended family (*Moore*) and even includes non-related people who provide support for one another (*Moreno*). In the plurality opinion in *Moore v. East Cleveland*, Justice Powell explained that the Constitution protects the sanctity of the family because the institution of the family is so deeply rooted in the nation's history and tradition that its existence is essential to our way of life. Although families are nowhere mentioned explicitly in the Constitution itself, the fundamental nature of family life makes it one of the areas of protected liberty which is immunized from "arbitrary impositions and purposeless restraints." This is a classic "substantive due process" position. Family rights are "natural" rights, and the state may not interfere with them unless there are exceptionally good reasons for doing so. Seen in the light of such a statement, the individual Court rulings that deal with marriage, procreation, child-bearing, the privacy of the marriage relationship, the right to make various choices for one's children, all fall into a pattern.

The basic function of the family is child care and child-raising, and the Court recognizes the importance of parental control over this process (*Yoder*). Parents make decisions in the best interests of their children (*Yoder*, *Parham v. JR*, *HL v. Matheson*). Natural families are not perfect (*Santosky*), but they are better for children than are state institutions, foster parents or social workers; children should not be removed from their natural families except under extreme circumstances.

Although families are private groups, the reproductive and socialization functions they perform are so important to the state that it attempts to regulate some aspects of family life. The Supreme Court has recognized that circumstances may demand state intervention, but it has insisted that intrusion in the internal affairs of the family be cautious and limited. Neglect and child abuse justify the removal of children from the home and even the severing of parental ties (*Santosky*, *Lassiter*), but the biological connections between parents and children are constitutionally protected and interference with them requires careful procedures. When families fail, children are not properly socialized and are likely to become criminals. (*Eddings v. Oklahoma*).

The traditional view that the family should have primary authority over the child has increasingly clashed with state policies requiring that parents function in prescribed ways. The state has a large stake in ensuring that socialization be properly performed. It has, indeed, taken over many parts of the socialization process. The parent's views, values and child-raising practices may thus clash with public programs designed to improve the level of child care.

The idea of family life as a private sphere and a private government conflicts with the fact that the state has always placed conditions on marriage, controlled divorce and used its police powers to ensure proper family functioning, even to the extent of passing criminal laws to enforce compliance with its will. In recent years, legislative programs have gone beyond minimal regulation to strengthen and support family units. Students of family policy have begun to suspect that even beneficent programs affect the manner in which families function, often in ways that were not predicted, and that the proliferation of government policies enacted to keep the supposedly sinking family afloat often make the vessel only the more unseaworthy.[14] Government activity has been especially suspect in the field of child care and support because child care bureaucracies and welfare workers have occasionally been overly aggressive in removing children from their "unsuitable" homes and have engaged in endless bureaucratic squabblings over theories of child placement that have prevented the reuniting of natural families or permanent placements by adoption.[15] Exposés of the poor quality of care offered in juvenile homes, mental hospitals and foster homes have made it clear that unsatisfactory or even abusive parents may often be preferable to public institutions. When these criticisms are assimilated to the law's preference for the natural family, it is not surprising to find the Justices applying constitutional principles to require a high standard of proof of abuse or neglect before they allow the state to separate children from their families or to terminate parental rights. It is also consistent with this high valuation of the natural home and parents to reject proposals for the separate representation of children's rights. It is better to assume that parents will usually do what is good for their children than to introduce further divisive elements into the family relationship.

In its concern for this fundamental institution, the Court has been in accord both with public opinion and with officials in the executive and legislative branches of the government who have been dismayed by reports that American families are in trouble and have been alarmed by census figures that show a rapid rate of change in many kinds of family and marital relationships. But in spite of its acceptance of much of the traditional ideology, the Court itself has been accused of contributing to family instability by its desegregation and school prayer decisions, its legalization of abortion and contraception and its objection to the censorship of books. As it has found more and more family-related cases on its docket, the Court has become cautious about handing down decisions that might further destabilize the family.

Some adjustment in the law has been unavoidable. Where older legal rules (legitimacy classifications, pregnancy leave, laws affecting the status of women) have been challenged on grounds of equal protection, the Justices have made adjustments to bring the law in line with current notions about equality, but have done so slowly and deliberately. They have also been reluctant to adopt new doctrines or to bring new kinds of groups under the protection of the Constitution when this kind of decision might disturb family structure. In this latter group of cases, we see the Court rejecting arguments that the right to privacy covers sexual freedom and non-marital cohabitation. In due process cases the Court has refused to extend constitutional protection to what it regards as radical new theories of "psychological parenting" and has been willing to move only tentatively in the area of "children's rights." Overall, the pattern seems to be one of accepting some changes but refusing to reach out to make decisions that might result in further disruption of family relationships.

A few decisions, however, seem to be more closely related to personal preferences for particular family forms than they do to the Court's tradition of conservatism and self-restraint. The *Village of Belle Terre v. Boraas* and *Moore v. City of East Cleveland* decisions are difficult to reconcile in terms of doctrine alone. In *Boraas* the Court upheld the power of the city to enact zoning regulations and approved a single-family zoning ordinance designed to protect middle-class family, neighborhood and property values. In *Moore* it rejected a similar zoning ordinance, holding that it interfered with an accepted form of family organization—the extended family. The *Boraas* decision allowed the local community to protect itself not only against boarding houses and group homes, but also against non-marital cohabitation and incursions by students and "hippie" communitarians that might disrupt the harmony of traditional family living patterns. The Justices did not regard the student "family" in *Boraas* as a family at all, but saw it as a household composed of a loose combination of unrelated individuals. The extended family in *Moore*, on the other hand, was a familar and congenial living arrangement. Although zoning ordinances similar to those enacted by the Village of Belle Terre are common, they often have more to do with the preferences and prejudices of neighborhoods than they do with practical zoning concerns such as population density, access to schools, traffic and noise. A large extended family can disrupt a quiet, single-family suburb as much or more than a group of unrelated individuals.

The zoning cases pitted families and quasi-families against the state's regulatory power. In other kinds of cases, the Court found itself trying to settle conflicts of rights within the family as an entity. The parental rights termination cases illustrate this kind of conflict, as do cases involving parental consent before minors can have abortions. As far as the children themselves are concerned, law and tradition make their rights subordinate to collective "family rights" and their decisions subordinate to the will of their parents, but especially where older children are concerned, there are clearly occasions for exceptions to this principle.

Procedural due process cases would seem to offer less room for the expression of judicial preferences, but here as well as in the more unstructured substantive due process and equal protection cases, the Justices make revealing choices. A trio of decisions, *Lassiter*, *Santosky* and *Streeter*, all presented problems of procedural due process but were decided on the basis of three different bodies of doctrine. The right to counsel guaranteed by the Sixth and Fourteenth amendments requires the appointment of counsel for all indigents accused of serious crime. But because Abby Gail Lassiter was not in danger of losing her physical liberty, she was not entitled to representation by court-appointed counsel; parental rights termination hearings are not always unfair because the parent is unrepresented. In *Santosky*, however, the Court held that the termination of parental rights was so drastic a step that the finding of facts indicating abuse or neglect of the children must be based on "clear and convincing" evidence, a standard of proof much stricter than that of "a preponderance of the evidence," the standard that had been required by state law. But the factual differences between the parents in these two cases may help explain these decisions. Ms. Lassiter was serving a long sentence for second degree murder, and her retention of parental rights was more or less a formality, in conflict with the social agency's desire to find a permanent home for her son. In *Santosky*, however, although the children had been removed from the home for some years, the Court wanted to be certain that formal termination of parental rights would not be made for frivolous or unconvincing reasons, or without a clear showing of parental abuse. A third case, *Little v. Streeter*, also seems in conflict with the *Lassiter* decision, inasmuch as the Court sustained Streeter's argument that the state should pay for blood tests to establish that he had *not* fathered a child, while it denied Lassiter's argument that the public should provide her with legal representation in her fight to retain parental rights. Here again, the important differences lie in factors other than those discussed in the appellate opinions. The paternity case should be considered in the light of the whole range of legitimacy decisions through which the Court has been working, and in the context of the growing public demand that non-marital parents be held legally responsible for the support of their offspring—a general change of direction toward regularizing the role of unmarried parents and forcing them to support their children.

The differences in these cases suggest that much of the underlying decisional motivation may lie in the Court's family ideology rather than in the constitutional doctrines themselves. In a sense, all of these decisions are part of the "revival of substantive due process" that commentators trace back to *Griswold v. Connecticut* and *Roe v. Wade,* or even to the earlier *Meyer* and *Pierce* decisions.[16] Although other constitutional bases are invoked in these opinions, and only Justice Powell's argument in *Moore* makes this point explicitly, all of the decisions deal with questions of fundamental values. The Equal Protection cases, insofar as they establish some classifications as acceptable and some as unacceptable, involve issues of substance, not simply problems of line-drawing. Classifications that are far from irrational, as Professors Kenneth L. Karst and Harold W. Horowitz have pointed out, may be held unconstitutional because they produce inequities that do not fit the American ideal of equality.[17] When the Court holds that a classification cannot be used in a way that restricts the exercise of fundamental freedoms, it has decided that the legislature may not impair fundamental rights.

The procedural due process cases also reflect judgments about fundamental values, because more procedure and more due process are required in some situations than in others. Here the question is not whether a hearing can be fair if held without a lawyer or without a certain standard of proof, but whether some rights are so important that they must be protected by scrupulous procedures, whereas others are less valuable and do not need extraordinary safeguards.

Although most of these cases came to the Court with due process and equal protection claims, some raised questions under other clauses of the Constitution. It is often possible to see that the more important underlying concern relates to the family. *Wisconsin v. Yoder*, for example, is not as much a freedom of religion case as it is a conflict between state and community over who should socialize the children—a quintessential family issue. *Ingraham v. Wright* was argued and decided on cruel and unusual punishment (Eighth Amendment) grounds, but it presented a related problem, a conflict between the state and the parents over the discipline of children in school.[18] The important point made in *Ginsberg v. New York*, a decision upholding legislation forbidding the sale of "soft-core" pornography to minors under seventeen, was that the state may act to help parents protect and control their children and supervise their reading.[19] This is also the important issue in a more recent case, *Board of Education of Island Trees Union School District v. Pico*. Decisions that secure rights to privacy invariably deal with the claims in a context of reproductive choice or family privacy. It has been quite correctly noted that the Court has been very reluctant to use this doctrine to confer broad rights to sexual freedom or non-marital cohabitation.[20]

Family cases thus come to the Court clothed in a number of different constitutional garments. They also present a very random sampling of the whole range of family-related legal problems in state and federal courts. Some of the difficulty the Justices have had in seeing these problems in relation to one another has been the grab-bag quality of their provenance: the cases do not come to the Court in an orderly sequence, but in a haphazard series of unrelated appeals. Another part of the difficulty has been that the power of stereotypes embedded in the belief systems of individual Justices makes it difficult, under some circumstances, for them to see the panorama of events without coloring it with hues from their own histories and psychologies.

Supreme Court Justices are not unaware of the need to recognize and discount personal bias in decision-making. If it were possible for the members of the Court to stand back and make an effort at self-conscious appraisal of the particular images of the family which they have internalized, the Justices might be freer to develop new rules that both conserve traditional family values and allow adaptation of the older family ideology to families that are not frozen into a single mold, but are themselves constantly adapting to changing circumstances. Family policy in the nation at the present time is of great concern to everybody, but there has been much confusion and conflict over the direction in which it should go. As it is, the Court's work in this area has done little to clarify the issues or articulate principles around which a new consensus could be formed, a consensus that recognizes the reality and permanence of certain kinds of social change.

When it does its best work, the Supreme Court conserves traditional values while adjusting legal and constitutional doctrines to new situations. It clarifies issues and facilitates the solution of problems by articulating governing principles and then demonstrating how they can be applied to new realities; it updates rules and at the same time indicates new directions for the law to take that are consistent with governing constitutional theory.

In the family cases the Supreme Court's accomplishment has been mixed. Where the gap between old stereotypes and legal doctrine and new social facts has been so great that it could no longer be ignored, the Court has made clear, relevant changes. In the legitimacy and abortion decisions, it overturned old policies that were too rigid, declaring old laws unconstitutional and allowing a new level of political and legal adjustments to take place.

Where reproduction and gender are both at issue, the Court's work has been especially unsatisfactory and confusing; it has not been able to see necessary distinctions between gender and reproduction or between "real" and socially defined differences between men and women, and has tended to confuse stereotypes with actualities. The pregnancy disability cases illustrate this failing. Congress eventually stepped in to overrule the Court's decisions, recognizing that pregnancy disability rules kept women from working in situations where their economic status required them to work to support themselves, their children or their families.

Cases involving the schools have found the Court protecting parental authority over children and the socialization process, although the cases have been decided under constitutional doctrines that obscure the political conflicts raging around the public school system.

In a few marginal cases the Court has resisted state and federal legislation defining "families" too narrowly. Claims by new kinds of family configurations to the protections and status of traditional families are looming but have not yet been faced.

New and very troublesome questions of public policy are beginning to arise in cases dealing with child support. Here the needs of children often coincide with the postulate that men and women should be financially as well as morally responsible for biological acts that bring children into the world. But there are also practical reservations about tough child support laws and the methods that can be used to make moral obligations binding on recalcitrant parents. There is some presentiment that it will be increasingly necessary to use public funds to ensure adequate care for children, especially those being raised by single parents. Conflicting ideological perspectives lie behind many of these policy alternatives. The Court still accepts biology as creating preeminently significant family ties and has tried to protect the biological family more strongly than other types of relationships.

Finally, the Court has not provided careful analytical thinking about the roles of professionals providing family services and about where they fit in conflicts between parents, children and the state.

In much of the political conflict over family issues, there is an assumption that the governmental system itself is dependent on accepted family forms, that the character traits needed for free self-government, the moral outlook necessary for successful democracy, are a product of training in certain types of families.[21] According to this view, although it has been constitutionally invisible, the traditional American family is almost a pre-condition underlying more formal constitutional arrangements. The Court is now finding itself called on to give constitutional protection to family values that have always before been taken as given. The values it is championing, however, are in the courts in part because they are changing. There is always a lag between Supreme Court decisions, constitutional law and the contemporary course of events. It is perhaps not inaccurate to say that the function of constitutional decision-making is to tame and assimilate social change that has already occurred. In a sense the Court always engages in rear-guard actions, fighting battles over ways of life that have already been partly lost.[22] If this is true, the real meaning of the Supreme Court's engagement in the battle over the family is that it signifies that the war is already over.

Notes

INTRODUCTION

1. *Hoyt v. Florida*, 368 U.S. 57 (1961).
2. See Irene Diamond, ed., *Families, Politics and Public Policy* (New York: Longman, 1983); Sylvia A. Law, "Rethinking Sex and the Constitution," *University of Pennsylvania Law Review* (June 1984): 955–1040.
3. *Roberts v. City of Boston*, 5 Cushing 198 (1849).

CHAPTER 1

1. Walter Lippmann, *Public Opinion* (Reprint of 1922 ed.; New York: Macmillan, 1960), p. 90.
2. Judith Mitchell, *Woman's Estate* (New York: Pantheon Books, 1971), p. 148.
3. Laurence H. Tribe, *American Constitutional Law* (Mineola, N.Y.: Foundation Press, 1978), p. 989.
4. Arthur Selwyn Miller, "The Concept of the 'Living Constitution'," in *Social Change and Fundamental Law* (Westport, Conn.: Greenwood Press, 1977), quoting Ralph Waldo Emerson, p. 350.
5. *Brown v. Board of Education*, 347 U.S. 483 (1954).
6. *Loving v. Virginia*, 388 U.S. 1 (1967).
7. *Levy v. Louisiana*, 391 U.S. 68 (1968).
8. *Griswold v. Connecticut*, 381 U.S. 497 (1965); *Roe v. Wade*, 410 U.S. 113 (1973); and see *Doe v. Commonwealth's Attorney for the City of Richmond*, 403 F. Supp. 1199 (1975). Thomas C. Grey, "Eros, Civilization

and the Burger Court," *Law and Contemporary Problems* 43 (Summer 1980): 83–101, discusses some of these cases.

9. Charles Reich, "The New Property," *Yale Law Journal* 73 (April 1964): 733, 771–74; *Goldberg v. Kelly*, 397 U.S. 25 (1970).

10. See *Stanley v. Illinois*, 405 U.S. 645 (1972); *Parham v. JR*, 442 U.S. 584 (1979); *Santosky v. Kramer*, 102 S.Ct. 1388 (1982).

11. Gerald Gunther, *Cases and Materials on Constitutional Law*, 10th ed. (Mineola, N.Y.: Foundation Press, 1980), pp. 502–503.

12. *Burns Baking Co. v. Bryan*, 264 U.S. 504 (1924), Brandeis opinion.

13. Cf. *Carey v. Population Services*, 431 U.S. 678 (1977).

14. *Griswold v. Connecticut*, 381 U.S. 497 (1965); see C. Thomas Dienes, *Law, Politics and Birth Control* (Urbana: University of Illinois Press, 1972).

15. Eva R. Rubin, *Abortion, Politics and the Courts* (Westport, Conn.: Greenwood Press, 1982); Karen O'Connor, *Women's Organizations' Use of the Courts* (Lexington, Mass.: Lexington Books, 1980).

16. Jack Greenberg, *Judicial Process and Social Change, Constitutional Litigation* (St. Paul, Minn.: West Publishing Co., 1977); Aryeh Neier, *Only Judgment: The Limits of Litigation in Social Change* (Middletown, Conn.: Wesleyan University Press, 1982).

17. Arlene S. Skolnick and Jerome H. Skolnick, eds., *Family in Transition* (Boston: Little, Brown, 1971), pp. 7–8.

18. F. L. Morton, "Sexual Equality and the Family in Tocqueville's *Democracy in America*," *Canadian Journal of Political Science* 17, no. 2 (June 1984): 309–24. Robert L. Griswold, *Family and Divorce in California, 1850–1890, Victorian Illusions and Everyday Realities* (Albany: State University of New York Press, 1982) describes family realities and myths in the context of divorce proceedings.

19. *Reynolds v. United States*, 98 U.S. 244 (1878); *Maynard v. Hill*, 125 U.S. 190 (1888); *Meyer v. Nebraska*, 262 U.S. 1042 (1923); *Pierce v. Society of Sisters*, 268 U.S. 510 (1925).

20. *Reynolds v. United States* (1878).

21. *Skinner v. Oklahoma*, 316 U.S. 53 (1942); *Loving v. Virginia* (1967).

22. *Prince v. Massachusetts*, 321 U.S. 158 (1943); *Griswold v. Connecticut*, 381 U.S. 479 (1965).

23. *Loving v. Virginia* (1967); *Zablocki v. Redhail*, 434 U.S. 374 (1978); *Skinner v. Oklahoma* (1942); *Griswold v. Connecticut* (1965); *Roe v. Wade* (1973).

24. *State v. Rhodes*, 61 N.C. 453 (1868).

25. *Maynard v. Hill* (1888).

26. *Griswold v. Connecticut* (1965), p. 486.

27. *Poe v. Ullman*, 367 U.S. 497 (1962), p. 551–52.

28. *Parham v. JR*, 442 U.S. 584 (1979), p. 602.

29. *Meyer v. Nebraska*, 262 U.S. 390 (1922), p. 401.

30. See Carl F. Kaestle, *Pillars of the Republic, Common Schools and American Society, 1780–1860* (New York: Hill and Wang, 1983), ch. 5, for a description of the dominant Protestant family ideology of this period. Griswold, cited above in note 18, also explores the ideology and the realities of nineteenth-century family life.

31. Jessie Barnard, *The Future of Motherhood* (New York/London: Penguin Books, 1974), pp. 3–6.

32. *Bradwell v. Illinois*, 83 U.S. 130 (1873); *Minor v. Happersett*, 88 U.S. 162, (1875); *Reed v. Reed*, 404 U.S. 71 (1971).

Haig Basmajian, "Sexism in the Language of Legislatures and Courts," in Allean P. Nilson et al., eds., *Sexism and Language* (Urbana, Ill.: National Council of Teachers of English, 1977), pp. 77–104. Basmajian's article analyzes the language in legislative debate and judicial opinions and uses it to illustrate attitudes toward women.

Ruth B. Cowan, "Women's Rights Through Litigation: An Examination of the American Civil Liberties Union Women's Rights Project, 1971–1976," *Columbia Human Rights Law Review* 8 (Spring-Summer 1976): 373–412, describes the litigation campaign to change judicial attitudes.

33. *Reynolds v. United States; Belle Terre v. Boraas*, 416 U.S. (1974).

34. *Belle Terre v. Boraas; Smith v. Organization of Foster Families for Equality and Reform*, 431 U.S. 816 (1977).

35. *Santosky v. Kramer* (1982); *Eddings v. Oklahoma*, 102 S.Ct. 869 (1982); *Smith v. Organization of Foster Families for Equality and Reform*, 431 U.S. 816 (1977).

36. Robert H. Mnookin, *Child, Family and State, Problems and Materials on Children and the Law* (Boston: Little, Brown, 1978), pp. 515–16.

37. Christopher Lasch, *Haven in a Heartless World: The Family Besieged* (New York: Basic Books, 1977), p. xiv.

38. Edward Shorter, *The Making of the Modern Family* (New York: Basic Books, 1977), p. 7.

39. Jane Flax, "Contemporary American Families: Decline or Transformation?" in Irene Diamond, ed., *Families, Politics and Public Policy* (New York: Longman, 1983), pp. 21–40. Flax believes that the most important changes occurring in family patterns are related to divorce, women's employment and the increasing number of families headed by women. For an interesting theory about the meaning of these trends, see Elizabeth Nickles and Laura Ashcraft, *The Coming Matriarchy* (New York: Seaview Books, 1981).

40. *The State of Families 1984–85* (New York: Family Service America, 1984), pp. 7–15, 23, 32, 60, 72–77. See also U.S. Department of Commerce, Bureau of the Census, Current Population Reports, Series P–20.

41. Harry D. Krause, *Family Law* (St. Paul, Minn.: West Publishing Co., 1976), p. 305.

42. Rollin M. Perkins, *Criminal Law*, 3d ed. (Mineola, N.Y.: Foundation Press, 1982), p. 455.

43. On the disabilities placed on illegitimate children, see generally Harry D. Krause, *Illegitimacy: Law and Social Policy* (Indianapolis: Bobbs-Merrill, 1971).

44. Sandra L. Hofferth and Kristin A. Moore, "Women's Employment and Marriage," in Ralph E. Smith, ed., *The Subtle Revolution* (Washington, D.C.: Urban Institute, 1979), pp. 108–10. "Runaway Wives," *Psychology Today* (May 1975): 45.

45. Andrew Hacker, "Farewell to the Family?" *New York Review of Books*, March 18, 1982, pp. 37–44, discusses socialization by peers.

46. Kristin A. Moore, "Government Policies Related to Teenage Family Formation and Functioning: An Inventory," in Theodora Ooms, ed., *Teenage Pregnancy in a Family Context* (Philadelphia: Temple University Press, 1981), pp. 165–213.

CHAPTER 2

1. Quoted by Justice Douglas in *Levy v. Louisiana*, 391 U.S. 68 (1968), p. 72 n.6.

2. Harry D. Krause, *Family Law in a Nutshell* (St. Paul, Minn.: West Publishing Co., 1977), pp. 4–5. *Ex parte Burrus*, 136 U.S. 500 (1889), p. 503.

3. Harry D. Krause, *Family Law* (St. Paul, Minn.: West Publishing Co., 1976), p. 415.

4. "Comment: Extent of a Parent's Duty of Support," in *Selected Essays on Family Law* (Brooklyn, N.Y.: Foundation Press, 1950), p. 1072; Horace H. Robbins and Francis Deak, "The Familial Property Rights of Illegitimate Children: A Comparative Study," in *Selected Essays*, pp. 728–29, 736–37; Frederick Pollock and Frederic William Maitland, *The History of English Law*, 2d ed. (Washington, D.C.: Lawyers' Literary Club, 1959), v. 2, pp. 396–99.

5. "Parent's Duty of Support," p. 1072.

6. Robbins and Deak, "Property Rights of Illegitimate Children," p. 737.

7. *Encyclopedia Britannica*, v. 15, "Legitimacy and Illegitimacy," p. 879 (1957 ed.).

8. *Gomez v. Perez*, 409 U.S. 435 (1973).

9. "Parent's Duty of Support," p. 1072.

10. Harry D. Krause, *Illegitimacy: Law and Social Policy* (Indianapolis: Bobbs-Merrill, 1971), pp. 269–72; see also Harry D. Krause, "Equal Protection for the Illegitimate," *Michigan Law Review* 65 (January 1967): 477–506.

For sociological and historical discussions of illegitimacy, see Peter Laslett, Karla Oosterveen and Richard M. Smith, *Bastardy and Its Comparative History* (Cambridge: Harvard University Press, 1980); Shirley Foster Hartley, *Illegitimacy* (Berkeley: University of California Press, 1975).

11. For descriptions of the treatment of unmarried mothers, see Carol Glassman, "Women and the Welfare System," pp. 102–15, in Robin Morgan, ed., *Sisterhood Is Powerful* (New York: Vintage, 1970), and Letty Cottin Pogrebin, *Family Politics* (New York: McGraw-Hill, 1983), ch. 8.

12. Krause, *Illegitimacy*, p. 17. Stuart J. Stein, "Common Law Marriage, Its History and Certain Contemporary Problems," *Journal of Family Law* 9 (1970): 271–99. Stein counts fifteen states as recognizing common law marriage in 1970, but other states presume that a valid marriage has taken place.

13. U.S. Department of Commerce, Bureau of the Census, *Statistical Abstract of the United States, 1980*, Table 95: Births to Unmarried Women by Race and Age of Mother, 1950–1978. *Statistical Abstract of the United States, 1981*, Table 98: Births to Unmarried Women by Race and Age of Mother, 1950–1979, p. 65.

See also Theodora Ooms, ed., *Teenage Pregnancy in a Family Context: Implications for Policy* (Philadelphia: Temple University Press, 1981), especially introduction and ch. 2.

14. Krause, *Family Law*, 1983, p. 938.

15. See note 13 above.

16. Krause, *Illegitimacy*, p. 258.

17. *Ibid.*, p. 260. See also Justice White, dissenting in *Parham v. Hughes*, 441 U.S. 347 (1979), p. 367 n.140.

18. U.S. Congress, Senate, Committee on Labor and Human Resources, *Broken Families*, Hearings before the Subcommittee on Family and Human Resources, 98th Cong., 1st sess., March 22 and 24, 1983, pp. 85, 205–7.

19. Karen DeCrow, *Sexist Justice* (New York: Random House, 1974), p. 232. See also Aleta Wallach and Patricia Tenoso, "A Vindication of the Rights of Unmarried Mothers and Their Children: An Analysis of the Institution of Illegitimacy, Equal Protection and the Uniform Parentage Act," *University of Kansas Law Review* 23 (Fall 1974): 23–90.

20. See Robert L. Stenger, "Expanding the Constitutional Rights of Illegitimate Children, 1968–80," *Journal of Family Law* 19 (May (1981)): 407–44. This article gives a detailed analysis of the cases through 1980.

21. Gerald Gunther, *Cases and Materials on Constitutional Law*, 10th ed. (Mineola, N.Y.: Foundation Press, 1980), pp. 897–98.

22. Stenger, "Expanding the Constitutional Rights," *passim*.

23. 391 U.S. 68 (1968); *Quilloin v. Walcott*, 434 U.S. 246 (1978); *Caban*

v. Mohammad, 441 U.S. 380 (1979); *Parham v. Hughes*, 441 U.S. 347 (1979); *Lehr v. Robertson*, 103 S.Ct. 2985 (1983).

24. John C. Gray, Jr., and David Rudovsky, "The Court Acknowledges the Illegitimate: Levy v. Louisiana and Glona v. American Guarantee and Liability Insurance Co.," *University of Pennsylvania Law Review* 118 (November 1969): 1–39.

25. Harry D. Krause, "Equal Protection for the Illegitimate," *Michigan Law Review* 65 (January 1967): 499.

26. Pollock and Maitland, *History of English Law*, II, 366–85.

27. *Glona v. American Guarantee & Insurance Co.*, 391 U.S. 73 (1968).

28. *Ibid.*, at pp. 74–75.

29. *Ibid.*

30. Krause, *Illegitimacy*, pp. 173–74.

31. *Trimble v. Gordon*, 430 U.S. 702 (1977).

32. Justice Harlan, dissenting in *Levy v. Louisiana*, at p. 80.

33. *Labine v. Vincent*, 401 U.S. 536 (1971).

34. *Gomez v. Perez*, 409 U.S. 435 (1973).

35. *Mills v. Hableutzel*, 456 U.S. 91 (1982).

36. *Pickett v. Brown*, 103 S.Ct. 2199 (1983).

37. *Mills v. Hableutzel*, 456 U.S. 91, Justice O'Connor concurring at p. 104.

38. Uniform Parentage Act, *The Book of the States* (Lexington, Ky.: Council of State Governments, 1982–1983), v. 24, p. 88. Ten states had ratified by 1983. The Uniform Parentage Act is discussed from a feminist perspective in Wallach and Tenoso, "Vindication of the Rights," above, n. 16. See also Krause, *Family Law* (1983).

39. *Mills v. Hableutzel*, 456 U.S. 91 (1982), Justice O'Connor concurring.

40. Jerome A. Barron, "Notice to the Unwed Father and Termination of Parental Rights: Implementing Stanley v. Illinois," in Sanford N. Katz, ed., *The Youngest Minority: Lawyers in Defense of Children* (Chicago: American Bar Association Section on Family Law, 1977), v. 2, pp. 22–41.

41. *Stanley v. Illinois*, 405 U.S. 645 (1972).

42. The cases are *Murray v. Department of Agriculture* (1973), *Vlandis v. Kline* (1973), *Cleveland v. LaFleur* (1974) and *Weinberger v. Salfi* (1975). See "Note: Irrebuttable Presumption Doctrine in the Supreme Court," *Harvard Law Review* 87 (May 1974): 1534–56; "Note: Irrebuttable Presumptions: An Illusory Analysis," *Stanford Law Review* 27 (January 1975): 449.

43. Walter Wadlington, Charles H. Whitebread and Samuel M. Davis, *Children in the Legal System, Cases and Materials* (Mineola, N.Y.: Foundation Press, 1983), pp. 130–31. See also Barron, "Notice to the Unwed Father," pp. 22–41.

44. Wadlington et al., *Children in the Legal System*, pp. 130–31.

45. *Quilloin v. Walcott*, 434 U.S. 246 (1978).

46. Justice Marshall cited *Meyer v. Nebraska, Wisconsin v. Yoder, Stanley v. Illinois, Prince v. Massachusetts, Smith v. Organization of Foster Families* and *Cleveland Board of Education v. La Fleur*.

47. *Caban v. Mohammad*, 441 U.S. 380 (1979).

48. *Parham v. Hughes*, 441 U.S. 347 (1979); Justice Powell concurring at p. 360.

49. *Ibid.*

50. *Parham v. Hughes*, p. 352.

51. White footnote, 441 U.S. p. 367 n. 14.

52. Steven P. Erie, Martin Rein and Barbara Wiget, "Women and the Reagan Revolution: Thermidor for the Social Welfare Economy," in Irene Diamond, ed., *Families, Politics, and Public Policy* (New York: Longman, 1983). The authors cite research done by Heather L. Ross and Isabel V. Sawhill, *Time of Transition* (Washington, D.C.: Urban Institute, 1975), and Frank Levy, "Labor Force Dynamics and the Distribution of Employability," Urban Institute Working Paper, No. 1269–02 (Washington, D.C.: Urban Institute, January 1980).

53. *Lehr v. Robertson*, 103 S.Ct. 2985 (1983).

54. Harry D. Krause, "Child-Support Enforcement: Legislative Tasks for the Early 1980's," in Judith Cassetty, ed., *The Parental Child-Support Obligation* (Lexington, Mass.: Lexington Books, 1983), pp. 243–55.

55. Kenneth R. Redden, *Federal Regulation of the Family*. (Charlottesville, Va.: Michie Co., 1982). Uniform Reciprocal Enforcement of Support Act and Revised Uniform Reciprocal Enforcement of Support Act are discussed, section 5.6 C, pp. 102–105.

56. Sanford N. Katz, "A Historical Perspective on Child Support Laws in the United States," in Cassetty, ed., *The Parental Child-Support Obligation*, pp. 17–21; Krause, *Family Law* (1983), pp. 939–41.

57. Redden, *Federal Regulation of the Family*, discusses the Parent Locator Service, section 5.2 ABCD, pp. 87–92.

58. *Ibid.*, p. 88.

59. *Congressional Quarterly Weekly Report*, April 28, 1984, p. 992 (HR 4325). Child Support Enforcement Amendments of 1984. P.L. 98–378, 98 Stat. 1305. See also U.S. Department of Health and Human Services, Office of Child Support Enforcement, *Handbook on Child Support Enforcement* (1984).

60. Judy Mann, "Child Support," *Washington Post*, January 18, 1984, C 1. *Congressional Quarterly Weekly Report*, April 28, 1984, p. 992.

61. Judith Cassetty, "Emerging Issues in Child-Support Policy and Practice," in Cassetty, ed., *The Parental Child-Support Obligation*, p. 3.

62. Krause, *Family Law in a Nutshell*, pp. 166–67.

63. *Lehr v. Robertson*, 103 S.Ct. 2985 (1983).

64. *Zablocki v. Redhail*, 434 U.S. 374 (1978).

65. Quoting Dr. Ron Haskins, Associate Director of the Bush Institute for Child and Family Policy, "Symposium to Deal with Enforcement of Child Support," Interview, *Chapel Hill Newspaper*, April 16, 1984. See also Irwin Garfinkel, David Betson, Thomas Corbett and Sherwood K. Zink, "A Proposal for Comprehensive Reform of the Child-Support System in Wisconsin," in Cassetty, ed., *The Parental Child-Support Obligation*, pp. 263–82.

66. Laurence Tribe, *American Constitutional Law* (Mineola, N.Y.: Foundation Press, 1978), pp. 1057, 1090.

67. Stenger, "Expanding the Constitutional Rights of Children," pp. 441–45. The cases are hard to tabulate because they deal with such diverse uses of the classification. It is probably accurate to describe the case law as requiring that "statutes making distinctions between legitimate and illegitimate children must be narrowly drawn and closely related to real problems of proof." Wadlington et al., *Children in the Legal System*, p. 122.

68. *Labine v. Vincent*, 401 U.S. 532 (1971).

69. *Trimble v. Gordon*, 430 U.S. 762 (1977).

70. *Matthews v. Lucas*, 427 U.S. 495 (1976); *Norton v. Mathews*, 427 U.S. 524 (1976); *Califano v. Boles*, 443 U.S. 282 (1979).

71. *Califano v. Boles*, 443 U.S. 282 (1979).

72. Robert A. Burt, "The Constitution of the Family," *Supreme Court Review* (1979): 329–95. See also Justice Rehnquist dissenting in *Trimble v. Gordon*, at pp. 777–86.

73. Nan D. Hunter, "Child Support Law and Policy: The Systematic Imposition of Costs on Women," *Harvard Women's Law Journal* 6 (Spring 1983): 1–29.

CHAPTER 3

1. Kingsley Davis, "Illegitimacy and the Social Structure," *American Journal of Sociology* 45 (September 1939): 215.

2. Rosalind Pollack Petchevsky, "Anti-abortion, Anti-feminism and the Rise of the New Right," *Feminist Studies* 7 (Summer 1981): 221.

3. Kristin Luker, *Abortion and the Politics of Motherhood* (Berkeley: University of California Press, 1984), pp. 159–75.

4. *Ibid.*, p. 162.

5. *Ibid.*, p. 165.

6. Beverly Wildung Harrison, *Our Right to Choose: Toward a New Ethic of Abortion* (Boston: Beacon Press, 1983), p. 163.

7. Fred M. Frohock, *Abortion: A Case Study in Law and Morals* (Westport, Conn.: Greenwood Press, 1983), pp. 76–77.

8. James Reed, *Birth Control and American Society: From Private Vice to Public Virtue* (Princeton, N.J.: Princeton University Press, 1978), ch. 3.

9. *Ibid.*, pp. 44, 45.

10. Edward Shorter, *A History of Women's Bodies* (New York: Basic Books, 1982), pp. 191–224; James C. Mohr, *Abortion in America* (New York: Oxford University Press, 1978), pp. 74–85.

11. Mohr, *Abortion in America*, ch. 9.

12. Luker, *Abortion and the Politics of Motherhood*, pp. 32–35.

13. Zillah Eisenstein, "State, Patriarchal Family and Working Mothers," in Irene Diamond, ed., *Families, Politics and Public Policy* (New York: Longman, 1983), pp. 52–56.

14. Reed, *Birth Control and American Society*, pp. 208–10, 370–71.

15. Justice O'Connor's opinion in *City of Akron v. Akron Center for Reproductive Health*, 103 S.Ct. 2481 (1983), p. 2507. See Sylvia A. Law, "Rethinking Sex and the Constitution," *University of Pennsylvania Law Review* 132 (June 1984): 1023–24 n.245.

16. Luker, *Abortion and the Politics of Motherhood*, pp. 16–39; Shorter, *A History of Women's Bodies*, pp. 223–24.

17. *Betts v. Brady*, 316 U.S. 455 (1942).

18. Law, "Rethinking Sex and the Constitution," p. 981.

19. *Ibid.*

20. *Prince v. Massachusetts*, 321 U.S. 158 (1944).

21. *Griswold v. Connecticut*, 381 U.S. 497 (1965); *Eisenstadt v. Baird*, 405 U.S. 438 (1972).

22. *Doe v. Commonwealth's Attorney for the City of Richmond*, 425 U.S. 901 (1976).

23. *Poe v. Ullman*, 367 U.S. 497 (1961), Justice Harlan dissenting.

24. NOW Bill of Rights, quoted in Robin Morgan, ed., *Sisterhood Is Powerful* (New York: Vintage Books, 1970), pp. 512–14.

25. Lucinda Cisler, "Unfinished Business: Birth Control and Women's Liberation," in Robin Morgan, ed., *Sisterhood Is Powerful* (New York: Vintage Books, 1970), pp. 245–88.

26. Janice Goodman, Rhonda Copelon Schoenbrod and Nancy Stearns, "Roe and Doe: Where Do We Go from Here?" *Women's Rights Law Reporter* 1 (Spring 1973): 29.

27. Equal protection was argued very narrowly in the early cases. Eva R. Rubin, *Abortion, Politics and the Courts* (Westport, Conn.: Greenwood Press, 1982), pp. 49–50. Abortion was not seen as an issue of sex equality; see Law, "Rethinking Sex and the Constitution," pp. 973, 985 n.114, 115.

28. *Truax v. Corrigan*, 257 U.S. 312 (1921).

29. *Lindsley v. Carbonic Natural Gas Co.*, 220 U.S. 61, 78–79 (1911). The classification issue is discussed in Robert J. Harris, *The Quest for Equality: The Constitution, Congress and the Supreme Court* (Baton Rouge: Louisiana State University Press, 1960).

30. *Hoyt v. Florida*, 368 U.S. 57 (1961); *Rostker v. Goldberg*, 453 U.S. 57 (1981).

31. Ann E. Freedman, "Sex Equality, Sex Differences and the Supreme Court" *Yale Law Journal* 92 (May 1984): 913–68.

32. Law, "Rethinking Sex and the Constitution," p. 958.

33. *Ibid.*, pp. 962–63.

34. *Ibid.*, p. 969.

35. *Ibid.*, pp. 1008–1009.

36. Luker, *Abortion and the Politics of Motherhood*, pp. 45–54.

37. Judith Blake, "Abortion and Public Opinion: The 1960–1970 Decade," *Science* 171 (February 1971): 540–49; John E. Jackson and Maris A. Vinovskis, "Public Opinion, Elections and the Single Issue," in Gilbert Y. Steiner, ed., *The Abortion Dispute and the American System* (Washington, D.C.: Brookings Institute, 1983), pp. 64–81.

38. Lawrence M. Friedman, "The Conflict Over Constitutional Legitimacy," in Steiner, ed., *The Abortion Dispute and the American System*, p. 22.

39. *Doe v. Bolton*, 410 U.S. 179 (1973).

40. *Furman v. Georgia*, 408 U.S. 238 (1972).

41. Petchevsky, "Anti-Abortion, Anti-feminism and the Rise of the New Right," pp. 213–20.

42. Harrison, *Our Right to Choose*, p. 38.

43. *Planned Parenthood of Central Missouri v. Danforth*, 428 U.S. 52 (1976).

44. Three decisions: *Bellotti v. Baird* (1979); *HL v. Matheson* (1981), *City of Akron v. Akron Center for Reproductive Health* (1983).

45. *Maher v. Roe*, 432 U.S. 464 (1977); *Beal v. Doe*, 432 U.S. 438 (1977); *Harris v. McRae*, 448 U.S. 297 (1980).

46. Justice Marshall dissenting in *Beal v. Doe*, at p. 456.

47. *City of Akron v. Akron Center for Reproductive Health*, 103 S.Ct. 2481 (1983).

CHAPTER 4

1. Margaret Mead, "Women's Rights: A Cultural Dilemma," in *Women's Role in Contemporary Society: The Report of the New York Commission on Human Rights* (New York: Discus Books, 1972), p. 176.

2. Katharine T. Bartlett, "Pregnancy and the Constitution: The

Uniqueness Trap," *California Law Review* 62 (December 1974): 1532–66, discusses the stereotypes about women that underlie the Supreme Court's handling of pregnancy disability cases.

3. Mirra Komarofsky, "Cultural and Psychohistorical Background of Women's Status in America," in *Women's Role in Contemporary Society*, pp. 63–64.

4. The following sources deal with stereotyping: Arthur G. Miller, "Historical and Contemporary Perspectives on Stereotyping," in *In the Eye of the Beholder* (New York: Praeger, 1982), pp. 27–28; Richard E. Nisbett and Timothy DeCamp Wilson, "Telling More Than We Can Know: Verbal Reports on Mental Processes," *Psychological Review* 84 (May 1977): 231–59; Donald T. Campbell, "Stereotypes and the Perceptions of Group Differences," *American Psychologist* 22 (October 1967): 817–29.

5. *Reed v. Reed*, 404 U.S. 71 (1971); *Frontiero v. Richardson*, 411 U.S. 677 (1973).

6. From an editorial, *New York Herald*, 1850. Reprinted in Eleanor Flexner, *Century of Struggle* (New York: Atheneum Press, 1972), pp. 81–82.

7. Haig Basmajian, "Sexism in the Language of Legislatures and Courts," in Allean P. Nilson et al., eds., *Sexism and Language* (Urbana, Ill., National Council of Teachers of English, 1977), pp. 77–104; see also Elizabeth Nickles and Laura Ashcraft, *The Coming Matriarchy* (New York: Seaview Books, 1981).

8. *Hoyt v. Florida*, 368 U.S. 57 (1961).

9. *Congressional Quarterly*, "Employment in America" (Washington, D.C.: Congressional Quarterly, 1983), pp. 8–9.

10. Changes in the employment of women are documented in the bibliography under "Women and Employment."

11. Sheila B. Kamerman, Alfred J. Kahn and Paul Kingston, *Maternity Policies and Working Women* (New York: Columbia University Press, 1983), pp. 8–9.

12. Eileen Boris and Peter Bardaglio, "The Transformation of Patriarchy: The Historic Role of the State," in Irene Diamond, ed., *Families, Politics and Public Policy* (New York: Longman, 1983), p. 80. For a summary of the situation prior to 1971, see Elizabeth Duncan Koontz, "Childbirth and Childrearing Leave: Job Related Benefits," *New York Law Forum* 17, no. 2 (1971): 480–502. See also Valerie K. Oppenheimer, "A Sociologist's Skepticism," in *Corporate Lib* (Baltimore: Johns Hopkins, University Press, 1973), pp. 30–39, and Ralph E. Smith, ed., *The Subtle Revolution* (Washington, D.C.: Urban Institute, 1979).

13. *Cleveland Board of Education v. La Fleur*, 414 U.S. 632, 642 n.9, states that the records in the courts below indicate that one of the

reasons for teacher pregnancy rules seems to have been the insulation of schoolchildren from the sight of pregnant women.

14. Edward Shorter, *A History of Women's Bodies* (New York: Basic Books, 1982), pp. 288–89.

15. Kristin A. Moore and Sandra L. Hofferth, "Women and Their Children," in Smith, ed., *The Subtle Revolution*, p. 152.

16. Statistics on percentage of women in workforce, 1974: 42.2 percent in 1974.

17. *Congress and the Nation*, vol. 5 (Washington, D.C.: Congressional Quarterly, 1981), pp. 795–96.

18. Kamerman et al., *Maternity Policies and Working Women*, p. 37.

19. Trudy Hayden, "Punishing Pregnancy: Discrimination in Education, Employment and Credit," in Barbara A. Babcock et al., *Sex Discrimination and the Law* (Boston: Little, Brown, 1975).

20. *Cleveland Board of Education v. La Fleur*, 414 U.S. 632 (1974).

21. Karen O'Connor, *Women's Organizations' Use of the Courts* (Lexington, Mass.: Lexington Books, 1980).

22. *Cohen v. Chesterfield County School Board*, 414 U.S. 632 (1974).

23. *Cleveland Board of Education v. La Fleur*, 414 U.S. 632, 639 n.8 lists the mandatory maternity leave cases.

24. O'Connor, *Women's Organizations' Use*, p. 110.

25. *Roe v. Wade*, 410 U.S. 113 (1973).

26. "Note: The Irrebuttable Presumption Doctrine in the Supreme Court," *Harvard Law Review* 87 (May 1974): 1534–56; "Note: Irrebuttable Presumptions: An Illusory Analysis," *Stanford Law Review* 27 (January 1975): 449–73.

27. The *Reed* and *Frontiero* cases, cited above, note 5.

28. *Cleveland Board of Education v. La Fleur*, at 647 n.13.

29. *Cohen v. Chesterfield County School Board*, 474 F2d 395 (4th cir. 1973).

30. David L. Kirp and Dorothy Robyn, "Pregnancy, Justice and the Justices," *Texas Law Review* 57 (August 1979): 947–64.

31. Nan D. Hunter, "Women and Child Support," in Diamond, ed., *Families, Politics and Public Policy*, pp. 213–15.

32. Dorothy Haener, "Maternity and Other Fringe Benefits," in *Women's Role in Contemporary Society*, pp. 364–79.

33. *Congress and the Nation*, Congressional Quarterly Service, vol. 5, pp. 795–96: "Pregnancy Disability."

34. *Geduldig v. Aiello*, 417 U.S. 484 (1974). See, on this case, Diane L. Zimmerman, "Comment: Geduldig v. Aiello: Pregnancy Classifications and the Definition of Sex Discrimination," *Columbia Law Review* 75 (March 1975): 441–82.

35. *Geduldig v. Aiello*, 417 U.S. 484, p. 496.

36. *Ibid.*, p. 497 n.20.

37. *Ibid.*, pp. 492–96.

38. Kirp and Robyn, "Pregnancy, Justice and the Justices," p. 955.

39. U.S. Congress, Senate, Committee on Human Resources S. Report 95–331, 95th Cong., 1st sess., 1977. S. 995, Amending Title VII, Civil Rights Act of 1964.

40. Bob Woodward and Scott Armstrong, *The Brethen* (New York: Simon and Schuster, 1979), p. 255.

41. *General Electric Co. v. Gilbert*, 429 U.S. 125 (1976).

42. 429 U.S. 125, p. 136.

43. Dissent at pp. 146–60.

44. *Nashville Gas Co. v. Satty*, 434 U.S. 136, 1977. See, on this and the Gilbert case, Ellen T. Taylor, "Comment: Differential Treatment of Pregnancy in Employment: The Impact of G.E. Co. v. Gilbert and Nashville Gas v. Satty," *Harvard Civil Rights-Civil Liberties Law Review* (Summer 1978): 717–50.

45. "Pregnancy Disability," *Congress and the Nation*, vol. 5, pp. 796–97.

46. U.S. Code Congressional and Administrative News, 95th Cong., 2d sess., 1978, vol. 5. Legislative History, Civil Rights Act of 1964, pp. 4749–55 (St. Paul, Minn.: West Publishing Co., 1979). The Pregnancy Disability Act was an amendment to the Civil Rights Act of 1964, passed in 1978.

47. Justice Brennan dissenting in *G.E. v. Gilbert*, at pp. 159–60.

48. *Newport News Shipbuilding and Dry Dock Co. v. EEOC*, 103 S.Ct. 2622 (1983).

49. Senate Report 95–331, quoted in the Opinion of the Court at 2628, 2629 n.17, 20.

50. Ruby Ray Seward, *The American Family: A Demographic History* (Beverly Hills, Calif.: Sage Publications, 1978), pp. 170–71.

51. Jane Flax. "Contemporary American Families: Decline or Transformation," in Diamond, ed., *Families, Politics and Public Policy*, pp. 26–27.

52. Sandra L. Hofferth and Kristin A. Moore, "Women's Employment and Marriage," in Smith, ed., *The Subtle Revolution*, pp. 108–10.

53. Babcock et al., "Statistical Patterns of Divorce," *Sex Discrimination and the Law*, pp. 677–78.

CHAPTER 5

1. U.S. Senate, Committee on Labor and Human Resources, Report on S.1090, "Adolescent Family Life," July 21, 1981. The purpose of the Adolescent Family Life Bill was "to promote self discipline and chastity

and other positive, family centered approaches to the problems of adolescent promiscuity and adolescent pregnancy."

The Committee report stated that the birth rate was declining in the population generally, but figures available by 1978 showed the incidence of teenage sex was rising, and compared the number of births and the abortion rate. The Committee Report (p. 2) also stated that the illegitimacy rate was about 50 percent for those nineteen or under having babies.

2. *Carey v. Population Services International*, 431 U.S. 678 (1977); *Michael M. v. Sonoma County Court*, 450 U.S. 462 (1981); *HL v. Matheson*, 450 U.S. 379 (1981).

3. Alan Guttmacher Institute, *Eleven Million Teenagers: What Can Be Done About the Epidemic of Adolescent Pregnancies in the United States?* (New York: Planned Parenthood of America, 1976). See Maris A. Vinovskis, "An 'Epidemic' of Adolescent Pregnancy? Some Historical Considerations," *Journal of Family History* 6 (Summer 1981): 208.

4. Senate Report on S.1090, p. 2; Anne L. Harper, "Teenage Sexuality and Public Policy: An Agenda for Gender Education," in Irene Diamond, ed., *Families, Politics and Public Policy* (New York: Longman, 1983), pp. 220–35.

5. Edward Shorter, *The Making of the Modern Family* (New York: Basic Books, Harper Torchbooks Edition, 1975), pp. 108–19. But see contra Ira L. Reiss, "The Sexual Renaissance: A Summary and Analysis," *Journal of Social Issues* 22 (April 1966): 123–37. See also Kenneth L. Cannon and Richard Long, "Premarital Sexual Behavior in the Sixties," in Marvin B. Sussman, *Sourcebook in Marriage and the Family*, 4th ed. (Boston: Houghton Mifflin, 1974).

6. Shorter, *The Making of the Modern Family*, p. 81.

7. *Ibid.*, p. 84.

8. Alan Guttmacher Institute, *Teenage Pregnancy: The Problem That Hasn't Gone Away* (New York: Planned Parenthood of America, 1981), p. 20. See John F. Kantner and Melvin Zelnik, "Sexual Activity, Contraceptive Use and Pregnancy Among Metropolitan Area Teenagers, 1971–1979," *Family Planning Perspectives* 12 (September/October 1980): 230–37.

9. See Andrew Hacker's long essay review, "Farewell to the Family?" *New York Review of Books*, March 18, 1982, pp. 37–44.

10. Alan Guttmacher Institute, *Eleven Million Teenagers*, pp. 7–20.

11. Anne L. Harper, "Teenage Sexuality and Public Policy," in Diamond, ed., *Families, Politics and Public Policy*, pp. 220–21.

12. Alan Guttmacher Institute, *Teenage Pregnancy*, p. 9.

13. Report on S.1090, p. 2.

14. Alan Guttmacher Institute, *Teenage Pregnancy*, p. 11.

15. Report on S. 1090, p. 2.

16. William Raspberry, "U.S. Teen-Agers and Sex," *Washington Post*, March 15, 1985, A 21. See also Barbara Ehrenreich, "Family Feud on the Left: The Social Issue Game," *Nation*, March 13, 1982, pp. 289, 303–306.

17. Ehrenreich, "Family Feud," p. 289; Shelah Gilbert Leader, "Fiscal Policy and Family Structure," in Diamond, ed., *Families, Politics and Public Policy*, p. 139.

18. See Kristin Luker, *Abortion and the Politics of Motherhood* (Berkeley: University of California Press, 1984), pp. 159–75.

19. *Carey v. Population Services International*, 431 U.S. 678 (1977), at pp. 695–96.

20. *Griswold v. Connecticut*, 381 U.S. 479 (1965); *Roe v. Wade* 410 U.S. 113 (1973); *Eisenstadt v. Baird*, 405 U.S. 438 (1972).

21. Justice White concurring, p. 703.

22. Opinion of the Court, p. 695.

23. Justice Stevens concurring, p. 715.

24. Justice Rehnquist dissenting, p. 717.

25. *Michael M. v. Sonoma County Court* (1981).

26. Arnold H. Loewy, "Returned to the Pedestal: The Supreme Court and Gender Classification Cases: 1980 Term," *North Carolina Law Review* 60 (October 1981): 99.

27. Brennan opinion, p. 495 n.10.

28. Robert L. Griswold, *Family and Divorce in California, 1850–1890* (Albany: State University of New York Press, 1982), pp. 70–75. Griswold cites Nancy Cott, "Passionlessness: An Interpretation of Victorian Sexual Ideology, 1790–1850," *Signs* 3 (Fall 1975): 15–29.

29. Leo Kanowitz, *Women and the Law* (Albuquerque: University of New Mexico Press, 1969), pp. 18–25.

30. *Ibid.*, pp. 20–1.

31. Karen DeCrow, *Sexist Justice* (New York: Random House, 1974), p. 266.

32. Haig Basmajian, "Sexism in the Language of Legislatures and Courts," in Allean P. Nilson et al., eds., *Sexism and Language* (Urbana, Ill.: National Council of Teachers of English, 1977), pp. 77–104, discusses some of the stereotypes about women in legislation and judicial opinions.

33. Justice Blackmun concurring, pp. 481–87.

34. Justice Stephens dissenting, pp. 496–502.

35. Justice Brennan dissenting, pp. 488–96.

36. See N.C. General Statutes 14–27.4, Subsection (a)(2).

37. Loewy, "Returned to the Pedestal," p. 99.

38. Justice Stevens dissenting, p. 496.

39. Dissenting opinion, Justice Brennan, p. 494 n.8.

40. *Planned Parenthood of Central Missouri v. Danforth*, 428 U.S. 52 (1976).

41. *Bellotti v. Baird* (Bellotti II), 443 U.S. 662 (1979).

42. Walter Wadlington, Charles H. Whitebread and Samuel M. Davis, *Children in the Legal System, Cases and Materials* (Mineola, N.Y.: Foundation Press, 1983), pp. 893–94.

43. Utah statute, Utah Code, Ann. sec. 76–7–304 (1974); Utah Code, Ann. sec. 76–7–304 (2) 1978.

44. *HL v. Matheson*, dissenting opinion, p. 425.

45. R. D. Laing and David Cooper, among others, have discussed the conflicts within families and their psychological effects on family members. R. D. Laing and A. Esterson, *Sanity, Madness and the Family: Families of Schizophrenics* (Harmondsworth, Middlesex, England: Penguin Books, 1964); R. D. Laing, *The Politics of the Family* (New York: Vintage/Random House, 1972); David Cooper, *The Death of the Family* (New York: Vintage Books, 1971). For interviews illustrating parental concern about minors and abortion, see Fred M. Frohock, *Abortion: A Case Study in Law and Morals* (Westport, Conn.: Greenwood Press, 1983), pp. 73–75, 85.

46. Nadine Cohodas, "Alternatives to Abortion. Federal Abortion Alternatives Cut by Reagan Administration" (CQ Special Report), *Congressional Quarterly Weekly Report*, November 17, 1984, pp. 2949–55.

47. *Ibid.*, p. 2952.

48. The proposed Family Protection Act was discussed in *Congressional Quarterly Weekly Report*, October 3, 1981, p. 1916. The chief sponsors of this bill were Senators Roger W. Jepsen (R., Iowa) and Paul Laxalt (R., Nev.). In the House, Representative Albert Lee Smith, Jr. (R., Ala.) sponsored the bill.

49. Senator Denton's legislation is discussed in Harper, "Teenage Sexuality," pp. 226–28. The Family Life Bill (S.1090) was introduced in April 1981. The stated purpose of the legislation was: "To promote self-discipline and chastity and other positive, family centered approaches to the problem of adolescent promiscuity and adolescent pregnancy." The Adolescent Family Life Program has been in effect since 1981.

50. "Teen-Age Birth Control Rule Implemented," *Washington Post*, January 27, 1983, A 1; Jeremiah A. Denton, Jr., "Parents Ought to Know," *Washington Post*, March 2, 1983, A 23; "Rule Requiring Parental Notification for Contraceptives Is Rejected Again," *Washington Post*, July 9, 1983, A 1.

51. *Planned Parenthood Federation of America, Inc. v. Heckler*, 52 LW 2128 (1983). See also *N.Y. v. Heckler*, Court of Appeals, 2d Circuit, 52 LW 2243 (1983).

52. "Revised 'Baby Doe' Rule Offered," (Raleigh) *News and Observer*, July 1, 1983, 7A; Gordon B. Avery, "Big Brother in the Nursery," *Washington Post*, March 23, 1983, A 25; Juan Williams, "Government Child-Care Spending Down by 14 Percent, Group Finds," *Washington Post*, October 3, 1983, A 4; "HHS Orders Treatment for 'Baby Doe' Infants", *Washington Post*, April 16, 1985, A 17. Congress authorized the new regulations by adding provisions to child abuse laws. States must implement the regulations by October 9, 1985, or lose child abuse grants.

53. *City of Akron v. Akron Center for Reproductive Health, Inc.*, 103 S.Ct. 2481 (1983); *Planned Parenthood Association v. Ashcroft*, 103 S.Ct. 2517 (1983); *Simopoulos v. Virginia*, 103 S.Ct. 2532 (1983).

CHAPTER 6

1. Carl F. Kaestle, *Pillars of the Republic: Common Schools and American Society, 1780–1860* (New York: Hill and Wang, 1983), p. 158.

2. *Wisconsin v. Yoder*, 406 U.S. 205 (1972).

3. *Meyer v. Nebraska*, 262 U.S. 390 (1923).

4. *Pierce v. Society of Sisters*, 268 U.S. 510 (1925).

5. Two early school cases are *Cumming v. Board of Education*, 175 U.S. 528 (1899), and *Gong Lum v. Rice*, 275 U.S. 78 (1927).

6. Anson Phelps Stokes, *Church and State in the United States*, 3 vols. (New York: Harper, 1950), v. 2, pp. 738–39.

7. *Meyer v. Nebraska*, p. 402.

8. Stokes, *Church and State*, v. 2, p. 737.

9. See *Pierce v. Society of Sisters, passim*.

10. Stephen Arons, "The Separation of School and State: Pierce Reconsidered," *Harvard Education Review* 46, no. 1 (February 1976): 76–104.

11. *Everson v. Board of Education*, 330 U.S. 1 (1947).

12. *Meyer v. Nebraska*, p. 402.

13. *Reynolds v. United States*, 98 U.S. 145 (1879), *Prince v. Massachusetts*, 321 U.S. 158 (1944), *Braunfeld v. Brown*, 366 U.S. 599 (1961).

14. Richard C. Cortner, *The Supreme Court and Civil Liberties Policy* (Palo Alto, Calif.: Mayfield, 1975), pp. 158–70; Stephen T. Knudsen, "The Education of the Amish Child," *University of California Law Review* 62, no. 5 (December 1974): 1506–31.

15. *Garber v. Kansas*, 389 U.S. 51 (1967).

16. *Wisconsin v. Yoder*, p. 225.

17. Richard C. Cortner, *The Supreme Court*, pp. 160–62.

18. *Sherbert v. Verner*, 376 U.S. 398 (1963).

19. See cases in note 13.

20. See *People ex rel Wallace v. Labrenz*, 104 N.E. 2d 769 (1952).

21. Opinion of the Court, pp. 213–14, 231–33.

22. Quoting *Brown v. Board of Education*, p. 238.

23. *Tinker v. Des Moines*, 393 U.S. 503 (1969).

24. *Wisconsin v. Yoder*, Douglas dissenting, p. 241.

25. Brigitte Berger and Peter L. Berger. *The War Over the Family* (Garden City, N.Y.: Anchor Press/ Doubleday, 1984), pp. 199, 210–11, 212–14.

26. Unpublished memo and brief, Memorandum to Hon. Rufus L. Edmisten, Attorney General of North Carolina, November 3, 1977. William B. Ball, the Harrisburg attorney who represented the Amish in the *Yoder* litigation, set out the legal argument for deregulating religious schools.

27. Kaestle, *Pillars of the Republic*, ch. 5. On changing attitudes toward the school system, see Colin Greer, *The Great School Legend* (New York: Basic Books, 1972); Michael S. Katz, *A History of Compulsory Education Laws* (Bloomington, Ind.: Phi Delta Kappa Educational Foundation, 1976); Diane Ravitch, *The Revisionists Revised: A Critique of the Radical Attack on the Schools* (New York: Basic Books, 1978).

28. Kaestle, *Pillars of the Republic*, p. 101.

29. Joel Spring, ''The Evolving Political Structure of American Schooling,'' in Robert B. Everhart, ed., *The Public School Monopoly*, (San Francisco: Pacific Institute for Public Policy Research, 1982), pp. 89–95.

30. Virginia Davis Nordin and William Lloyd Turner, ''More than Segregation Academies: The Growing Protestant Fundamentalist Schools,'' *Phi Delta Kappan* (February 1980): 391–94.

31. *Ibid.*

32. Tim LaHaye, *The Battle for the Family* (Old Tappan, N.J.: Fleming H. Revell Co., 1982), pp. 87–88.

33. See *Medeiros v. Kiyosaki*, 478 P.2d 314 (1970). Supreme Court of Hawaii (parents' rights to withdraw children from sex education classes).

34. *Tinker v. Des Moines*, 393 U.S. 503 (1969); *Goss v. Lopez*, 419 U.S. 565 (1975).

35. *Ingraham v. Wright*, 430 U.S. 651 (1977).

36. *Board of Education of Island Trees Union Free School District v. Pico*, 102 S.Ct. 2799 (1982).

37. See *New Jersey v. TLO*, 105 S.Ct. 733, at pp. 742, 749, 752.

38. See Brennan opinion, p. 2806, Burger opinion, dissenting, p. 2819.

39. Both the opinion of the Court and the dissent cite *Ambach v. Norwich*, 441 U.S. 68, p. 77 (1979), as establishing this principle.

40. Because there had been a summary judgment by the District Court, all the Supreme Court was required to decide was whether the Court of Appeals had been correct in holding that there were material issues of fact that should have gone to trial.

41. *Island Trees*, p. 2810.

42. Dissent, *Island Trees*, p. 2819.

43. *Island Trees*, Rehnquist dissenting, p. 2829.

44. *New Jersey v. TLO*, 105 S.Ct. 733, 1985.

45. *Ibid.*, at p. 744; citing *Terry v. Ohio*, 392 U.S. 1 (1969).

46. Blackmun dissent, *New Jersey v. TLO*, at p. 749.

47. *Ibid.*, at p. 747.

48. *Ingraham v. Wright*, 430 U.S. 651 (1977).

49. *Mueller v. Allen*, 103 S.Ct. 3062 (1983). This decision was the first sign that the Court might relax its antagonistic attitude toward financial aid to religious schools. The Establishment Clause cases decided in the last ten years do not entirely preclude a change in direction.

CHAPTER 7

1. Betty E. Cogswell and Marvin B. Sussman, "Changing Family and Marriage Forms: Complications for Human Service Systems," in Marvin B. Sussman, ed., *Sourcebook in Marriage and the Family*, 4th ed. (Boston: Houghton Mifflin, 1974), p. 95.

2. Robert A. Burt, "The Constitution of the Family," *Supreme Court Review* (1979): 329–95 (Chicago: University of Chicago Press, 1980).

3. *Moore v. City of East Cleveland, Ohio*, 431 U.S. 494 (1977).

4. *Moore v. City of East Cleveland, Ohio*, at p. 503.

5. *Reynolds v. U.S.*, 98 U.S. 145 (1878).

6. *Loving v. Virginia*, 388 U.S. 1 (1967).

7. State regulations of marriage, see Harry D. Krause, *Family Law: Cases, Comments and Questions*. 2d ed. (St. Paul, Minn.: West Publishing Co., 1983), ch. 1.

8. *Moore v. City of East Cleveland*, pp. 503–504.

9. *Moore v. City of East Cleveland*, p. 504 n.13, 14, citing J. Harvie Wilkinson and G. Edward White, "Constitutional Protection for Personal Lifestyles," *Cornell Law Review* 62 (March 1977): 563–625.

10. *Moore v. City of East Cleveland*, p. 504.

11. Hyman Rodman, "Lower-Class Family Behavior," in Arlene S. and Jerome H. Skolnick, eds., *Family in Transition* (Boston: Little, Brown, 1971), pp. 410–13.

12. Jacobus ten Broek, "Present Status and Constitutionality of the Family Law of the Poor," in Joel F. Handler, ed., *Family Law and the Poor*, (Westport, Conn.: Greenwood Press, 1971), pp. 145–213.

13. *Ibid.*, p. 207.

14. Charles Reich,, "Individual Rights and Social Welfare: The Emerging Legal Issues," *Yale Law Journal* 74 (June 1965): 1256; "Symposium: Law of the Poor," *California Law Review* 54 (May 1965): 319.

15. Aryeh Neier, *Only Judgment: The Limits of Litigation in Social Change* (Middletown, Conn.: Wesleyan University Press, 1982), ch. 8. Jack Greenberg, *Judicial Process and Social Change* (St. Paul, Minn.: West Publishing Co., 1977), ch. 3.

16. *King v. Smith*, 392 U.S. 309 (1968).

17. *Shapiro v. Thompson*, 394 U.S. 618 (1969); *Goldberg v. Kelly*, 397 U.S. 25 (1970); *Wheeler v. Montgomery*, 397 U.S. 280 (1970).

18. *Dandridge v. Williams*, 397 U.S. 471, 1970 (1970).

19. *Wyman v. James*, 400 U.S. 399 (1971).

20. *U.S. Department of Agriculture v. Moreno*, 413 U.S. 528; *U.S.D.A. v. Murray*, 413 U.S. 508 (1973).

21. *New Jersey Welfare Rights Organization v. Cahill*, 411 U.S. 619 (1973).

22. Quoting Dr. Ron Haskins, Associate Director of the Bush Institute for Child and Family Policy, "Symposium to Deal with Enforcement of Child Support," interview, *Chapel Hill Newspaper*, April 16, 1984.

23. *Ibid*.

24. *Zablocki v. Redhail*, 434 U.S. 374 (1978).

25. *Ibid*.

26. *Ibid*., p. 386.

27. *Ibid*., p. 387.

28. *Ibid*., p. 404.

29. *Ibid*., p. 390.

30. *Beal v. Doe*, 432 U.S. 438 (1977), *Maher v. Roe*, 432 U.S. 464 (1977).

31. See the much publicized case of *Marvin v. Marvin*, 557 P2d. 106 (1977), Supreme Court of California.

32. Larry I. Palmer, "Adoption: A Plea for Realistic Constitutional Decision-making," *Columbia Human Rights Law Review* 11 (Spring-Summer 1980): 1–49; Gilbert Y. Steiner, *The Futility of Family Policy* (Washington, D.C.: Brookings Institute, 1981), p. 130.

33. Joseph Goldstein, Anna Freud and Albert J. Solnit, *Beyond the Best Interests of the Child* (New York: Free Press, 1973).

34. *Smith v. Organization of Foster Families for Equality and Reform*, 431 U.S. 816 (1977), p. 843.

35. *Smith v. OFFER*, p. 843.

36. *Ibid*., p. 845.

37. *Caban v. Mohammad*, 441 U.S. 380 (1979); *Quilloin v. Walcott*, 434 U.S. 246 (1978); and *Lehr v. Robertson*, 103 S.Ct. 2985 (1983).

38. *Lehr v. Robertson*, p. 2999.

39. Richard F. Babcock, *The Zoning Game* (Madison: University of Wisconsin Press, 1966).

40. 272 U.S. 365 (1926).

41. Babcock, *The Zoning Game*, p. 4.

42. *Village of Belle Terre v. Boraas*, 416 U.S. 1 (1974).

43. *Ibid.*, p. 9.

44. *Public Utilities Commission v. Pollak*, 343 U.S. 451 (1952).

45. See *City of Santa Barbara v. Adamson*, 610 P.2d 436 (1980), and cases discussed in the opinions.

46. *Moore v. City of East Cleveland*, pp. 505–506.

47. *Hollenbaugh v. Carnegie Free Library*, 578 F2d 1374 (1978); *cert. denied*, 439 U.S. 1052 (1978).

48. See *City of Santa Barbara v. Adamson*, above, note 45.

CHAPTER 8

1. *Eddings v. Oklahoma*, 102 S.Ct. 869 (1982), evidence submitted in mitigation, death penalty argument.

2. David Rothman, *The Discovery of Asylum* (Boston: Little, Brown, 1971), pp. 65–68; Robert H. Mnookin, *Child, Family and State: Problems and Materials on Children and the Law* (Boston: Little, Brown, 1978), p. 515.

3. *Smith v. Organization of Foster Families for Equality and Reform*, 431 U.S. 816 (1977), *Parham v. JR*, 442 U.S. 584 (1979), *Santosky v. Kramer*, 455 U.S. 745 (1982).

4. *Smith v. OFFER*, p. 843.

5. *Ibid.*, p. 843.

6. *Parham v. JR*, p. 602.

7. *Ibid.*, p. 621, Stewart concurring.

8. *Ibid.*, p. 603.

9. *Ibid.* See cases cited on p. 602.

10. *Smith v. OFFER*, p. 844.

11. *Parham v. JR*, p. 602.

12. *Parham v. JR*, p. 603. It has been pointed out that Blackstone and Kent have been quoted out of context for some of these statements. See Walter Wadlington, Charles H. Whitebread and Samuel M. Davis, *Children and the Legal System, Cases and Materials* (Mineola, N.Y.: Foundation Press, 1983), p. 182.

13. *Santosky v. Kramer*, pp. 753–54.

14. *Parham v. JR*, p. 598.

15. *Parham v. JR*, p. 599.

16. Lloyd de Mause, "The Evolution of Childhood," in *The History of Childhood* (New York: Psychohistory Press, 1974), pp. 1–75.

17. Murray A. Straus, Richard J. Gelles and Suzanne K. Steinmetz, *Behind Closed Doors: Violence in the American Family* (Garden City, N.Y.: Anchor Press/Doubleday, 1981). "Survey Hints at Scope of Family Violence," (Raleigh) *News and Observer*, April 23, 1984, p. 8A.

18. Kenneth Keniston and the Carnegie Council on Children, *All Our*

Children: The American Family Under Pressure (New York and London: Harcourt Brace Jovanovich, Harvest Book ed., 1977), p. 183.

19. Sir William Blackstone, *Commentaries on the Laws of England*, 4th ed., James DeWitt Andrews, ed. (Chicago: Callaghan and Co., 1899), Book I, ch. 16.

20. Sanford N. Katz, in *The Youngest Minority*, vol. 2, American Bar Association, Section on Family Law (Chicago: ABA Press, 1977), pp. 4–5.

21. *Ibid.*

22. See Justice Brennan dissenting in *Parham v. JR*, 442 U.S. 584, pp. 628–29 (1979).

23. Sanford N. Katz, "Foster Parents Versus Agencies: A Case Study in the Judicial Application of the 'Best Interests of the Child' Doctrine," *Michigan Law Review* 65 (November 1966): 145–70.

24. Beatrice Gross and Ronald Gross, eds., *The Children's Rights Movement: Overcoming the Oppression of Young People* (Garden City, N.Y.: Anchor Press/Doubleday, 1977); David Gottlieb, ed., *Children's Liberation* (Englewood Cliffs, N.J.: Prentice-Hall, 1973); Bruce R. Stewart, "Recognizing the Competing Interests of Parent and Child," *School Law Bulletin* 13 (April 1982): 1–9. See the following cases: *In re Gault*, 387 U.S. 1 (1967); *Tinker v. Des Moines School District*, 393 U.S. 503 (1969); *Goss v. Lopez*, 419 U.S. 565 (1975); *Breed v. Jones*, 421 U.S. 519 (1975).

25. *Planned Parenthood of Central Missouri v. Danforth*, 428 U.S. 52 (1976).

26. *Bellotti v. Baird*, 443 U.S. 622 (1979).

27. *Roe v. Wade*, 410 U.S. 113 (1973).

28. *HL v. Matheson*, 450 U.S. 398 (1981).

29. *Smith v. Organization of Foster Families for Equality and Reform*, 431 U.S. 816, 827–28 (1977). See, generally, Gilbert Y. Steiner, *The Futility of Family Policy* (Washington, D.C.: Brookings Institute, 1981), ch. 5.

30. Joseph Goldstein, Anna Freud and Albert J. Solnit, *Beyond the Best Interests of the Child* (New York: Free Press, 1973).

31. *Mathews v. Eldridge*, 424 U.S. 319, 335 (1976).

32. *Smith v. OFFER* (1977).

33. Keniston, *All Our Children*, p. 189.

34. *Parham v. JR*, 442 U.S. 584 (1979).

35. Keniston, *All Our Children*, p. 193.

36. *Ibid.*; Fred R. Mabbut, "Juveniles, Mental Hospital Commitment and Civil Rights: The Case of Parham v. J.R.," *Journal of Family Law* 19 (November 1980): 27–64.

37. Katz, *The Youngest Minority*, vol. 2, pp. 4–5.

38. Keniston, *All Our Children*, p. 192; Curt R. Bartol, "Parens Patriae: Poltergeist of Mental Health Law," In Richard A.L. Gambitta et al.,

eds., *Governing Through Courts* (Beverly Hills, Calif., Sage Publications, 1981), pp. 132–48.

39. *Parham v. JR*, pp. 602, 604.

40. *Ibid.*, p. 602, Justice Stewart concurring, p. 621.

41. Justice Brennan dissenting, pp. 628–29; Mabbut, "Juveniles, Mental Hospital Commitment and Civil Rights", pp. 55–59.

42. *Parham v. JR*, p. 598.

43. Marsha Garrison, "Why Terminate Parental Rights?" *Stanford Law Review* 35 (February 1983): 423–96.

44. *Lassiter v. Department of Social Services of Durham County, North Carolina*, 453 U.S. 927 (1981).

45. In 1981, shortly after the Lassiter decision, the North Carolina legislature amended the General Statutes to provide counsel to indigent parents at termination proceedings automatically, unless waived. See G.S. 7-A–289.23, 289.27, 289.30, 415(a). See also *In re Clark*, 303 N.C. 592, 281 S.E. 47, 1981.

46. *Little v. Streeter*, 452 U.S. 1 (1981).

47. *Boddie v. Connecticut*, 401 U.S. 371 (1971).

48. Margaret Emanuel Schmid, "Note: Due Process—The Indigent Parent's Right to State-Furnished Counsel in Parental Status Termination Proceedings: An Examination of the Supreme Court's Methodology." *Wake Forest Law Review* 17 (December 1981): 961–89, at p. 986. Schmid identifies the problem of the balancing approach as focusing on "the subjective value of various interests rather than on the requirements for a fair hearing" (p. 989).

49. *Santosky v. Kramer*, 102 S.Ct. 1388 (1982).

50. *Mathews v. Eldridge*, 424 U.S. 319, 335 (1976).

51. *Santosky*, 1397–98; see Krause, *Family Law*, p. 1062, on termination proceedings.

52. Katz, *The Youngest Minority*, vol. 2, pp. 4–5.

53. Keniston, *All Our Children*, pp. 185–86.

54. *Ibid.* ch. 9.

CHAPTER 9

1. Walter Lippmann, *Public Opinion* (New York: Macmillan, 1922; reprint ed., Macmillan Paperbacks, 1960), p. 31.

2. Brigitte Berger and Peter L. Berger. *The War Over the Family* (Garden City, N.Y.: Anchor Press/Doubleday, 1984); Tim LaHaye, *The Battle for the Family* (Old Tappan, N.J.: Fleming H. Revell Co., 1982); Gilbert Y. Steiner, *The Futility of Family Policy* (Washington, D.C.: Brookings Institute, 1981).

3. Donald L. Horowitz, *The Courts and Social Policy* (Washington, D.C.: Brookings Institute, 1977), pp. 45–51.

4. Mark De Wolfe Howe, ed., *Holmes-Pollock Letters*, 2d ed. (Cambridge: Belknap Press, 1961), Holmes to Pollock, May 25, 1906.

5. Quoted in Max Lerner, ed., *The Mind and Faith of Justice Holmes* (New York: Modern Library, 1943), p. 400.

6. *Hoyt v. Florida*, 368 U.S. 57 (1961).

7. See Gerald Gunther, *Cases and Materials on Constitutional Law* (Mineola, N.Y.: Foundation Press, 1980), pp. 674–75.

8. Laurence Tribe, *American Constitutional Law* (Mineola, N.Y.: Foundation Press, 1978), p. 1065.

9. Sylvia A. Law, "Rethinking Sex and the Constitution," *University of Pennsylvania Law Review* 132 (June 1984): 955–1040.

10. See ch. 2.

11. Hyman Rodman, "Lower-Class Family Behavior," in Arlene S. Skolnick and Jerome H. Skolnick, eds., *Family in Transition* (Boston: Little, Brown, 1981), p. 410.

12. 431 U.S. 678 (1977), Stevens opinion, at p. 713.

13. See, for example, R. D. Laing and A. Esterson, *Sanity, Madness and the Family* (Harmondsworth, Middlesex, England: Penguin Books, 1964); David Cooper, *The Death of the Family* (New York: Vintage Books, 1971).

14. See Berger and Berger, *The War Over the Family*, ch. 9.

15. See Steiner, *The Futility of Family Policy*, pp. 137–41.

16. Gunther, *Constitutional Law*, pp. 570–71 ff.

17. Kenneth L. Karst and Harold W. Horowitz, "Reitman v. Mulkey: A Telophase of Substantive Equal Protection," *Supreme Court Review* (1967): 39–80.

18. *Ingraham v. Wright*, 430 U.S. 651 (1977).

19. *Ginsberg v. New York*, 390 U.S. 629 (1968); 102 S.Ct. 2799, (1982).

20. Thomas C. Grey, "Eros, Civilization and the Burger Court," *Law and Contemporary Problems* 43, no. 3 (1980): 83–100. See the discussion of this issue in Ronald Dworkin, *New York Review of Books*, November 8, 1984.

21. Berger and Berger, *The War Over the Family*, ch. 8.

22. Arthur S. Miller, *The Supreme Court and American Capitalism* (New York: Free Press, 1968), p. 230.

Bibliography

Some excellent new work on family and reproductive issues has been done by feminist scholars, lawyers and political scientists. These books and articles give new perspectives on old problems. I found the articles by Zillah Eisenstein, Jane Flax, Ann E. Freedman, Sylvia A. Law and Rosalind P. Petchevsky and the books by Beverly W. Harrison and Kristin Luker especially enlightening.

I have relied very heavily on Harry D. Krause's books on illegitimacy and family law. I found the article by Robert A. Burt in *The Supreme Court Review* (1979) provocative and his description of one of the roles of courts as that of "provoking and prolonging orderly conflict" very useful. Andrew Hacker's long review of family books in *The New York Review of Books*, the essay "Rethinking the Family" by Arlene S. and Jerome Skolnick, and Lawrence M. Friedman's article on *Roe v. Wade* in Gilbert Y. Steiner's volume *The Abortion Dispute and the American System* all gave me a great deal to think about. None of these authors should be held responsible for my conclusions, however.

GENERAL STUDIES ON THE FAMILY

Berger, Brigitte, and Peter L. Berger. *The War Over the Family*, Garden City, N.Y.: Anchor Press/Doubleday, 1984.

Diamond, Irene, ed. *Families, Politics and Public Policy*. New York: Longman, 1983.

Family Service America. *The State of Families 1984–85*. New York: Family
    Service America, 1984.

Flax, Jane. "Contemporary American Families: Decline or Transfor-
    mation." In Irene Diamond, ed. *Families, Politics and Public Policy*,
    pp. 21–40.

Goode, William J. *Readings on the Family and Society*. Englewood Cliffs,
    N.J.: Prentice-Hall, 1964.

Hacker, Andrew. "Farewell to the Family?" *New York Review of Books*,
    March 18, 1982.

Keniston, Kenneth, and The Carnegie Council on Children. *All Our
    Children: The American Family Under Pressure*. New York: Harcourt
    Brace Jovanovich (Harvest Book ed.), 1977.

LaHaye, Tim. *The Battle for the Family*. Old Tappan, N.J.: Fleming H.
    Revell Co., 1982.

Laing, R. D., and A. Esterson. *Sanity, Madness and the Family: Families
    of Schizophrenics*. Harmondsworth, Middlesex, England: Penguin
    Books, 1964.

Lasch, Christopher. *Haven in a Heartless World: The Family Besieged*. New
    York: Basic Books, 1977.

Pogrebin, Letty Cottin. *Family Politics*. New York: McGraw-Hill, 1983.

Seward, Ruby Ray. *The American Family: A Demographic History*. Beverly
    Hills, Calif.: Sage Publications, 1978.

Shorter, Edward. *The Making of the Modern Family*. New York: Basic
    Books, 1975.

Skolnick, Arlene S., and Jerome H. Skolnick, eds. *Family in Transition*.
    Boston: Little, Brown, 1971.

Sussman, Marvin B., ed. *Sourcebook in Marriage and the Family*. 4th ed.
    Boston: Houghton Mifflin, 1974.

U.S. Department of Commerce, Bureau of the Census. *Current Popu-
    lation Reports*, Series P–20.

STEREOTYPES AND FAMILY IDEOLOGY

Barnard, Jessie. *The Future of Motherhood*. New York: Penguin Books,
    1974.

Basmajian, Haig. "Sexism in the Language of Legislatures and Courts."
    In Allean P. Nilson et al., eds. *Sexism and Language*. Urbana, Ill.:
    National Council of Teachers of English, 1977.

Boris, Eileen, and Peter Bardaglio. "The Transformation of Patriarchy:
    The Historic Role of the State." In Irene Diamond, ed. *Families,
    Politics and Public Policy*. New York: Longman, 1983.

Campbell, Donald T. "Stereotypes and the Perceptions of Group Dif-
    ferences." *American Psychologist* 22 (October 1967): 817–29.

Cott, Nancy. "Passionlessness: An Interpretation of Victorian Sexual Ideology, 1790–1850." *Signs* 3 (Fall 1975): 15–29.

DeCrow, Karen. *Sexist Justice*. New York: Random House, 1974.

Griswold, Robert L. *Family and Divorce in California, 1850–1890: Victorian Illusions and Everyday Realities*. Albany: State University of New York Press, 1982.

Kaestle, Carl F. *Pillars of the Republic: Common Schools and American Society, 1780–1860*. New York: Hill and Wang, 1983.

Kanowitz, Leo. *Women and the Law*. Albuquerque, N.M.: University of New Mexico Press, 1969.

Lippmann, Walter. *Public Opinion*. Reprint of the 1922 ed. New York: Macmillan Paperbacks, 1960.

Loewy, Arnold H. "Returned to the Pedestal: The Supreme Court and Gender Classification Cases: 1980 Term." *North Carolina Law Review* 60 (October 1981): 87–101.

Miller, Arthur G. "Historical and Contemporary Perspectives on Stereotyping." In Arthur G. Miller, ed. *In the Eye of the Beholder*. New York: Praeger, 1982.

Mitchell, Judith. *Woman's Estate*. New York: Pantheon Books, 1971.

Morton, F. L. "Sexual Equality and the Family in Tocqueville's Democracy in America." *Canadian Journal of Political Science* 17 (June 1984): 309–24.

Nisbett, Richard E., and Timothy DeCamp Wilson. "Telling More Than We Can Know: Verbal Reports on Mental Processes." *Psychological Review* 84 (May 1977): 231–59.

CHILDREN AND PARENTS

Barron, Jerome A. "Notice to the Unwed Father and Termination of Parental Rights: Implementing Stanley v. Illinois." In Sanford N. Katz, ed. *The Youngest Minority: Lawyers in Defense of Children*. Chicago: American Bar Association Press, 1977, v. 2, pp. 22–41.

Cannon, Kenneth L., and Richard Long. "Premarital Sexual Behavior in the Sixties." In Marvin B. Sussman, ed. *Sourcebook in Marriage and the Family*. 4th ed. Boston: Houghton Mifflin, 1974.

Cassetty, Judith. "Emerging Issues in Child-Support Policy and Practice." In Judith Cassetty, ed. *The Parental Child-Support Obligation: Research, Practice, and Social Policy*. Lexington, Mass.: Lexington Books, 1983.

"Comment: Extent of a Parent's Duty of Support." In *Selected Essays on Family Law*. Brooklyn: Foundation Press, 1950, pp. 1070–74.

Davis, Kingsley. "Illegitimacy and the Social Structure." *American Journal of Sociology* 45 (September 1939): 215–33.

de Mause, Lloyd. "The Evolution of Childhood." In *The History of Child-hood*. New York: Psychohistory Press, 1974, pp. 1–75.

Garfinkel, Irwin, David Betson, Thomas Corbett and Sherwood K. Zink. "A Proposal for Comprehensive Reform of the Child-Support System in Wisconsin." In Judith Cassetty, ed. *The Parental Child-Support Obligation*, pp. 263–82.

Garrison, Marsha. "Why Terminate Parental Rights?" *Stanford Law Review* 35 (February 1983): 423–96.

Goldstein, Joseph, Anna Freud and Albert J. Solnit. *Beyond the Best Interests of the Child*. New York: Free Press, 1973.

Gottlieb, David, ed. *Children's Liberation*. Englewood Cliffs, N.J.: Prentice-Hall, 1973.

Gray, John C., Jr., and David Rudovsky. "The Court Acknowledges the Illegitimate: Levy v. Louisiana and Glona v. American Guarantee and Liability Insurance Co." *University of Pennsylvania Law Review* 118 (November 1969): 1–39.

Gross, Beatrice, and Ronald Gross, eds. *The Children's Rights Movement: Overcoming the Oppression of Young People*. Garden City, N.Y.: Anchor Press/Doubleday, 1977.

Hartley, Shirley Foster. *Illegitimacy*. Berkeley: University of California Press, 1975.

Hunter, Nan D. "Child Support Law and Policy: The Systematic Imposition of Costs on Women." *Harvard Women's Law Journal* 6 (Spring 1983): 1–29.

———. "Women and Child Support." In Irene Diamond, ed. *Families, Politics and Public Policy*, pp. 213–15.

Katz, Sanford N. "A Historical Perspective on Child Support Laws in the United States." In Judith Cassetty, ed. *The Parental Child-Support Obligation*, pp. 17–21.

———, ed. *The Youngest Minority*. 2 vols. Chicago: American Bar Association Press, 1977.

Krause, Harry D. "Equal Protection for the Illegitimate." *Michigan Law Review* 65 (January 1967): 477–506.

———. *Illegitimacy: Law and Social Policy*. Indianapolis: Bobbs-Merrill, 1971.

Laslett, Peter, Karla Oosterveen and Richard M. Smith. *Bastardy and Its Comparative History*. Cambridge: Harvard University Press, 1980.

Mabbut, Fred R. "Juveniles, Mental Hospital Commitment and Civil Rights: The Case of Parham v. J.R." *Journal of Family Law* 19 (November 1980): 27–64.

Robbins, Horace H., and Francis Deak. "The Familial Rights of Illegitimate Children." In *Selected Essays on Family Law*. Brooklyn: Foundation Press, 1950, pp. 728–49.

Stenger, Robert L. "Expanding the Constitutional Rights of Illegitimate Children, 1968–80." *Journal of Family Law* 19 (May 1981): 407–44.

Straus, Murray A., Richard J. Gelles and Suzanne K. Steinmetz. *Behind Closed Doors: Violence in the American Family.* Garden City, N.Y.: Anchor Press/Doubleday, 1981.

Wallach, Aleta, and Patricia Tenoso. "A Vindication of the Rights of Unmarried Mothers and Their Children: An Analysis of the Institution of Illegitimacy, Equal Protection and the Uniform Parentage Act." *University of Kansas Law Review* 23 (1974): 23–90.

WOMEN AND EMPLOYMENT

Babcock, Barbara A., Ann Freedman, Eleanor Holmes Norton and Susan Ross. *Sex Discrimination and the Law.* Boston: Little, Brown, 1975.

Bartlett, Katharine T. "Pregnancy and the Constitution: The Uniqueness Trap." *California Law Review* 62 (December 1974): 1532–66.

Congressional Quarterly. *Employment in America.* Washington, D.C.: Congressional Quarterly, 1983.

Eisenstein, Zillah. "State, Patriarchal Family and Working Mothers." In Irene Diamond, ed. *Family, Politics and Public Policy,* pp. 41–58.

Erie, Steven P., Martin Rein and Barbara Wiget. "Women and the Reagan Revolution: Thermidor for the Social Welfare Economy." In Irene Diamond, ed. *Family, Politics and Public Policy,* pp. 94–119.

Evans, Sarah. *Personal Politics.* New York: Random House, 1980.

Flexner, Eleanor. *Century of Struggle.* New York: Atheneum Press, 1972.

Giraldo, Z. I. *Public Policy and the Family: Wives and Mothers in the Work Force.* Lexington, Mass.: Lexington Books, 1980.

Glassman, Carol. "Women and the Welfare System." In Robin Morgan, ed. *Sisterhood Is Powerful.* New York: Vintage/Random House, 1970.

Haener, Dorothy. "Maternity and Other Fringe Benefits." In *Women's Role in Contemporary Society,* pp. 364–79.

Kamerman, Sheila B., Alfred J. Kahn and Paul Kingston. *Maternity Policies and Working Women.* New York: Columbia University Press, 1983.

Kirp, David L., and Dorothy Robyn. "Pregnancy, Justice and the Justices." *Texas Law Review* 57 (August 1979): 947–64.

Koontz, Elizabeth. "Childbirth and Childrearing Leave: Job Related Benefits." *New York Law Forum* 17, no. 2 (1971): 480–502.

Levitan, Sar A., and Richard S. Belous. "Working Wives and Mothers:

What Happens to Family Life." *Monthly Labor Review* 104 (September 1981): 26–31.

Moore, Kristin A., and Sandra L. Hofferth. "Women and Their Children." In Ralph E. Smith, ed. *The Subtle Revolution*. Washington, D.C.: Urban Institute, 1979, pp. 125–59.

————. "Women's Employment and Marriage." In Smith, ed. *The Subtle Revolution*, pp. 108–10.

Smith, Ralph E., ed. *The Subtle Revolution*. Washington, D.C.: Urban Institute, 1979.

Taylor, Ellen T. "Comment: Differential Treatment of Pregnancy in Employment: The Impact of G.E. Co. v. Gilbert and Nashville Gas v. Satty." *Harvard Civil Rights-Civil Liberties Law Review* 13 (Summer 1978): 717–50.

"Women's Role in Contemporary Society." *The Report of the New York Commission on Human Rights, September 21–25, 1970*. New York: Discus Books, 1972.

Zelman, Patricia G. *Women, Work and National Policy: The Kennedy-Johnson Years*. Ann Arbor, Mich.: UMI Research Press, 1981.

Zimmerman, Diane L. "Comment: Geduldig v. Aiello: Pregnancy Classifications and the Definition of Sex Discrimination." *Columbia Law Review* 75 (March 1975): 441–82.

SEX AND REPRODUCTION

Alan Guttmacher Institute. *Eleven Million Teenagers: What Can Be Done About the Epidemic of Adolescent Pregnancies in the United States?* New York: Planned Parenthood of America, 1976.

————. *Teenage Pregnancy: The Problem That Hasn't Gone Away*. New York: Planned Parenthood of America, 1981.

Blake, Judith. "Abortion and Public Opinion: The 1960–1970 Decade." *Science* 171 (February 1971): 540–49.

Brown, Wendy. "Reproductive Freedom and the Right to Privacy: A Paradox for Feminists." In Irene Diamond, ed. *Family, Politics and Public Policy*, pp. 322–38.

Dienes, C. Thomas. *Law, Politics and Birth Control*. Urbana: University of Illinois Press, 1972.

Ely, John Hart. "The Wages of Crying Wolf: A Comment on Roe v. Wade." *Yale Law Journal* 82 (April 1973): 920–49.

Fox, Greer Litton. "The Family's Role in Adolescent Sexual Behavior." In Theodora Ooms, ed. *Teenage Pregnancy*, pp. 73–125.

Freedman, Anne. "Sex Equality, Sex Differences and the Supreme Court." *Yale Law Journal* 92 (May 1984): 913–68.

Frohock, Fred M. *Abortion: A Case Study in Law and Morals*. Westport, Conn.: Greenwood Press, 1983.

Goodman, Janice, Rhonda Copelon Schoenbrod and Nancy Stearns. "Roe and Doe: Where Do We Go from Here?" *Women's Rights Law Reporter* 1 (Spring 1973): 2–38.

Gordon, Linda. *Woman's Body, Woman's Right*. New York: Penguin Books, 1977.

Harper, Anne L. "Teenage Sexuality and Public Policy: An Agenda for Gender Education." In Irene Diamond, ed. *Families, Politics and Public Policy*, pp. 220–35.

Harrison, Beverly Wildung. *Our Right to Choose: Toward a New Ethic of Abortion*. Boston: Beacon Press, 1983.

Jackson, John E., and Maris A. Vinovskis. "Public Opinion, Elections and the Single Issue." In Gilbert Y. Steiner, ed. *The Abortion Dispute and the American System*, pp. 64–81.

Jones, Audrey E., and Paul J. Placek. "Teenage Women in the United States: Sex, Contraception, Pregnancy, Fertility and Maternal and Infant Health." In Ooms, ed. *Teenage Pregnancy*, pp. 49–72.

Kantner, John F., and Melvin Zelnik. "Sexual Activity, Contraceptive Use and Pregnancy Among Metropolitan Area Teenagers, 1971–1979." *Family Planning Perspectives* 12 (September/October 1980): 230–37.

Law, Sylvia A. "Rethinking Sex and the Constitution." *University of Pennsylvania Law Review* 132 (June 1984): 955–1040.

Luker, Kristin. *Abortion and the Politics of Motherhood*. Berkeley: University of California Press, 1984.

Mohr, James C. *Abortion in America*. New York: Oxford University Press, 1978.

Ooms, Theodora, ed. *Teenage Pregnancy in a Family Context: Implications for Policy*. Philadelphia: Temple University Press, 1981.

Petchevsky, Rosalind Pollack. "Anti-abortion, Anti-feminism and the Rise of the New Right." *Feminist Studies* 7 (Summer 1981): 206–46.

Reed, James. *Birth Control and American Society: From Private Vice to Public Virtue*. Princeton, N.J.: Princeton University Press, 1978.

Regan, Donald H. "Rewriting Roe v. Wade." *Michigan Law Review* 77 (August 1979): 1569–1646.

Reiss, Ira L. "The Sexual Renaissance: A Summary and Analysis." *Journal of Social Issues* 22 (April 1966): 123–37.

Rubin, Eva R. *Abortion, Politics and the Courts*. Westport, Conn.: Greenwood Press, 1982.

Shorter, Edward. *A History of Women's Bodies*. New York: Basic Books, 1982.

Steiner, Gilbert Y., ed. *The Abortion Dispute and the American System*. Washington, D.C.: Brookings Institute, 1983.

Thomson, Judith Jarvis. "A Defense of Abortion." *Philosophy and Public Affairs* 1 (Fall 1971): 47–66.

Vinovskis, Maris A. "An 'Epidemic' of Adolescent Pregnancy? Some Historical Considerations," *Journal of Family History* 6 (Summer 1981): 208.

EDUCATION AND SOCIALIZATION

Arons, Stephen. "The Separation of School and State: Pierce Reconsidered." *Harvard Education Review* 46 (February 1976): 76–104.

Everhart, Robert B., ed. *The Public School Monopoly*. San Francisco: Pacific Institute for Public Policy Research, 1982.

Greer, Colin. *The Great School Legend*. New York: Basic Books, 1972.

Kaestle, Carl F. *Pillars of the Republic: Common Schools and American Society, 1780–1860*. New York: Hill and Wang, 1983.

Katz, Michael S. *A History of Compulsory Education Laws*. Bloomington, Ind.: Phi Delta Kappa Educational Foundation, 1976.

Knudsen, Stephen T. "The Education of the Amish Child." *University of California Law Review* 62, no. 5 (December 1974): 1506–31.

Nordin, Virginia Davis, and William Lloyd Turner. "More Than Segregation Academies; The Growing Protestant Fundamentalist Schools." *Phi Delta Kappan* (February 1980): 391–94.

Ravitch, Diane. *The Revisionists Revised: A Critique of the Radical Attack on the Schools*. New York: Basic Books, 1978.

Spring, Joel. "The Evolving Political Structure of American Schooling." In Robert B. Everhart, ed. *The Public School Monopoly*, pp. 89–95.

Stewart, Bruce R. "Recognizing the Competing Interests of Parent and Child." *School Law Bulletin* 13 (April 1982): 1–9.

Stokes, Anson Phelps. *Church and State in the United States*. 3 vols. New York: Harper, 1950.

ALTERNATE LIFE STYLES

Cogswell, Betty E., and Marvin B. Sussman. "Changing Family and Marriage Forms: Complications for Human Service Systems." In Marvin B. Sussman, ed. 4th ed. *Sourcebook in Marriage and the Family*. Boston: Houghton Mifflin, 1974, pp. 90–99.

"Comment: Homosexuals' Right to Marry: A Constitutional Test and a Legislative Solution." *University of Pennsylvania Law Review* 128 (1979): pp. 193–216.

Crutchfield, Charles F. "Non-Marital Relationships and Their Impact on the Institution of Marriage and the Traditional Family Structure." *Journal of Family Law* 19 (1980–1981): 247–61.

Grey, Thomas C. "Eros, Civilization and the Burger Court." *Law and Contemporary Problems* 43, no. 3 (Summer 1980): 83–101.

Karst, Kenneth L. "The Freedom of Intimate Association." *Yale Law Journal* 89 (March 1980): 624–92.

Kearn, Patricia, and Kathleen Ridolfi. "Note: The Fourteenth Amendment's Protection of a Woman's Right to Be a Single Parent Through Artificial Insemination by a Donor." *Womens' Rights Reporter* 7 (Spring 1982): 251–84.

Lorio, Kathryn Venturatos. "Alternate Means of Reproduction: Virgin Territory for Legislation." *Louisiana Law Review* 44 (July 1984): 1641–76.

Madison, George W. "Marital and Non-Marital Relationships: The Right to Alternate Lifestyles." *Columbia Human Rights Law Review* 11 (Spring-Summer 1979): 189–226.

Martin, Julia H., and Donna J. Tolson. "Family Composition in Virginia: Female Headed Families, 1970–1980." *Newsletter*, Institute of Government, University of Virginia. July 1983.

Rodman, Hyman. "Lower-Class Family Behavior." In Arlene S. and Jerome H. Skolnick, eds. *Family in Transition*, pp. 410–13.

Stinnett, Nick, and Craig W. Birdsong. *The Family and Alternate Life Styles*. Chicago: Nelson-Hall, 1978.

Sussman, Marvin B., and Lee Burchinal. "Kin Family Network: Unheralded Structure in Current Conceptualization of Family Functioning." In Marvin B. Sussman, ed. *Sourcebook in Marriage and the Family*, pp. 170–76.

Vincent, Clark E. "Mental Health and the Family." In Marvin B. Sussman, ed. *Sourcebook in Marriage and the Family*, pp. 279–99.

Wadlington, Walter. "Artificial Conception: The Challenge for Family Law." *Virginia Law Review* 69 (1983): 465–514.

Wexler, Joan G. "Rethinking the Modification of Child Custody Decrees." *Yale Law Journal* 94 (March 1985): 757–820.

Wilkinson, J. Harvie, and G. Edward White. "Constitutional Protection for Personal Lifestyles." *Cornell Law Review* 62 (March 1977): 563–625.

Willemsen, Michael A. "Justice Tobriner and the Tolerance of Evolving Lifestyles." *Hastings Law Journal* 29 (September 1977): 73–97.

LEGAL AND CONSTITUTIONAL ISSUES

Baer, Judith. *Equality Under the Constitution: Reclaiming the Fourteenth Amendment*. Ithaca, N.Y.: Cornell University Press, 1983.

Blackstone, Sir William. *Commentaries on the Laws of England*. James
    DeWitt Andrews, ed. 4th ed. Chicago: Callaghan and Co., 1899.
Burt, Robert A. "The Constitution of the Family." *Supreme Court Review*
    (1979): 329–95.
Cortner, Richard C. *The Supreme Court and Civil Liberties Policy*. Palo
    Alto, Calif.: Mayfield, 1975.
Cowan, Ruth B. "Women's Rights Through Litigation: An Examination
    of the American Civil Liberties Union Women's Rights Project,
    1971–1976." *Columbia Human Rights Law Review* 8 (Spring-Sum-
    mer 1976): 373–412.
Greenberg, Jack. *Judicial Process and Social Change, Constitutional Litiga-
    tion*. St. Paul, Minn.: West Publishing Co., 1977.
Gunther, Gerald. *Cases and Materials on Constitutional Law*. 10th ed.
    Mineola, N.Y.: Foundation Press, 1980.
Harris, Robert J. *The Quest for Equality: The Constitution, Congress and the
    Supreme Court*. Baton Rouge: Louisiana State University Press,
    1960.
Horowitz, Donald L. *The Courts and Social Policy*. Washington, D.C.:
    Brookings Institute, 1977.
Howe, Mark De Wolfe, ed. *Holmes-Pollock Letters*. 2d ed. Cambridge:
    Belknap Press, 1961.
Karst, Kenneth L., and Harold W. Horowitz. "Reitman v. Mulkey: A
    Telophase of Substantive Equal Protection." *Supreme Court Re-
    view* 1967: 39–80.
Krause, Harry. *Family Law: Cases, Comments and Questions*. 2d ed. St.
    Paul, Minn.: West Publishing Co., 1983.
Lerner, Max, ed. *The Mind and Faith of Justice Holmes*. New York: Modern
    Library, 1943.
Miller, Arthur Selwyn. "The Concept of the 'Living Constitution'." In
    Arthur S. Miller, *Social Change and Fundamental Law*. Westport,
    Conn.: Greenwood Press, 1977.
————. *The Supreme Court and American Capitalism*. New York: Free
    Press, 1968.
Mnookin, Robert H. *Child, Family and State: Problems and Materials on
    Children and the Law*. Boston: Little, Brown, 1978.
Neier, Aryeh. *Only Judgment: The Limits of Litigation in Social Change*.
    Middletown, Conn.: Wesleyan University Press, 1982.
"Note: The Irrebuttable Presumption Doctrine in the Supreme Court."
    Harvard Law Review 87 (May 1974): 1534–56.
"Note: Irrebuttable Presumptions: An Illusory Analysis." *Stanford Law
    Review* 27 (January 1975): 449–73.
O'Connor, Karen. *Women's Organizations' Use of the Courts*. Lexington,
    Mass.: Lexington Books, 1980.

Perkins, Rollin M. *Criminal Law*. 3d ed. Mineola, N.Y.: Foundation Press, 1982.

Pollock, Frederick, and Frederic William Maitland. *The History of English Law, Before the Time of Edward I*. Washington, D.C.: Lawyers' Literary Club, 1959.

Reich, Charles. "Individual Rights and Social Welfare: The Emerging Legal Issues." *Yale Law Journal* 74 (June 1965): 1244–1357.

―――. "The New Property." *Yale Law Journal* 73 (April 1964): 733–74.

Schmid, Margaret Emanuel. "Note: Due Process—The Indigent Parent's Right to State-Furnished Counsel in Parental Status Termination Proceedings—An Examination of the Supreme Court's Methodology." *Wake Forest Law Review* 17 (December 1981): 961–89.

"Symposium: Law of the Poor." *California Law Review* 54 (May 1966).

ten Broek, Jacobus. "Present Status and Constitutionality of the Family Law of the Poor." In Joel F. Handler, ed. *Family Law and the Poor*. Westport, Conn.: Greenwood Press, 1971.

Tribe, Laurence. *American Constitutional Law*. Mineola, N.Y.: Foundation Press, 1978.

Wadlington, Walter, Charles H. Whitebread and Samuel M. Davis. *Children in the Legal System, Cases and Materials*. Mineola, N.Y.: Foundation Press, 1983.

Woodward, Bob, and Scott Armstrong. *The Brethren*. New York: Simon and Schuster, 1979.

GOVERNMENT POLICIES

Babcock, Richard F. *The Zoning Game*. Madison: University of Wisconsin Press, 1966.

Cassetty, Judith, ed. *The Parental Child-Support Obligation*. Lexington, Mass.: Lexington Books, 1983.

Cohodas, Nadine. "Alternatives to Abortion. Federal Abortion Alternatives Cut by Reagan Administration." *Congressional Quarterly Weekly Report*, November 17, 1984, pp. 2949–55.

Ehrenreich, Barbara. "Family Feud on the Left: The Social Issue Game." *Nation*, March 13, 1982, pp. 289, 303–306.

Gambitta, Richard A.L., et al., eds. *Governing Through Courts*. Beverly Hills, Calif.: Sage Publications, 1981.

Gusfield, Joseph R. *Symbolic Crusade*. Urbana: University of Illinois Press, 1963.

Katz, Sanford N. "Foster Parents Versus Agencies: A Case Study in the Judicial Application of the 'Best Interests of the Child' Doctrine." *Michigan Law Review* 65 (November 1966): 145–70.

Moore, Kristin A. "Government Policies Related to Teenage Family
    Formation and Functioning: An Inventory." In Ooms, ed. *Teen-
    age Pregnancy*, pp. 165–213.
Palmer, Larry I. "Adoption: A Plea for Realistic Constitutional Decision-
    making." *Columbia Human Rights Law Review* 11 (Spring-Summer
    1980): 1–49.
Redden, Kenneth R. *Federal Regulation of the Family*. Charlottesville, Va.:
    Michie Co., 1982.
Siegel, Reva B. "Note: Employment Equality Under the Pregnancy Dis-
    ability Act of 1978." *Yale Law Journal* 94 (March 1985): 929–56.
Steiner, Gilbert Y. *The Futility of Family Policy*. Washington, D.C.: Brook-
    ings Institute, 1981.

Index of Cases

Index

Home visits, 148
Homosexuals, 22, 115, 154
Horowitz, Harold W., 195
Housing: programs, 151; single
   family, 157–58
Humanistic philosophy, 133

Ideology, 11, 36, 79–80, 112, 119,
   131, 156, 165, 175, 179, 187, 192,
   195, 197, 198; public school, 134.
   See also Family ideology
Illegitimacy, vii, 25, 148, 186, 187;
   classifications, 14, 187, 192; law
   of, 28–38;
Illinois, child custody legislation,
   39
Income tax refunds, 49
Indigents, 177, 179, 180
Inheritance, 35–36, 38, 51–52, 187,
   190
Institutionalization, 13, 26
Internal Revenue Service, 49
Irrebuttable presumptions, 39, 40,
   84, 95, 149. *See also* Due process

Javits, Jacob, 93
Jefferson, Thomas, 28
Jews, Orthodox, 125
Judges, federal, 11
Judicial decision-making, bias in,
   196–97
Juries, i-iii, 185
Justice, juvenile, 167
Juvenile homes, 192

Kaestle, Carl F., 119
Kanowitz, Leo, 106
Karst, Kenneth L., 195
Kent, James, 16, 174
Krause, Harry D., 22–23, 50
Koop, C. Everett, 116

La Haye, Tim, 133, 183
Lasch, Christopher, 21

Lassiter, Abby Gail, 176, 194
Law, Sylvia, 62, 67–68, 186
Legitimacy classifications. *See*
   Classifications, legislative
Legitimation, 43–46
Liberals, attitudes toward family
   problems, 100–101
Liberty, 27, 55, 64, 159
Life styles, alternate, 41, 154, 158,
   159–60, 184, 187
Lippmann, Walter, 11, 183
Litigation of social issues, iii, 13,
   14, 65, 134, 147–48, 167, 183–84
Living arrangements, non-mari-
   tal, 146, 157, 193, 196
Loewy, Arnold H., 108–9
Louisiana, wrongful death stat-
   ute, 32–35
Lutherans, 121, 123

McReynolds, James C., 18, 123
Marital status, classification by, 41–
   47. *See also* Classifications,
   legislative
Marriage, 11, 16–17, 21–22, 147,
   157, 164, 166, 190, 191; ceremonial, 148, 150; interracial, 144;
   middle-class, 53; rate of, 100; restrictions on, 144, 153; right to,
   17, 50, 144, 152–54, 158
Marshall, Thurgood, 98, 102; dissenting in *Beal v. Doe*, 75; dissenting in *HL v. Matheson*, 111;
   dissenting (to denial of *certiorari*), in *Hollenbaugh v. Carnegie
   Free Library*, 160; dissenting in
   Lehr v. Robertson, 47, 157; concurring in *Moore v. City of East
   Cleveland*, 146; opinion in *Quilloin v. Walcott*, 41; dissenting in
   Parham v. JR, 174; dissenting in
   Village of Belle Terre v. Boraas, 158;

About the Author

EVA R. RUBIN is Associate Professor of Political Science and Public Administration at North Carolina State University, Raleigh. She has previously written *Abortion, Politics and the Courts* (Greenwood Press, 1982).

DUE DATE

Al